From

The Women's Press Ltd
34 Great Sutton Street, London EC1V 0DX

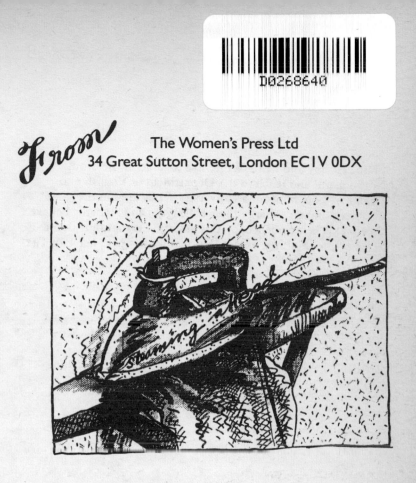

Elaine Hobby and Chris White live together in Beeston, Nottingham, and teach in the Department of English and Drama at Loughborough University. They are not the same person (although some of their colleagues and students believe they are). Their evidence for this assertion is that they don't agree about anything, except that neither has paid her Poll Tax.

What Lesbians do in Books

Elaine Hobby and
Chris White, editors

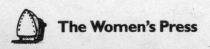 **The Women's Press**

First published by The Women's Press Limited 1991
A member of the Namara Group
34 Great Sutton Street, London EC1V 0DX

Collection copyright © Elaine Hobby and Chris White, 1991

Cataloguing in Publication Data is available
from the British Library

Typeset by Contour Typesetters, Southall, London
Printed and bound in Great Britain by
Cox & Wyman Ltd, Reading

For the women who made this book possible.

LESBIANS IN BOOKS

Lesbians in books: we are
exploring the shape of ourselves
past, present, future
a curve, a promise, a brick wall;
new thoughts, old beginnings.
Here
she has written a love story,
not well – but precious to me,
because she wrote it for us.
Here
she has written a book about gardening;
you would never guess this woman
green-booted, grey-haired, muddily corduroyed
    cheerful
is a lesbian, too, and is glad of it
seeing a lover's curve in that fall of alyssum.
There
is a poem written in anger, quite unambiguous;
there
is another, three centuries earlier
also (if you had only realised) quite unambiguous.
My lover, plaintive, playful
asks for rude books, and I provide them;
I thumb through, looking for the good bits
wanting to promote as much homosexuality as
    possible
in *my* bed.

Statistics are curious. 10–15 per cent of the population
are gay, maybe. 10–15 per cent of books published are
by women, maybe. Maybe libraries stock 40 per cent of
the books by women they could stock. (Stay with me;
this is all guesswork.) My sums say from this, there's
4,444 books by lesbians in my local library. Approxi-
mately, you understand.

And statistically (of course)
we have written about elephants and empires
herbs and housing regulations
magicians, music, maps
and the quality of mud in certain countries.

You will, perhaps, refute the 'we'
we are so unidentifiable
such an inconvenient minority, and you have no way
    of knowing
if one of us wrote that book your daughter is reading
on law, or lice, or loving.

We teach your grandchildren
we wash your dead,
we designed the toothpaste tube you held just half an
    hour ago
lesbians abseil in the house of lords
some bus routes are staffed entirely by lesbians.
But you do not know the face of your fear,
you will not look us in the eyes;
what we write is propaganda
and while you read it, and legislate against it
we are finding out more and more about ourselves
we are exploring our past and our present
and shaping our future, while you try to abolish it.

We wrote the book your daughter is reading
on law, or lice, or loving
and she will write, with others or alone
on violence, or the changing of the seasons
on her past
her present
her future.

Jan Sellers
February 1988

Contents

Jan Sellers   'Lesbians in Books'   vi

Elaine Hobby and Chris White   Introduction   1

1) LESBIAN BOOKS

Paulina Palmer   The Lesbian Feminist Thriller and
  Detective Novel   9

Liz Yorke   Primary Intensities: Lesbian Poetry and
  the Reading of Difference   28

Gillian Spraggs   Divine Visitations: Sappho's
  Poetry of Love   50

Chris White   'She Was Not Really Man at All': The
  Lesbian Practice and Politics of Edith Ellis   68

Lyndie Brimstone   Towards a New Cartography:
  Radclyffe Hall, Virginia Woolf and the Working
  of Common Land   86

2) LESBIANS READING

Gillian Hanscombe   Katherine Mansfield's Pear
  Tree   111

Gabriele Griffin   *The Chinese Garden*:
  A Cautionary Tale   134

Giti Thadani   Anamika   155

3) LESBIANS WRITING

Elaine Hobby   Katherine Philips:
  Seventeenth-Century Lesbian Poet   183

Patricia Duncker   Reading Genesis   205

Dorothea Smartt   From My Eyes ... Zamis Publishing
  Poetry 1984–1988   226

Caeia March   The Process of Writing
  Three Ply Yarn   239

Notes on Contributors   256

Bibliography   261

Index   274

INTRODUCTION
Chris White and Elaine Hobby

The title of *What Lesbians Do In Books* is a joke and a serious matter. Lesbians in books have long been silenced, exploited or parodied in (un)popular fiction and (un)populist 'science' and 'sociology'. Despite repeated attempts by lesbians to intervene in heterosexual accounts of the work of Katherine Philips and Katherine Mansfield, Virginia Woolf and Sappho – to name only the most obvious examples – *What Lesbians Do In Books* is the first British collection of explicitly lesbian essays on literature. This book takes on and displays what lesbians – as writers, campaigners, critics – *do* in books. The range represented in this collection – there are lesbians as writers and lesbians as readers, zamis publishing poetry and white lesbians publishing detective stories, lesbian remakings of the Garden of Eden and Sanskrit myth – emphasises the extraordinary diversity of such writings and approaches.

The first section of this collection, 'Lesbian Books', focuses on lesbian readings of lesbian texts. The writings and authors examined here are preoccupied in different ways with struggles to find a language and frame of reference in which to talk about lesbian culture, desire and identity, in diverse historical moments. The section opens in the present, with Paulina Palmer's essay on lesbian detective fiction and thrillers, which explores the ways in which these recent lesbian novels employ and remake the conventions of a predominantly heterosexual and male genre. Liz Yorke's work also engages with contemporary lesbian writings, shifting focus to poetry and its authors' attempts to develop new ways of figuring lesbian desire in a language that takes account of and works to expand understandings of female bodies and lesbian community. In different but complementary ways, Chris White and Lyndie Brimstone map an earlier period this century, investigating the ways in which Radclyffe Hall, Virginia Woolf and Edith Ellis related to and moved beyond contemporary sexology and concepts of 'inversion'. Gill Spraggs looks further back in time again, examining the erotics of Sappho's poetry and demonstrating the need for any account of past culture to take on board the very different understandings people have had of sexuality and desire if we are really to make sense of what they say.

'Lesbians Reading', the second section of this book, brings to texts what Gillian Hanscombe calls 'lesbian specs', that is, the reader's knowledge of cultural frameworks, languages and encodings. These 'lesbian specs' make it possible for the reader to decipher lesbian meanings and lesbian moments in texts that do not declare explicitly their lesbianism. Gillian Hanscombe's reading of a Katherine Mansfield short story demonstrates accordingly the change made to the possible meanings of the story if the reader allows for the existence of such hidden references. Gabriele Griffin's essay on Rosemary Manning's *The Chinese Garden* analyses a novel crucially concerned with cultural and specifically literary encodings of lesbianism. She fills out and explicates these embedded references, showing the ways in which *The Chinese Garden* conceals and yet reveals desire and experience which are lesbian but cannot be named as such. Finally, Giti Thadani's work on lesbian motifs in Sanskrit myth draws attention to the role of the reader in creating the meaning of texts. She shows that meaning is not fixed, stable and easily constituted, but fluid and always in the process of becoming. A lesbian reader, she demonstrates, can work towards meaning without recourse to simple, authoritative definitions or received mythologies.

The third section, 'Lesbians Writing', has many connections with both 'Lesbian Books' and 'Lesbians Reading'. The authors of these essays focus on the activities of lesbian writers themselves. Elaine Hobby and Patricia Duncker both examine the possibilities for writing lesbian desire in the world of the English revolution. Where Elaine Hobby's essay takes as its centre the activities of a

single seventeenth-century lesbian, Katherine Philips, and her poetry's eroticisation of domination and submission, Patricia Duncker's moves away from its historical beginnings, demonstrating quite other ways of writing and remaking a lesbian past. Dorothea Smartt and Caeia March, as writers of poetry and novels themselves, conclude this collection with their accounts of lesbian writers and writing today. Dorothea Smartt's bibliography compiles a history of recent London-based Blacklesbian poetry, indicating the connections between these authors and other political and cultural developments. Caeia March's essay tells the story of the writing and production of her novel *Three Ply Yarn*, showing the influence of diverse political and cultural concerns and events in its making.

In arranging *What Lesbians Do In Books* in these sections, we do not want to distract attention from quite other important connections, and significant differences, between the essays. Giti Thadani, Patricia Duncker, Elaine Hobby, Liz Yorke and Gillian Spraggs are all concerned, in various ways, with the importance of a God, gods, or goddesses in lesbian works. The significance of biography and biographical information is pertinent not only to Dorothea Smartt's and Caeia March's essays, but is also crucial to Gillian Hanscombe's and Chris White's. Giti Thadani, Liz Yorke, Patricia Duncker and Lyndie Brimstone are all, variously, pre-occupied with attempts to find a way of writing, 'writing as a lesbian', which refuses traditional (heterosexual? masculine?) constraints of unilinear development. Gillian Spraggs, Elaine Hobby and Chris White all take issue with Foucauldian accounts of the history of homosexuality. The limitations of the mainstream academic curriculum is a problem addressed by Paulina Palmer, Lyndie Brimstone, Gillian Hanscombe and Gabriele Griffin. In one form or another, all of these essays concern themselves with the relationship between lesbianism and feminism, and they do not, on the whole, agree with one another. For us as editors, this has been a crucial element in the making of this book: we believe that lesbianism has many histories and many practices, and we wanted *What Lesbians Do In Books* to demonstrate and thereby defend that variety.

What Lesbians Do In Books has been a long time in the making. The idea of this collection was first floated by the commissioning editor of Manchester University Press in April 1986. Two volumes were planned: one of lesbian work, one of essays by gay men (edited by Simon Shepherd and Mick Wallis), both to appear as part of the MUP's new Cultural Politics series. When Manchester University Press refused to publish the completed gay male anthology in 1988 (in the meantime, Section 28 had passed into law, and was being used as the excuse for a great variety of attacks on lesbians and gays), the Cultural Politics series collapsed as we, and other authors, withdrew our books in protest. (Simon Shepherd and Mick Wallis' book has now been published by Unwin Hyman in 1989, entitled *Coming On Strong: Gay Politics and Culture*.) This delayed the completion of a collection that has been slow-moving from the beginning: working on this book has repeatedly reminded us how very complex and demanding lesbian lives are, as the work on individual essays was interrupted by illnesses of authors, their children and parents, periods of unemployment and over-employment, and a multiplicity of personal and professional demands.

Throughout, the authors of the essays in this collection, and Jan Sellers, whose poem 'Lesbians in Books' was written specially for it, have kept its editors going. Despite the disasters and distractions that beset all our lives, they have continued to insist that they wanted the book to be finished, and have continued to respond with patience and intelligence to our niggling requests for expansions, deletions and explanations. From the beginning it was important to us that *What Lesbians Do In Books* not only be about what white lesbians do in books, and we have been excited by the ways in which our white contributors have engaged with questions of race. Despite extensive and repeated attempts, however, we have not succeeded in commissioning more than two essays by Black women for this collection. We know a great deal of work on books is being done by Blacklesbians in Britain today. We are not able to find many who had the time, or who would choose, to write for this collection.

As our search for a new publisher was bearing no fruit and this book looked likely never to see the light of day (as, we have learned, has been the fate of more than one planned anthology of lesbian literary criticism), Ros de Lanerolle (then) of The Women's Press sought us out. She and her colleagues have ensured that *What Lesbians Do in Books* has finally been done. This book is dedicated to those women with love, in recognition that they made it possible. The final coming to light of the book was ensured by the diligence and warmth of Kathy Gale (publishing director),

Katherine Bright-Holmes (editor), Judith Murray (who copy edited it and made many helpful suggestions), Elizabeth Wright (who collated the proofs); Liz Gibbs (publicity), Vicki Bzovy, Stella Kane (production); Morven Hueston, Sandra den Hertog (contracts and rights); Mary Hemming and Sarah Wasley (sales); and Jacqui McDonough and Stephen Parker of Namara Design (who drew the cover). Heartfelt thanks to them all. We should also like to acknowledge the unwavering support of Simon Shepherd, Mick Wallis (who thought of the title and was almost too embarrassed to tell us it), Elizabeth Boa (for help with the German), De Bromley and Deirdre O'Byrne.

1

Lesbian Books

THE LESBIAN FEMINIST THRILLER AND DETECTIVE NOVEL
Paulina Palmer

FOR CAMBRIDGE LESBIAN LINE

> She really should write a novel. Put it all in. Journalism can't begin to do justice to the personalities, the nuances of the past two weeks. 'Could write a thriller,' she says aloud. 'A feminist thriller.'
>
> Barbara Wilson, *Ambitious Women*, p.155.[1]

INTRODUCTION

Women who identify as lesbian do not, of course, write in a cultural vacuum. On the contrary, they spend much of their energies engaging intellectually with the ideas and forms of the dominant literary culture. In fact, one of the things that lesbians frequently do in books is to appropriate certain well-known genres of fiction, re-creating and revising them in a manner which aims to interrogate and subvert patriarchal, heterosexual codes of conduct. The lesbian feminist thriller and detective novel, exemplified by Rebecca O'Rourke's *Jumping the Cracks* and Mary Wings' *She Came Too Late*, provide interesting examples of this strategy.

The format of the thriller and detective novel holds certain obvious attractions for the lesbian writer. As Sally Munt points out in her pioneering study of the genre,[2] it gives the writer the opportunity to combine the representation of lesbian romance, which makes reference to relationships and sexual encounters between women, with the exploration of themes of a specifically feminist kind. The conflict between feminist principles and patriarchal value schemes is a topic which O'Rourke, Wings and other writers habitually treat. Foregrounding themes of female oppression and exploitation, they structure their novels around incidents of male violence, including battery, rape and child abuse.

The thriller and detective novel, however, while providing an attractive vehicle for the treatment of feminist themes, also confront the writer with certain problems and contradictions. The ideological perspectives associated with the genre constitute a stumbling block. Traditional versions of the detective novel by Agatha Christie and Dorothy L Sayers, as Cora Kaplan observes,[3] generally reveal a conservative approach to class and gender. In the case of crime novels by Mickey Spillane and Ian Fleming, the value system endorsed is emphatically racist and misogynistic. The lesbian writer may experience difficulty in transforming these oppressive attitudes.[4]

Another problem facing the writer of the lesbian thriller hinges on the figure of the investigator. Whether she takes as her model the tough male agent portrayed by Raymond Chandler and Dashiell Hammett or the more genteel female sleuth represented in the work of Agatha Christie and Josephine Tey, she finds that their attitudes conflict with feminist values. The tough male sleuth is notorious for his ruthlessness and his exploitative treatment of women. The female sleuth often displays a puritanical attitude to female sexuality, regarding it disapprovingly as a socially disruptive force. Both figures, moreover, are arrogant and elitist. The belief in the value of individual enterprise to which they subscribe, though in tune with the political climate of the 1980s and 1990s, is at odds with socialist and feminist principles of collectivity.

The strategies which lesbian writers utilise to solve these particular problems, and the devices they introduce to adapt and modify the conventions and character stereotypes they inherit, differ considerably from text to text. By discussing a selection of novels by O'Rourke, Wings and other contributors to the genre, I plan to examine some of these strategies and evaluate their success.

I also aim to give the reader an insight into the variety and inventiveness of lesbian feminist detective and crime fiction.

STRUCTURE AND SETTING

Critics of the traditional thriller conventionally make a distinction between two different kinds of fiction – *the detective novel* and *the crime novel*.[5] The detective novel, they point out, generally centres on the figure of the detective and 'the puzzle' (usually an act of deception) which, by collecting clues and interrogating suspects, she/he attempts to solve. The detective, her/his role as hero unquestioned, is often portrayed as a somewhat aloof figure who displays exceptionally acute powers of reasoning and observation. She/he solves the puzzle by noticing clues and interrogating suspects. Fiction of this kind tends to be ideologically conservative. It upholds the values of the status quo and frequently has as its location the elitist, enclosed realm of the country house, academic college or grand hotel. It also ends on a firm note of closure. The reader feels, on reaching the end of the novel, that the temporary break-down in law and order has been put to rights – and the world is once again a secure and just place to live in. Contributors to the mode include Agatha Christie, Sir Arthur Conan Doyle and Josephine Tey.

The crime novel, on the contrary, centres less on the detective's solving of 'the puzzle' than on character interest and problems of a psychological nature. The investigator, instead of being portrayed as a superior individual who possesses brilliant powers of deduction, may appear fallible and unsure. The crime novel frequently displays interesting ideological contradictions. Although in terms of gender it endorses a tough brand of masculinity, it may none the less be socially radical, questioning aspects of the law and establishment.

The urban setting associated with the mode offers scope for a critique of social injustice and acts of intrigue in politics and big business. Criticism is directed at urban institutions and, in some cases, at the capitalist economy itself. The investigator, though succeeding in solving the crime, cannot be described as setting the world to rights, since society is represented as inherently unstable and unjust. The fiction of Chandler, Hammett and, in the field of the spy thriller, John le Carré, exemplifies this particular mode.

The detective novel and the crime novel are, of course, less distinct in practice than they appear in theory. Writers of the lesbian thriller, like their precursors in the traditional genre, frequently bring together elements from both. Barbara Wilson, for example, in *Murder in the Collective*, successfully combines an intricate murder mystery (hinging on a double crime, involving a satisfying element of 'puzzle' and an impressive assortment of suspects) with a psychosocial exploration of lesbian sexuality, and the interaction of people of different races and sexual identifications.

However, despite its element of generalisation, the distinction between the detective novel and the crime novel is useful in discussing the lesbian thriller. The majority of writers, in fact, choose to model their fiction on the format of the crime novel, since this lends itself more easily than the detective novel to the treatment of feminist themes and perspectives. The focus it places on character interest and psychology gives the writer scope to explore lesbian sexuality and experience, while the radical aspects of the mode, such as the questioning of the social hierarchy and legal system, provide a space for a critique of patriarchal power and the discriminatory treatment of lesbians and blacks. The urban setting associated with the genre enables the writer to explore the attractions, problems, and dangers of lesbian life in the city. The lack of firm closure which novels written in the mode often reveal accords with the open-ended nature of the feminist novel, which tends to represent both subjectivity and society in terms of process and flux.

However, the format of the crime novel, while giving the writer of the lesbian thriller the opportunity to treat themes of lesbian urban life and sexual and racial politics, also confronts her with problems of an ideological kind. Sarah Dreher, Katherine V Forrest and Barbara Wilson, by making the victim of the murder enquiry both female and the target of male attack, may be criticised for reproducing and perpetuating two passive stereotypes of femininity – *woman as victim* and *woman as enigma*. In fact, the only difference between the situation of the murder victim in many lesbian crime novels and the murder victim in the traditional novel is that 'the case' which she represents is investigated by a female sleuth, not a male one. Certain lesbian crime novels, moreover, also reproduce another conventionally passive image of femininity – *woman as the object of psychiatric enquiry*. Forrest and

Wilson, like their precursors in the traditional genre,[6] conflate the power-imbued role of crime investigator with the equally dominant one of psychoanalyst. Dory, the teenage murder victim in Forrest's *Murder at the Nightwood Bar*, attends the clinic of the feminist psychiatrist Dr Marietta Hall who, after the girl's death, passes on information about her to Kate, the sleuth. In Wilson's *Sisters of the Road* the investigator Pam, by reading Trish's diary and its intimate confessions, delves into her past and reconstructs her troubled adolescence in the manner of a psychoanalyst.

The roles and positions assigned to woman in the lesbian feminist thriller are not, however, entirely stereotypical. The negative image of her as the passive object of male violence, assigned to the murder victim, is offset by the positive representation of her as survivor, adept in the art of self-defence, which is assigned to the figure of the investigator. The varied interpretations which writers give this role, along with the urban setting which often forms its context, are illustrated by the novels of O'Rourke and Wings.

O'Rourke in *Jumping the Cracks* skilfully exploits the themes of social injustice, urban crime, and psychological interest associated with the traditional thriller, to explore issues that are specifically lesbian feminist. The novel is distinctively British in both theme and location. Neatly constructed though the plot is, it is of secondary importance to interests of a sociological and psychological kind. The real topics of the novel are the scandal of unemployment and inadequate housing, the division between North and South, and the economic and social decline of urban life which are depressingly familiar features of contemporary Britain. The analysis of these topics comes to us filtered through the perception of O'Rourke's working-class hero, Rats. Rats, a native of Hull, has moved down to London in order to make a fresh start in life, socially and in terms of work. Her response to the penury and loneliness of life on the dole alternates between bouts of lethargy, when she takes refuge in alcohol and sleep, and periods of frenetic activity, when she looks for employment and tries to cement the broken relationship with her girlfriend Helen. She also investigates, with a persistence verging on the fanatical, the mystery of the corpse which she glimpsed one night dumped on the passenger seat of a car parked in a Hackney street.

The urban location of the crime, combined with the novel's title *Jumping the Cracks*, alerts us to the fact that the city functions in this case primarily as a place of menace. The characters comment on the prevalence of urban violence and the personal tragedies to which it can give rise.[7] Key locations which Rats visits in the course of her investigations include the River Thames, ominously presented as the last resort of suicides and murder victims, and the local cemetery. Like her famous precursors Charles Dickens and Conan Doyle, who focused on urban locations, O'Rourke excels in the description of the streets, alleys and waterways of London.

In contrast to O'Rourke, who foregrounds the bleak aspects of lesbian urban life, Wings imbues her hero Emma Victor and her adventures in Boston with glamour. The contrary perspectives adopted by the two writers are reflected in differences of style. Whereas O'Rourke gives the reader the pleasures of identification and social realism, Wings, by cleverly parodying the style and imagery of Chandler's crime fiction, offers a stylised display of wit and pastiche.

Unlike Rats, who is working class, penniless and lacking in confidence, Emma Victor is middle class, affluent and, as her name suggests, buoyantly triumphant. Exuding an aura of glamour which is typically American in style, she eats in expensive restaurants and is extremely fashion conscious. She revels in the shifting scenarios of sexual encounters, masquerades and hair-breadth escapes which Wings invents for her. In portraying Emma's professional life, Wings attempts to combine a focus on individual enterprise with an interest in feminist collectivity. Emma has in the past made appearances on TV but, when the novel opens, she is dutifully helping her less fortunate sisters by answering distress calls on the local women's hotline. The reader, it is interesting to note, is positioned to identify not with the characters who are portrayed as victims or dropouts (Julie, the murder victim, and Sue, who is hooked on drugs) but with the attractive, successful Emma. This strategy has the advantage of identifying feminism with success and self-fulfilment, but it is problematic in that it makes it appear exclusive and élitist. Emma (the investigator), Frances (her lover) and Stacy (the villain) form, in fact, a triad of strong-willed, professional women. In representing their relations with one another, Wings skilfully exploits the conventions of both the American crime novel and the British detective novel. Adopting the Sherlock Holmes/Moriarty and the George Smiley/Karla paradigm,[8] she portrays Emma as experiencing a sense of affinity with Stacy, the villain, and recognising her as her double. Emma perceives, on meeting Stacy, similarities of personality and style.[9] Moreover, like the heroes in the fiction of Len Deighton and Ian Fleming, Emma at one stage suspects her lover Frances of being in cahoots with Stacy and implicated in a plot against her life. The focus Wings places on antagonism and competition between intelligent, university-educated women recalls the fiction of P D James and Josephine Tey.

As I mentioned earlier, writers of the lesbian feminist thriller generally favour the format of the crime novel. They seldom structure their works on the ideologically conservative design of the detective novel. One writer who does make this unusual choice is Val McDermid. Her novel *Report for Murder* illustrates the difficulties which the form poses for the lesbian writer.

Report for Murder is set in the socially elitist, enclosed world of a girls' boarding school in Derbyshire. The plot hinges on the murder of Lorna Smith-Couper, a famous cellist, who has agreed to play at a gala fundraising event to be held on the premises. The headmistress of the school, Pamela Overton, summons the assistance of Lindsay Gordon, journalist and amateur detective, to solve the crime. Lindsay eventually achieves this task, using the time-honoured methods of observation of clues, deduction and interrogating suspects that are associated with the traditional detective novel.

McDermid makes a valiant attempt to modify and transform the conservative, anti-feminist resonances of the novel's location and plot. The girls' boarding school recalls other similar all-women institutions in traditional detective novels – for example, Leys College in Josephine Tey's *Miss Pym Disposes*. However, instead of discrediting the place by representing it as a den of female jealousy and rivalry, as Tey tends to do, McDermid presents it in a positive manner. She emphasises the intelligence and co-operative abilities of the female staff. However, she also makes a point of criticising the elitism and privilege which the system of private education embodies. Lindsay, the investigator, who holds socialist views and has received a state education, is the mouthpiece of this critique.

Another conservative feature of the detective novel which McDermid attempts to remedy is its representation of femininity as a source of 'problems' and 'social disruption'. The negative portrayal of Lorna Smith-Couper, the murder victim, does fit this misogynistic stereotype. However, it is counteracted by

McDermid's positive treatment of certain other female characters. Moreover, though the murderer is initially assumed to be female, he turns out in the end to be male. He is, in fact, a typical representative of patriarchal, capitalist values.

McDermid's attempts to transform the conservative aspects of the detective novel are not totally successful. The novel is heavily schematic in design while the portrayal of character is, on occasion, simplistic and unconvincing.

THE INVESTIGATOR

The investigator who features in the traditional thriller and detective novel is generally portrayed as a figure of paradox and contradiction. She/he functions as the hub of character interaction in the text but is simultaneously depicted as an isolate who displays attributes of individualism and self-sufficiency. Although she/he works for the establishment and seeks to impose law and order, she/he is something of an outlaw who exists on the perimeter of society. And, while she/he strives to uncover conspiracy and extirpate crime, in carrying out the investigations, she/he uses methods involving violence and deceit.

An element of contradiction is also apparent in the actual construction of the investigator's character. Although she/he appears at first sight to represent a unified subjectivity, her/his personality reveals, in fact, a marked discrepancy between role and identity, and often reflects the modernist tradition of the fractured self. Beneath the hard-boiled, defensive pose adopted by the investigator in American crime fiction such as Chandler's Marlowe lie qualities of sensitivity, anxiety and insecurity.[10] Moreover, as Christopher Rollason points out, the sleuth, in attempting to identify with the thought processes of the criminal in order to reconstruct her/his motives and deeds, is her/himself temporarily transformed into 'an unstable, incoherent subject'.[11] She/he functions, on a mental level, as the criminal's double.

The profile of the traditional investigator, outlined above, foregrounds some of the problems which confront the writer of the lesbian feminist thriller in creating her own particular version of the figure. The attributes of ruthlessness and violence, traditionally assigned to the investigator, contravene feminist principles and ideals. Her/his individualism and arrogant belief in her/his own superior mental abilities are, of course, antithetical to feminist concepts of co-operation and collectivity. It is interesting to note that the lesbian feminist thriller is a product of the 1980s, a period when, with Thatcher and Reagan in power, right-wing ideals of individual enterprise were in the ascendant.

Yet, although the ruthlessness and individualism conventionally attributed to the investigator confront the writer with difficulties, they also, in my view, help to account for the vitality of the lesbian feminist thriller and its current popularity. They encourage writers to confront and explore certain themes which, since they conflict with the orthodoxies of feminist politics, seldom receive discussion in the Women's Movement. These themes include antagonism and competition between women, and the problematic aspects of collective action and decision-making. An unresolved conflict between individualism and collectivity lies, in fact, at the heart of a number of these novels. One of the characters in Wilson's *Murder in the Collective* astutely observes that collective methods of working are ill suited to the investigation of crime. [12]

Writers of the lesbian feminist thriller, moreover, invent a number of different strategies to interrogate and qualify the attributes of self-sufficiency and individualism conventionally assigned to the investigator. They subject these attributes to scrutiny – and deconstruct and undermine them. They also develop the qualities of insecurity and anxiety, along with the emphasis on the fractured self, which, as mentioned above, characterise the traditional representation of the figure. And on occasion, by emphasising the investigator's dependence on certain other characters in the novel, they transform the murder investigation into a co-operative enterprise.

O'Rourke in *Jumping the Cracks* successfully re-models the discrepancy between role and identity which is a conventional feature of the investigator's personality, so as to explore the survival tactics which lesbians adopt in urban life. The methods which she uses to achieve a balance between concepts of individualism and collectivity also merit discussion.

Like the investigator in the American crime novel, Rats, the hero of O'Rourke's novel, conceals attributes of intelligence and sensitivity beneath a taciturn exterior. An introvert loner, she is sullen and uncommunicative in her relations with acquaintances and employers, hiding her lesbianism under a defensive mask. Her unprepossessing persona hides, moreover, qualities of courage, perception and a capacity for deep emotional commitment. She values her relationship with her lover Helen for the significant emotional stability which it provides – and temporarily goes to pieces when it collapses. Rats also displays other affinities with the investigator in the American crime novel. She is separated from the world of urban crime which she investigates and yet, since she earns a living from working in a seedy accommodation agency which turns out to belong to the villain Pershing, she is simultaneously implicated in it. The need for economic survival leads her on occasion to compromise her integrity by participating unwillingly in her employer's ruthless schemes.

Rats, who is the archetypal loner and has difficulty in maintaining personal relationships, epitomises the attributes of individualism and independence which are traditionally assigned to the figure of the investigator. Helen, her lover, is, on the contrary, a vehicle for ideas of feminist collectivity. She is extrovert, makes friends easily and expresses her belief in the value of co-operative action by successfully organising a campaign for improved housing. The contrast between the two characters, and the opposing interests which they represent, is psychologically convincing and dramatically vivid.

A more complex analysis of the tensions between individualism and collectivity is found in Wilson's *Murder in the Collective*. Wilson creates, in conjunction with an exciting crime story, a cogently argued debate on the strengths and weaknesses of collective organisation and action. Centering the narrative on two collective business enterprises, she explores the contradictions inherent in trying to implement principles of collectivity in a capitalist society committed to competition and individual success. The topic of collectivity is one which interests me personally. I have worked for a number of years on a lesbian line in East Anglia and have experience of both the positive and negative aspects of collective organisation. Like other feminists,[13] I criticise its structures and practices as inefficient and cumbersome but, at the same time, recognise the advantages of flexibility and continuity they undoubtedly possess. Wilson's representation of collectivity is, in my opinion, very fair. While illustrating its practical difficulties, she highlights its basic value.

As well as exploring the strengths and weaknesses of collective organisation, Wilson also foregrounds, in her portrayal of the amateur sleuth Pam Nilsen, the problems of the investigator's role.

The fraught experience of interrogating suspects jolts Pam into recognising the brutal aspects of the role and its incompatibility with feminist attitudes.

In her subsequently published novel *Sisters of the Road*[14] Wilson continues to interrogate and deconstruct the role of investigator, alerting the reader to its implications of power. At the start of the novel Pam Nilsen, again cast in the role of investigator, displays the attributes of arrogance and self-sufficiency which are conventionally assigned to the male sleuth. As the novel progresses, however, her pretensions to self-sufficiency and superior intelligence are slowly but surely deflated. She is portrayed as becoming increasingly dependent on other people both in her crime-investigating activities and in her personal life.

And, while deflating Pam's pretensions to self-sufficiency and infallibility, Wilson also undercuts her autonomy. Instead of portraying her as a unitary figure, she goes out of her way to depict her subjectivity as contradictory and heterogeneous. The relationship which Pam forms with Trish, the teenage companion of the murder victim whom she befriends, illustrates this particular point. Pam plays in relation to Trish the roles of sister, mentor and comforter. In the final pages of the novel Wilson unexpectedly collapses the distance between the two characters. Pam is brutally raped by Wayne, the villain who on a previous occasion sexually initiated and terrorised Trish, and thus she temporarily becomes Trish's double.

A more controversial representation of the lesbian investigator than O'Rourke's and Wilson's is Forrest's portrayal of Kate Delafield, the sleuth in *Murder at the Nightwood Bar*. Kate is a member of the Los Angeles police force, she has a butch persona and, in one disturbing episode, she is so angered by a man's aggressive behaviour that she momentarily loses control, attacks him with her fists and injures his nose.[15] These aspects of Kate's portrayal disconcert feminist critics. Munt, for example, appears uncomfortable with Kate's butch persona and with the contradictions of her being a lesbian cop (pp. 94–99). Since I interpret the novel in a more sympathetic light, I intend to reappraise these particular points.

The butch position which Kate exemplifies is, of course, a contentious issue among lesbian feminists. In the early years of the Women's Movement lesbians who adopted it were criticised for mimicking male codes of behaviour. Recently, however, the position has been revalued from a historical perspective. The American writer Joan Nestle comments perceptively:

> Butch-femme relationships, as I experienced them, were complex erotic statements, not phony heterosexual replicas. They were filled with a deeply Lesbian language of stance, dress, gesture, loving, courage and autonomy. None of the butch women I was with, and this includes a passing woman, ever presented themselves to me as men; they did announce themselves as tabooed women who were willing to identify their passion for other women by wearing clothes that symbolized the taking of responsibility. Part of this responsibility was sexual expertise. In the 1950s this courage to feel comfortable with arousing another woman became a political act.[16]

Nestle's comments, by shedding light on the complexities of the butch position, help to clarify Forrest's portrayal of Kate Delafield. Kate's lesbianism, despite the fact that she discreetly avoids mentioning it, is an open secret in the crime squad in which she works. Since she performs her job efficiently, her colleagues turn a blind eye to it, tolerating though not really accepting her lesbian orientation. It is also, she uneasily perceives, recognised by the visitors to the Nightwood Bar, the lesbian club which forms the centre of her detective investigation. The tensions of Kate's position, trapped as she is between the establishment world of the police force and the lesbian ghetto of the club, constitute the novel's central theme. It is the emphasis which Forrest places on Kate's butch persona, the signifier of her status as 'tabooed woman', which facilitates the exploration of these tensions – along with other important themes such as the irrational nature of homophobia, and the bigotry and stigmatisation which lesbians encounter. A positive feature of Forrest's novel is that, unlike Wilson and Wings who limit their analysis to the protected space of the middle-class feminist collective or friendship coterie where lesbianism is seen as socially acceptable, she explores themes of prejudice and discrimination not necessarily encountered there.

Another topic which Forrest discusses is the controversial one of *female violence*. Forrest deconstructs the position Kate occupies in the police force, teasing out its contradictions. Far from endorsing Kate's sudden violent outburst against the man, Forrest represents it as a symptom of personal conflict, reflecting the tensions between her role as police detective and 'her rage as a lesbian woman' (p. 109). The episode is, in fact, central to the novel's narrative design since it links Kate, on a symbolic plane, to the figure of the murderer who, in this particular novel, is female. Kate, though differing from the murderer in age, sexual orientation and ideological perspectives, shares with her a significant contradiction: she is a woman who, while priding herself on her integrity and sense of responsibility, reacts passionately to events and is capable of committing an act of violence.

Munt also criticises Forrest for taking a biologistic and essentialist approach to lesbianism (p. 98). Here I think she makes the error of attributing views expressed by Kate to the author. Kate's opinions are not presented uncritically but, on the contrary, are challenged by the other characters and subjected to debate.

SEX, RACE AND AGE

A standard component of the lesbian feminist detective and crime novel is, as I mentioned earlier, passages describing sexual relations and encounters between women. A focus on sex is, in fact, a distinctive feature of lesbian crime fiction, differentiating it from lesbian fiction of a more general kind in which it occurs less frequently. Contemporary writers such as Caeia March and Anna Wilson, reacting against the identification of lesbianism with the sex act and influenced by puritanical trends in the Women's Movement,[17] make scarcely any reference to lesbian sexual practice. They concentrate instead of themes of lesbian romance and woman-bonding. The reason that writers of lesbian crime fiction have escaped these repressive influences and feel free to introduce descriptions of sexual encounters into their novels lies, I suggest, in the area of genre and convention. The thriller is traditionally categorised as escapist entertainment and, as illustrated by the fiction of Ian Fleming and Martin Sands, frequently includes descriptions of sex. This gives the thriller writer a licence to focus on sexual practice which is denied to writers of other kinds of lesbian fiction. It is one which she understandably exploits.

In representing sexual encounters between women, the writer of the lesbian thriller draws on a variety of conflicting and contradictory cultural discourses. The most prominent is the conventional, power-imbued discourse of heterosexual relations. This is constructed around the polarised positions of masculine/ feminine and the antithesis of dominance/subordination. Motifs associated with it, such as dress codes, sexual objectification and 'the look', feature prominently in the novels of Forrest and Wings. The treatment of 'the look' by the two writers is particularly interesting. They transgress patriarchal gender conventions by portraying female characters appropriating the look. In Forrest's *Amateur City* Kate, who is attracted to Ellen, stares intently at her, causing her to behave and move self-consciously.[18] In Wings' *She Came Too Late* Emma, gazing appreciatively at Julie Arbeder, notices that 'she had a broad chest and the silk shirt was pulling slightly against her small breasts' (p. 13). However, as this quotation illustrates, the effect of the transgression is certainly not radical. Woman continues to be the focus of sexual objectification – though in this case she is objectified not by the male gaze but by that of the female character and reader. The look of Kate and Emma carry the narrative forward, and the reader, who is positioned to identify with it, shares in its implications of power.

The use which Wings makes of the motif of 'the look' is considerably more self-aware and subversive than Forrest's is. Wings humorously parodies the macho gaze of the traditional male sleuth and its capacity to objectify – as in Emma's enthusiastic description of Frances Cohen's figure: 'She had real hips, real lady's hips like two holsters hanging below her waist' (p. 37). Using devices of cliché and exaggeration, Wings alerts the reader to the contradictory brutality/absurdity of male fantasy projections of women.

The motif of 'the look', as well as carrying the usual sexual connotations, sometimes signifies in the lesbian thriller intellectual curiosity. The female sleuth, by insisting on investigating and 'looking into' the facts of the crime, transgresses patriarchal gender codes. By so doing, she risks punishment, including intimidation and physical assault. O'Rourke, in fact, cleverly uses the proverb 'Curiosity killed the cat' as a key structuring device in *Jumping the Cracks*. The villain Pershing, commenting on the persistent attempts he has made to intimidate and frighten Rats, quotes the proverb in a manner which is unpleasantly ominous and threatening (p. 102).

Another discourse which writers of the lesbian feminist thriller appropriate in representing sexual encounters between women is the discourse of mother/daughter relations in the pre-oedipal stage.[19] The importance of the theme of the pre-oedipal to the lesbian thriller has been noted by critics. Munt, discussing the attack on patriarchal power which typifies the genre, asks the pertinent question: 'I want to know what is the symbolic and psychoanalytic import of "murdering our fathers"? To retrieve that ideal and perfect union with our mothers perhaps . . . is that why I'm reading these books?' (p. 106). Munt's hypothesis that one of the pleasures which the lesbian thriller offers the reader is the analysis of love between women in terms of a displaced version of the mother/daughter bond is substantiated by reference to particular novels. Andrea Ross, a visitor to the Nightwood Bar, comments directly on the symbolic importance of the mother/daughter dyad. She describes Dory, the teenage murder victim, as subliminally engaged in 'looking for a mother lover'. She also tentatively suggests, 'I suspect sometimes we're just trying to get back to a safer time when we were our mothers' daughters. Back to when we were children and had no knowledge of men and how much they would control our lives' (p. 31). Andrea's notably idealised representation of mother/daughter relations as an untroubled haven of tranquillity, one which feminist psychoanalysts reject,[20] is contradicted, of course, by the actual events of the novel. In portraying Dory's relations with her biological mother Flora Quillin, and with her surrogate mother Dr Marietta Hall, Forrest foregrounds the destructive, power-ridden aspect of mother/daughter relations as well as the nurturing loving side.

Wings in *She Came Too Late* also depicts relations between women, both 'platonic' and sexual, in terms of a displaced version of the mother/daughter dyad. Emma, the investigator, admits to feeling 'an unrelenting, silly maternalism' towards Sue, an acquaintance who is hooked on drugs (p. 71). Wings' descriptions of Emma's love relationship with Frances Cohen alternates between power-ridden images verging on the sado/masochistic, and tender references to maternal nurturance. Emma's first physical encounter with Frances takes, in fact, the form of a humorous parody of the mother-daughter positions. Emma is pushed against Frances in a crowd of people, loses her balance – and discovers with astonishment and delight 'then she was on the floor and I was in her lap!' (p. 6).

Writers sometimes allude by implication to the theme of the mother/daughter dyad. O'Rourke in *Jumping the Cracks* describes the pleasures of sexual relationships not in terms of the dizzying excitement of orgasm, as male thriller writers such as Fleming do, but in terms of the female subject enjoying the luxury of dropping her self-protective mask, vulnerably weeping, and receiving comfort:

> Helen abandoned their earlier caution and reached out for Rats with both her arms. 'Oh my poor love, my poor, poor love. What a time you've been having.' In the face of such warmth Rats broke down and was comforted. (p. 91)

It is a luxury which Rats herself, and many lesbian readers whom the bigoted attitudes of society force to live closeted lives, seldom enjoy. This no doubt explains the powerful impact the episode makes.

The lesbian feminist detective and crime novel, while giving a fascinating insight into contemporary approaches to lesbian sexuality, also shows writers attempting to modify and transform the oppressive attitudes to race manifested by the traditional thriller. The latter is, in fact, notorious for its racism. Writers as different as Conan Doyle, Poe and Fleming, identifying white society with order and civilisation, assign the role of criminal to blacks, Asians and foreigners in general. The role carries disruptive and, on occasion, subhuman implications.

The attempt made by writers of the lesbian feminist thriller to challenge and transform these oppressive attitudes and stereotypes meets with varying degrees of success. 'Tokenism' is common. Forrest's *Murder at the Nightwood Bar* and Wings' *She Came Too Late*, though introducing positive representations of black female characters, give them relatively minor roles and show little interest in exploring their subjectivity. In contrast, other novels, such as Forrest's *Amateur City*, offer intelligent discussions of issues relating to race. The most complex and comprehensive analysis of the situation of blacks and women of colour is provided by Wilson in *Murder in the Collective*. The plot hinges on the Filipino resistance movement and the oppressive treatment of Filipino immigrants to the USA. June and Zee are assigned a significant role in the action and the problematic aspects of their situation explored in detail.

The majority of lesbian thriller writers, while making some attempt to challenge racist stereotypes, make little or no effort to challenge prejudices relating to age. The fashionable age for the lesbian investigator in the selection of novels discussed in this essay is around 30. Women above the age of 40 are either erased from the text (O'Rourke's *Jumping the Cracks* and Wilson's *Sisters of the Road*) or assigned minor roles (McDermid's *Report for Murder*) or the role of villain (Forrest's *Murder at the Nightwood Bar*). Older women, on the rare occasions when they do appear, tend to be described in terms of cliché. Pamela Overton, the middle-aged headmistress of the Derbyshire boarding school in McDermid's *Report for Murder*, is portrayed as (surprise, surprise!) 'an imposing woman in her late fifties' (p. 15). The most irritating strategy is the one adopted by Wings, who, while deleting women over 40, hypocritically pays lip service to the value of age, treating signs of ageing as fashionable. Emma Victor, intent as usual on advertising her feminist credentials, proudly announces to the reader that she possesses 'three nice wrinkles and a sprinkle of grey hair'! (p. 113)

There is one writer who is an exception in this respect, since she makes a deliberate effort to challenge prejudices relating to age. This is Sarah Dreher. In *Stoner McTavish*, [21] as well as gently mocking the prejudiced attitudes of her youthful investigator Stoner, she introduces several convincingly drawn representations of older women. These characters are, however, subsidiary and marginal actors in the narrative.

The propensity of writers of the lesbian detective and crime novel to erase or marginalise older and elderly women from their novels is, in actual fact, surprising. It runs counter to trends in contemporary lesbian fiction in general, where older women often play central roles, and is also at odds with detective fiction of the traditional kind. Christie's Miss Marple and Tey's Miss Pym each constitute the hub of the particular narrative in which they appear. Both characters, though dismissed by Kaplan on account of their conservative attitudes, display attributes of intelligence, strength and a degree of hard-won power. I have to admit that, as an older woman, I often gain more enjoyment from reading about their adventures than I do from reading about the exploits of the youthful investigators who appear in lesbian crime fiction.

The lesbian feminist detective and crime novel is, of course, still at an early stage of development – and perhaps in the future writers will start to address the topic of age. I look forward to seeing what they produce. Who knows, somebody may publish an equivalent to June Arnold's brilliantly witty *Sister Gin*,[22] which focuses on the lives of older women and reflects, in fact, an element of the thriller in its composition.

NOTES

1 Barbara Wilson, *Ambitious Women*, The Women's Press, London, 1983; Spinsters Ink, New York, 1982.

2 Sally Munt, 'The Investigators: Lesbian Crime Fiction', in Susannah Radstone, ed., *Sweet Dreams: Sexuality, Gender and Popular Fiction*, Lawrence & Wishart, London, 1988, pp. 92–95. Subsequent references are in the text.

3 'An Unsuitable Genre for a Feminist?', *Women's Review*, 8 (1986), pp. 18–19.

4 See Rosalind Coward and Linda Semple, 'Tracking Down the Past: Women and Detective Fiction', in Helen Carr, ed., *From My Guy to Sci Fi: Genre and Women's Writing in the Postmodern World*, Pandora, London, 1989, pp. 39–57.

5 Julian Symons, *Bloody Murder: From the Detective Story to the Crime Novel: A History*, Penguin, Harmondsworth, 1972, pp. 162–164. See also Jerry Palmer, *Thrillers: Genesis and Structure of a Popular Genre*, Edward Arnold, London, 1978, pp. 40–52.

6 See Gary Day, 'Investigating the Investigator: Hammett's Continental Op', in Brian Docherty, ed., *American Crime Fiction*, Macmillan, Basingstoke, 1988, p.45.

7 *Jumping the Cracks*, Virago, London, 1987, p. 100. Subsequent references are in the text.

8 See the detective stories of Conan Doyle and le Carré's *Smiley's People*, Hodder and Stoughton, London, 1980.

9 *She Came Too Late*, The Women's Press, London, 1986, p. 109. Subsequent references are in the text.

10 See Stephen Knight, '"A Hard Cheerfulness": An Introduction to Raymond Chandler', in Docherty, pp. 80–82.

11 'The Detective Myth in Edgar Allen Poe's Dupin Trilogy', in Docherty, p. 7.

12 Barbara Wilson, *Murder in the Collective*, The Women's Press, London, 1984, p. 132; Seal Press, Seattle, 1984.

13 See Jo Freeman, *The Politics of Women's Liberation: A Case Study of an Emerging Social Movement and Its Relation to the Policy Process*, Longman, London, 1975; and Joreen, 'The

Tyranny of Structurelessness', in Anne Koedt, Elen Levine and Anita Rapone, eds., *Radical Feminism*, Quadrangle, New York, 1973, pp. 285–289.

14 Barbara Wilson, *Sisters of the Road*, The Women's Press, London, 1986.

15 *Murder at the Nightwood Bar*, Pandora, London, 1987, p. 85; Naiad, Tallahassee, USA, 1987. Subsequent references are to the Pandora edition and are in the text.

16 Joan Nestle, 'Butch-Femme Relationships: Sexual Courage in the 1950s', *A Restricted Country*, Firebrand, New York, 1987, pp. 100–101.

17 See Nestle, 'My History with Censorship', *A Restricted Country*, p.149.

18 *Amateur City*, Pandora, London, 1987, p. 60; Naiad, USA, 1984.

19 See Joanna Ryan, 'Psychoanalysis and Women Loving Women', in Sue Cartledge and Ryan, eds., *Sex and Love: New Thoughts on Old Contradictions*, The Women's Press, London, 1983, pp. 196–209.

20 See Judith Kegan Gardiner, 'Mind Mother: Psychoanalysis and Feminism', in Gayle Greene and Coppélia Kahn, eds., *Making a Difference: Feminist Literary Criticism*, Methuen, London, 1985, pp. 113–145.

21 Sarah Dreher, *Stoner McTavish*, Pandora, London, 1987.

22 June Arnold, *Sister Gin*, The Women's Press, London, 1979.

PRIMARY INTENSITIES: LESBIAN POETRY AND THE READING OF DIFFERENCE
Liz Yorke

VALIDATING THE LESBIAN BODY

> It is, after all, always the meaning, the reading of difference that
> matters, and meaning is culturally engendered and sustained.
> Not to consider the body as some absolute (milk, blood, breasts,
> clitoris) for no 'body' is unmediated. Not body but the 'body' of
> psychosocial fabrications of difference. Or again, of sameness.
> Or again, of their relation.
>
> Rachel Blau DuPlessis[1]

In this essay, I explore the re-visionary strategies of a number of
women poets who are engaged in an attempt to construct a
language which adequately re-visions the body, sexuality and
libidinal trajectory of the lesbian woman. Coming to terms with
lesbian sexuality involves the poets in the political effort of
devising a pro-visional poetic strategy – as a means to make
explicit what has been excluded from patriarchal discourses. This
rethinking requires a major reorganisation of sexual, linguistic
and socio-symbolic systems, and, in addition, requires theorising
the female body as a positivity rather than a lack. I will draw on
Elizabeth Grosz's Irigarayan conceptualisations of the body as:

structured, inscribed, constituted and given meaning *socially* and *historically* – a body that exists as such only through its socio-linguistic construction. She [Irigaray] renders the concept of a 'pure' or 'natural' body meaningless. Power relations and systems of representations not only traverse the body and utilise its energies (as Kristeva claims) but actively constitute the body's very sensations, pleasures – the phenomenology of bodily experience.[2]

Recoding the lesbian body involves the poets in a strategic and transgressive effort to put in place new representations within language. Their effort is frequently directed towards countering the negative terms of Freudian and Lacanian accounts of the formation of a gendered identity. If gendered identity is not necessarily 'the result of biology, but of the *social and psychical meaning of the body*', then the way is open to reconceive of lesbian sexuality in terms other than the patriarchally given. Rather than seeing these poems as encoding a language of authentic female being, I shall analyse the fabrication of meaning that takes place within the mythical 'body' of a number of women's poems.

The language of poetry especially lends itself to the lesbian feminist poet's strategic and combative project, that is, the critique and revaluation of the coding of lesbian sexuality from different perspectives and locations within culture. Politically motivated lesbian poetry is interested in displacing inherited male models and myths through both a recoding of the relations between the self and 'the other' – and a positive revaluing of a female body whose sexuality is lived *in other terms*. A poetry not necessarily concerned with the 'exclusion' of men as such, but rather, in Rich's words, with 'that *primary presence of women to ourselves and each other* first described in prose by Mary Daly, and which is the crucible of a new language'.[3]

As well as breaking through the cultural taboo against the depiction of an affirming lesbian sexuality in art, these poems render historically visible *reconstructed representations* which endeavour to treat the primary intensity of lesbian eroticism with respect and reverence. In effect, the poems offer a position for the lesbian woman subject with which it is possible in delight and/or in anguish, to identify. The poet constructs a position or positions within language which offer lesbian women self-validating experiences. I see this poetry especially as offering a lesbian reader the validating experience of being able to recognise and realise her own position (or that of other women) *as an identity* in and through language. I use the term 'identity' in this special sense: identity is to be viewed as a desired position for the subject, constructed here so as to legitimate and validate particular lesbian viewpoints.

The poems included in this essay are chosen because they offer a legitimating, cleansing, recuperative version of lesbian erotic life and its corresponding dimensions of joy and loss. Crucially, they embody a refusal to collaborate with the coercive, almost palpable, interlocking construct of heterosexual ideology, language and law which would deny and/or misrepresent the wholesome validity of the lesbian trajectory of desire, as well as attempting to delegitimate and harass the lesbian subject.

Luce Irigaray, French feminist theorist, pays particular attention to the relation between mother and daughter, a relation inadequately theorised either in Freud or Lacan. She draws attention to the fact that, within western patriarchal cultures, women's relationships with their mothers, and with other women, are devalued. She argues that the little girl suffers 'narcissistic distress' because this primary 'carnal' relation to her mother is so censored, her own body is underestimated, even 'reviled', like her mother's (in Freudian and Lacanian psychoanalytic terms), as castrated. She argues that:

> a woman, if she cannot in one way or another, recuperate her first object (i.e. make real the possibility of keeping her first earliest libidinal attachments by displacing them onto an/Other), is always exiled from herself.[4]

How does she return from exile? How does a woman reclaim her 'self' and (as Irigaray puts it) *re-mark*, in language, her different economy of representation? Can she articulate an economy of desire that is not based on an assumption of the anatomical inferiority of the female and that will not concede anything to the hierarchy of values ordained within heterosexual phallocentric ideology? In particular, how does the lesbian poet put her relation to other women into words and inscribe the specificity of her desire within the symbolic? Is it possible to reconstitute herself as subject through the body, touch, words and gaze of the lesbian Other – within and despite, the debilitating and destructive systems of patriarchy? Adrienne Rich, in her poem 'Origins and History of Consciousness', explores this struggle:

> It was simple to meet you, simple to take your eyes
> into mine, saying: these are eyes I have known
> from the first . . . It was simple to touch you
> against the hacked background, the grain of what we
> had been, the choices, years . . . It was even simple
> to take each other's lives in our hands, as bodies.
>
> What is not simple: to wake from drowning
> from where the ocean beat inside us like an afterbirth
> into this common, acute particularity
> these two selves who walked half a lifetime untouching –
> to wake to something deceptively simple: a glass
> sweated with dew, a ring of the telephone, a scream
> of someone beaten up far down in the street
> causing each of us to listen to her own inward scream
>
> knowing the mind of the mugger and the mugged
> as any woman must who stands to survive this city,
> this century, this life . . .⁵

Rich does not here imagine an ideal separatist world in which women may ecstatically rejoice in their discovery of one another.⁶ Rather, she shows these women as actively struggling for survival, working together as lovers who trust each other. Lowered down an almost umbilical rope, they explore new ways of being in relationship. The metaphors of darkness and light point to a relationship in which contradictions and negativity are fully searched out and revealed. The women recognise each other, identify each other in the metaphoric darkness of the womb, and this new conception is for them an *illumination*. They are 'drenched in light' within the darkness. Their coming together is marked by a joyful ecstasy – sexual, spiritual, mystic – as each identifies the other in the non-dualist patterns of language Rich has taken so much care to construct:

> Trusting, untrusting,
> we lowered ourselves into this, let ourselves
> downward hand over hand as on a rope that quivered

over the unsearched . . . We did this. Conceived
of each other, conceived each other in a darkness
which I remember as drenched in light.

Each woman is desired by and desires both the m/Other, and her
woman lover as Other. Each woman participates in the symbolic
'conception' of the other: they are 'mothers' *birthing* each other
into language *through trust*. In Irigaray's words: 'We find ourselves
as we entrust ourselves to each other.'[7] Yet, at the same time, both
live in a world of darkness, crisis and painful contradictions, a
world where the 'inward scream' is matched by the scream of
'someone beaten up far down in the street' (p. 8).

In using these metaphors of conception, Rich draws on the
watery, oceanic, (heart) beating imagery of the womb/mother.
The metaphors of conception, darkness and drowning – the
suffocating panic of birth trauma – interconnect with metaphors
of illumination, of awakening, of being 'drenched in light'. The
women accept the mutual affirmation of the maternal gaze – and
the associated pattern that inevitably accompanies this relation:
the 'trusting, untrusting' that none the less enables the women to
'take each other's lives in our hands, as bodies'. The poet's use of
'us' indicates that both women simultaneously experience this
return to the maternal oceanic space of womb/water as well as
experiencing the exit from that space, the waking moment of
rebirth. Their return is not, therefore, to some idyllic place of
origin to re-establish contact and continuity with the mother but is,
rather, conceived as a frightening rebirth or spiritual awakening –
into a fuller understanding of the situation of women in
patriarchy.

The poem itself is deceptively simple. Paradoxically, the
mutually returned gaze between herself and her lover, of 'eyes I
have known from the first', may again be interpreted as signalling
the woman's recuperation of the gaze exchanged between infant
and mother. This symbolic desiring connection to the mother is
recalled as difficult and dangerous. Yet the women 'conceive' of
each other, recover each other from exile. This 'return' enables the
women to become 'two selves' in relation. The lives of the women,
together '*as bodies*' are present to each other, are able to revalue
each other. The women are no longer represented as *object* to the
male gaze, but as equally participating in a mirroring inter-
relationship:

> We did this. Conceived
> of each other, conceived each other in a darkness
> which I remember as drenched in light.

The all important adjunct 'of', differentiates active from passive mode, actor from acted upon, but the phrase 'each other' will not permit the patriarchal dualistic and hierarchical division into acting subject and acted on object: each *conceives* the other, is mother and daughter interchangeably, is both subject and object, is dark 'drenched' in light, reciprocally. As Irigaray puts it: 'Night and day are mingled in our gazes, our gestures, our bodies.'[8]

The mutuality and equality of this womanly mode of relating seem to be crucial to constructing an ideal, one which serves the utopian goal of building a 'gender/class/race-free' community for the social support and sexual and emotional enrichment of lesbian lives. At the same time and paradoxically, this seductive and inspiring utopian vision tends to deny, or seems to transcend, differences in economic power, class status and the experience of racial discrimination, not only within society, but also between one lesbian woman and another. It is necessary to be aware of the inbuilt contradictions of this position. It is also necessary to recognise that this effacement of the differences of race and class is a mid 1970s phenomenon which responded to the political urgencies of the time, those of forging an initial sense of solidarity between all women to set against the devastating fragmentation between women created by patriarchal social structures.

Today feminists face a somewhat different task, that of claiming and naming – sometimes celebrating, sometimes mourning – diversity and difference between women. Yet, the necessity for making this commitment to mutuality and equality – and creating a political and cultural context where such a relation may have a chance of being realised – remains important. We still have a political need to sustain and celebrate the woman-woman bond as between one subject and another subject, rather than conceding anything to the subject/object model typical of heterosexual patriarchy – spelt out for us by Simone de Beauvoir, so long ago.

The 'I' – 'I' of subject and subject in equal relationship, may be seen as a radical calling into question of the hierarchical structures of the nuclear family – or of any extended patriarchal family situation where institutionalised and conventional heterosexual modes of relating still prevail. This challenge to the hierarchies of patriarchy underlies Rich's poetic (as it does that of Irigaray). But, the ideal language that restores the object to speech and, in a sense, banishes the transcendent patriarchal 'I' to silence, is the language of desire: that is, a language that escapes from repression, that emerges from the desire-laden unconscious, from the world of the dream. A dream from which, while patriarchy still exists, the woman must wake – to the reality of 'a scream of someone beaten up', that chilling sound that echoes her 'own inward scream' (p. 8).

Lesbian feminist poets, writing from a position of otherness, as from a different psychic economy, have responded to this call, first voiced by Daly and Rich, to re-structure language. The poets have especially tried to re-order the heterosexual codes that structure sexual difference – often in terms that are potentially disruptive to the social contract. In the transformed psychic economy proposed by lesbian poets, in their poetic representations of the woman's body, it is often and precisely the genital anatomical difference from the male which is celebrated and desired as an empowering source of pleasure, rather than being reviled as 'castrated'. In their diverse attempts to counter patriarchal heterosexual cultural codes, they have frequently tried to make real the possibility for a woman to keep in consciousness her deepest attachments to the mother, and have celebrated and mourned this attachment in the transformed and transforming context of one woman's love for another.

To name publicly such lesbian attachment involves women in a difficult emotional and intellectual journey. In actual lived practice, the process of identification – through naming and claiming an identity, through revealing the lesbian trajectory of desire and thus bringing the unspoken to speech – is far from easy. Susan Griffin's poem 'The Woman Who Swims in Her Tears', explores the painful soul-searching and self-questioning that accompanied this lesbian relationship of the early 1970s. Rich, speaking of this poem and commenting on the difficulty of 'getting away' from male defined language, of naming for *the first time*, indicates the challenge and struggle it was, then, to find an appropriate language for lesbian sexuality: 'That poem has just never been written before; it condenses in one poem so much of a very long process that two women may go through in order to come together at all.'[9]

> The woman
> who slept beside the body of one
> other woman weeping,
> the women who wept.
> the women whose tears wet
>   each other's hair
> the woman who wrapped her legs
>   around another woman's thigh
>   and said I am afraid.
> the woman who put her head
>   in the
> place between the shoulder and breast
>   of the other woman and
>   said, 'Am I wrong?'[10]

An impersonal voice tells of 'the woman', 'the other woman', 'the body of one other woman'. This voice, used to speak of this sexually intimate context, creates tension at different levels: privacy/revelation; proximity/distance; private/public space; concern/reluctance to intrude. There is tension too in the vague reference to other 'women'. There may be an inclusive movement outwards to indicate a community of like women, but where? how many? is not clearly defined. Who speaks? Why is there this distancing, this difficult, effortful repetition, this mode of anxiety, distress, self-questioning? These tensions gesture towards a struggle against muteness; a struggle to overcome the impediments to speech, the doubts, resistances, uncertainties; the struggle of dealing with raw conflict, of contradiction; and they indicate also the especially intense process of honestly bringing to language that which has been rigorously excluded from it:

> So much defiance needed for the possible. All the labour of feminism. Casting away all the denials of female experience. The denial of what we *know* to be true. Unwrapping yards of bandages. Like the bandages wrapped around the dead. From our eyes. Ears. Hands. Skin. All we are complicit in hiding.[11]

To come out of hiding and cast away 'all the denials' requires validation of lesbian identity at the deepest levels. To accept and to claim an identity, a lesbian 'I', that culture has taught everyone to despise, requires a major revaluation of both personal and cultural values. How is this defiant 'I' to be constructed so as to emerge from the silences of self-censorship and cultural exclusion?[12]

Drawing on Irigaray's account of the female psyche, I have suggested that the lesbian woman realises the possibility of renewing her first earliest libidinal attachments by displacing them on to a lesbian Other.

To theorise this further, I must (briefly) refer to Lacan. In his earlier exposition, Lacan proposes two fields which together give birth to the subject: 'the subject in the field of the drive and the subject as he [she] appears in the field of the Other'.[13] The Other, in articulating the chain of signifiers which govern 'whatever may be made present of the subject', thus plays an essential part in the construction of subjectivity in relation to the drive or libido.[14] Lacan stresses that the process of '*making oneself*' necessitates '*loving oneself through the other*'. By 'making oneself heard' and 'making oneself seen',[15] one is involved in 'subject making' – that is, working towards but never actually unifying the one, the one who is the (always divided) and constantly fading 'I' of apparent identity, appropriated out of and constituted within language.[16]

If we pursue the logic of Lacanian psychoanalysis to a point beyond Lacan's own emphasis, the reciprocal articulation of their desires of/for each other should play a part in the construction of the lesbian 'I'. I see the lesbian woman as learning to love and identify herself in the affirming field of meaning of the lesbian Other. I want to make the further suggestion that it is, at the deepest levels, the mirroring discourse of the lesbian *lover* which enables the lesbian subject to *make* her self, to identify herself so as to be seen and to be heard – to defiantly accept the costs and take the risks.

It is through receiving the deep acceptances of the reciprocal pleasures of lesbian love, that is, in the fullest dimensions of the physical, spiritual and sexual responses of her lover, that the lesbian woman is able to confirm the validity and integrity of her lesbian identity. In the context of poetry, this mirroring discourse may be seen as conveyed in the language of words or it may be conveyed in the gestural languages of the body or non-verbally, through the use of sexually or emotionally charged images.

Olga Broumas' fine poem 'Innocence' is especially interesting in this respect.[17] This poem draws its inspiration from body spirituality being developed by feminist women of many different faiths, who are exploring their spirituality and sexuality in theological terms.[18] In this poem, it is in the 'mirroring' symmetrical relation between (unlike) lesbian lovers – that is, in the reciprocal relation between 'Love, Love' and their 'merging shadows', Queen and Jester – that the lesbian sexual relation is ecstatically celebrated. This poem specifically validates each woman's lesbian sexuality, each woman's lesbian body, as being in and of God, the women's bodies being created in the image of God.

The poem images God herself as participating in the Love-making between the two women, the inventive and physically embodied hand of God appearing to produce *extra pleasure*. This manifest hand that is itself active in the sexual communion of the women, both is and is not, in and of them. She, God herself, is imaged as also around them, as the wind. This theology of the body dramatically counters fundamentalist (heterosexual and patriarchal) Christian pieties by representing religious ecstasy as of the body as well as the spirit, and, by representing the sexuality of the lesbian women as not merely without sin, but as divine and sacred in itself – as an aspect of God incarnate.

> God
> appears
>
> among us, elusive, the extra
> hand none of us – Love, Love, Jester, Queen –
> can quite locate, fix, or escape. Extra
> hand, extra
> pleasure. A hand
> with the glide of a tongue, a hand
> precise as an eyelid, a hand with a sense
> of smell, a hand that will dance
> to its liquid moan.
> God's hand
>
> loose on the four of us like a wind
> on the grassy hills of the South.

God is Love, physically embodied in, around and between these lesbian women – as they reciprocally give and receive the pleasures of sexual Love:

Manita's Love
opens herself to me, my sharp
Jester's tongue, my
cartwheels of pleasure. The Queen's own pearl
at my fingertips, and Manita pealing

my Jester's bells on our four
small steeples, as Sunday dawns

In this playful and complex reworking of the idea of church bells ringing in celebration, the nipples? clitoral bodies? of the women, as it were, become the 'small steeples' of the church of Love where God herself is worshipped.[19] In mutual joy, the 'Jester's bells' ring out their sexual ecstasy for all to hear – 'as Sunday dawns'. In the closing lines of this challenging poem, God herself affirms and applauds the innocence of this spiritual/sexual relation by clapping with her one hand, that is, by making an 'audible' sign from an approving Other, as one who herself participates in creating their lesbian identity, and who signals her acceptance and recognition of their sexual pleasure. Broumas, in using this 'impossible' Zen figuration, the 'sound' of one hand that 'claps and claps', creates a paradox within her poem: the sound, like lesbian sexuality itself, is both there and not there. Lesbian sexuality has been one of the most deafening silences of history and, even now, when it is spoken out and celebrated, it is a voice that is frequently simply *not heard*. A wry twist then, given the paradoxical hypocrisy of our cultural forms.

In the poem, this one hand seems to signal unconditional acceptance of lesbian sexuality, and is imaged by the poet as a part of God's creative 'making' of the lesbian sexual relation. This unconditional acceptance is also part of the poet's reconstruction of lesbian identity – in her creation of an affirming field of meaning for the lesbian reader, whether she is sexually active or not.

I want now to consider the specific position of black lesbian women. An affirming field of meaning is important to the white lesbian – but even if she suffers discrimination at work, at home, in social life, in religious life and elsewhere – she at least has access to 'skin privilege'. It must be even more important to the black lesbian woman who experiences, in addition to all the oppressive situations that can arise for the white lesbian, pernicious systematic racial and economic discrimination, sexual devaluation specific to black women and manifold overt and covert exclusions from certain fields of work, education and health care. There are no easy parallels to be drawn between black and white lesbian experience, though certain overlapping areas of oppression can be discerned.

It is also difficult to engage in any discussion of the dynamics of the bond between black mothers and their daughters according to the white western models formulated by Freud, Lacan and white French feminists. The limitations of this body of theory begin to be acutely felt wherever child-rearing practice does not conform to the typical western patterns of the patriarchal nuclear family. Black women, as mothers, have a pivotal and powerful role in many black families, but the mother is rarely sole carer for the child as in the white middle-class pattern. Black family networks have taken very different forms. In America, the extended family systems of Africa could not survive in their old patterns through the centuries of slavery and then through sustained racial and economic oppression. In the situations typical of today, the black mother is, of necessity, called upon to work to support her family – the grandmother, aunt, sister, cousin or any significant other of the extended family or circle of friends – may well be the one, or the one among many, to take care of her children. The child's relation to the mother is thus altered in important ways. The question arises: is Lacanian or post-Lacanian theory relevant in this changed context?

In her poem 'Black Mother Woman', Audre Lorde examines the nature of the conflict between herself and her own very powerful mother as a key figure in the relational process of self-definition.[20] The poet does not deny the difficulties of the relationship and it is clear that the political stance taken up by Audre Lorde is very different to that of her parents.

As daughter, the poet acknowledges the sharp edge of the mother's discipline: 'I cannot recall you gentle.'[21] Despite this, through the mother's pride, the daughter is able to recognise the love that is hidden in the silence of the not spoken, but which is, none the less, conveyed to her in more subtle ways. The poet acknowledges both the centrality of her respect and love for her mother's 'aged spirit', as well as her sense of distance and difference from her. She bears witness to her mother's long suffering acceptance of oppression, in these ambivalent lines:

> When strangers come and compliment me
> your aged spirit takes a bow
> jingling with pride
> but once you hid that secret
> in the center of furies
> hanging me
> with deep breasts and wiry hair
> with your own split flesh
> and long suffering eyes
> buried in myths of little worth.

In effect, the poet defines herself as other to her mother, in taking up a position very different from any her mother might have chosen. Yet, despite this, the daughter recognises the 'core of love' that enables the daughter to stand *as herself*:

> I have peeled away your anger
> down to the core of love
> and look mother
> I Am
> a dark temple where your true spirit rises
> beautiful
> and tough as chestnut
> stanchion against your nightmare of weakness
> and if my eyes conceal
> a squadron of conflicting rebellions
> I learned from you
> to define myself
> through your denials.

Alicia Ostriker has noted that 'this pattern of angry division and visionary reunion is especially important, in fact almost universal, among black and third-world women poets.'[22] She locates its source to the 'ambivalence of maternal attachment, associated with ambivalent views of the mother as power figure'.[23] The 'magically strong' bond between mother and daughter gives rise to these moving tributes to the black mother's strength and power-lessness. As a poet, Audre Lorde resists glossing over the anger, pain and sense of difference experienced by black people: '*I have a duty to speak the truth as I see it and to share not just my triumphs, not just the things that felt good, but the pain, the intense, often unmitigating pain.*'[24] This pain she experiences as the outcome of white supremacist racism, and of sexism, heterosexism, and homophobia – some of which, most hurtfully, emerges from black culture itself.[25] However, Lorde suggests that the courage to stand against all oppressive definition must come from love: 'what was beautiful had to serve the purpose of changing my life or I would have died.'[26] Lorde affirms the necessity to feel deeply, to feel joy, to love deeply as a crucial element of social protest: she bears witness to love above all:

> We define ourselves as lovers, as people who love each other all over again; we become new again. These poems insist that you can't separate loving from fighting, from dying, from hurting, but love is triumphant. It is powerful and strong, and I feel I grow a great deal in all of my emotions, especially in the capacity to love.
> The love expressed between women is particular and powerful, because we have had to love in order to live; love has been our survival.

In her poem 'Recreation', Audre Lorde affirms the possibility of identity re-creation through lesbian love-making: the lovers, 'moving through our word countries', affirm the 'coming-together' of each other's body – which is a poem.[27] This 'coming-together' is crucial to their creativity and writing, as to poetry, but is also crucial to the process of identifying each subjectivity to the other – through the signifying body of words. The categories: woman/ poem/flesh; you/me; earth/body; outside/inside – fuse, boundaries between them collapse into each other and lose their categorical specificity: the poem creates a woman-identified locus/field/'country' where the erotic 'flesh' may 'blossom' into 'the poem you make of me':

> . . . as your body moves
> under my hands
> charged and waiting
> we cut the leash
> you create me against your thighs
> hilly with images
> moving through our word countries
> my body

writes into your flesh
the poem
you make of me.

Touching you I catch midnight
as moon fires set in my throat
I love you flesh into blossom
I made you
and take you made
into me.

Lorde, in her essay, 'Uses of the Erotic: The Erotic as Power', sees
the erotic as a powerful resource, one that is 'firmly rooted in the
power of our unexpressed or unrecognised feeling'.[28] As in the
work of Olga Broumas and Adrienne Rich, the deepest erotic
passion of love is not merely a sensual, but is also a spiritual joy.
For Lorde, the erotic is 'a well of replenishing and provocative
force' (p. 54) and a source of 'power and information' (p. 53) – the
sharing of its joys being a provocative 'assertion of the lifeforce of
women' (p. 55). Lorde comments: 'Our erotic knowledge empowers
us, becomes a lens through which we scrutinize all aspects of our
existence, forcing us to evaluate those aspects honestly in terms of
their relative meaning within our lives' (p. 57). Representing the
lesbian sexual body, the sensual-emotional relationship, the
material geography of female pleasure in positive terms, becomes
a political strategy – the poet strives to generate a celebratory
mode of writing in which this empowering significance may be
found.

Thus it is at the level of erotic sexual pleasure that lesbian
difference makes itself most clearly apparent. The lesbian libidinal
economy is neither identifiable by a man nor can it be seen as
referrable to any masculine economy. Informing all of Adrienne
Rich's *The Dream of a Common Language* is her understanding of
the political – and spiritual – importance of this libidinal
connection between women at the level of the (textual) body:

I want to travel with you to every sacred mountain
smoking within like the sibyl stooped over her tripod,
I want to reach for your hand as we scale the path,
to feel your arteries glowing in my clasp,
never failing to note the small, jewel-like flower
unfamiliar to us, nameless till we rename her[29]

Libidinal difference, the 'smoking within' of lesbian sexual desire, is at the heart of this poem. The lesbian desire for physical connection to the other woman; the wish 'to feel' the (arterial) pulsing life of her blood; her body; the wish 'to travel' together; to 'scale the path' together. Again, in representing the contiguities and reciprocities of the woman-woman relation, in making visible the lesbian libidinal difference from the heterosexual trajectory, the poet's words 'burn' with the energy of libidinal and spiritual commitment to the lesbian 'path' which is to be undertaken outside the libidinal economies of the masculine symbolic order. It is the bodily presence of each to the other that empowers the women to rename 'the small jewel-like flower' of Poem XI, a flower that recalls Lorde's image of 'flesh into blossom';[30] and Olga Broumas' exotic lines from her revised myth, 'Leda and Her Swan': 'Scarlet/liturgies shake our room, amaryllis blooms/in your upper thighs, water lily/on mine, fervent delta'.[31]

In 'The Floating Poem, Unnumbered', from Adrienne Rich's *The Dream of a Common Language*, the image of the vaginal 'rose-wet cave' takes on a comparable value to Lorde's 'blossom'; and Broumas' 'amaryllis' or 'water lily' – as signifier of perfection, of the 'innocence and wisdom' of a sanctified and holy place. The 'Floating Poem', like Broumas' poem 'Innocence' is much influenced by the women's spirituality movement.[33] Its title (and possibly the title of her book) is taken from the zero card of the Tarot. This card, with no number and no specific place on the path, is, in effect, a floating card designated 'O', which, according to Vicki Noble, 'represents innocence, without ideas of sin or transgression', and is 'free to speak the truth without punishment or censorship, because we trust in the absolute innocence of her motivation'.[33] The poem, like the card, is resonant with infinitely joyful, carefree spontaneity, just as in Broumas' poem 'Innocence', it finds the route to 'pure wisdom' – here, to the 'innocence and wisdom' of the body of woman:

> Whatever happens with us, your body
> will haunt mine – tender, delicate
> your lovemaking, like the half-curled frond
> of the fiddlehead fern in forests
> just washed by sun . . .[34]

This superbly erotic language of touch, of tongue – of searching for and of reaching – which recognises the tender mutuality of the women, names, validates and dignifies the lesbian sexual bodily relation. Rich not only makes available what was previously 'unspeakable', censored, unwritten, and named only in patriarchal terms – but also transforms the codes in which this relation is signified, as a vital part of her re-visionary poetic. Once published and public this poem again becomes a self-conscious and urgent breaking through of the cultural taboo against the depiction of lesbian sensuality/sexuality in art. This language functions to displace the homophobic messages of obscenity, of disgust that bombard the lesbian from masculinist (and pornographic) culture. Viewed unromantically as an artistic revaluation of an always-already socialised bodily relation, the poem renders historically visible a reconstructed representation concerned with treating the primary intensity of lesbian eroticism with respect and reverence. In this context, Lorde's vulnerable and courageous 'Love Poem', eventually published in 1971, is comparable in its strategy, a strategy Rich recognises. She identifies (draws attention to) Lorde's poem, thus differentiating and confirming her position, and identifies with it – as a self-conscious choice. Rich comments in 'An Interview: Audre Lorde and Adrienne Rich', 'It was incredible. Like defiance. It was glorious.'[35]

> Speak earth and bless me with what is richest
> make sky flow honey out of my hips
> rigid as mountains
> spread over a valley
> carved out by the mouth of rain
>
> And I knew when I entered her I was
> high wind in her forests hollow
> fingers whispering sound
> honey flowed
> from the split cup
> impaled on a lance of tongues[36]

The warrior woman is an image very dear to Lorde, from which she derives the evocative symbolism of the mouth/tongue/word/speech – imagery which is intrinsically linked to the warrior imagery of the lance/sword/knives. Often in her work, words and languages become 'weapons' which are employed in the fight for the survival of black integrity. Ancestral myths and images drawn from Black African folklore form a vital part of Afro-American culture – and Audre Lorde powerfully develops this cultural project of reclamation in a feminist direction. Her use of these symbolic images gathers significance as we read, creating a symbolic network which resonates through many poems. In the poem 'Dahomey' for instance, we find the *fas* of the Nigerian god Shango, spelled out by a woman: 'I speak/ whatever language is needed/ to sharpen the knives of my tongue.'[37]

These images also link to Lorde's political desire to retain the concept of intrapsychic bisexuality: '*I have always wanted to be both man and woman, to incorporate the strongest and richest part of my mother and father within/into me – to share valleys and mountains upon my body the way the earth does in hills and peaks.*'[38]

These poets' refusal to submit to the coercive force of a condemnatory community, the challenge they offer to the pejorative clinical terminology of deviance – as well as their resistance to heterosexual ideology and practice mark a particular choice – to publicly and defiantly identify as lesbian, despite that identity being socially stigmatised. Perhaps inevitably, their challenge to heterosexual (medical or psychoanalytic) discursive practices finds as its locus or field the woman's erotic body – as the site of representation to be contested. These poets take responsibility for rewriting the codes informing lesbian social and sexual relations; for reformulating how 'the body', as locus in a network of relations, may be articulated. Thus, rather than accepting the conferred (despised) identity given within hostile but normative prescriptive discourses, the poets transform the codes, the categories: they change the rules. They offer another position for the lesbian subject to take up, to identify with, as a self-conscious cultural choice. Representing lesbians as normal rather than deviant; as sexually healthy rather than sexually 'sick'; as women whose behaviour is permissible rather than illegitimate – the poems, in effect, protest the privileged status of much judgmental prohibition concerning the lesbian and her 'unacceptable' erotic drives. Instead, they offer a legitimating, cleansing vision of her erotic life and its corresponding dimensions of joy and pain. The poets are involved in a process of producing, out of the erotic body's libidinal difference, social and political meanings unpoliced, uncensored, by a heterosexual patriarchy, validations which are woven into their poetry.

NOTES

1 The quotation is from Rachel Blau DuPlessis' essay. 'For the Etruscans' (1979), in Elaine Showalter, ed., *The New Feminist Criticism: Essays on Women, Literature and Theory*, Virago, London, 1986, p. 273.

2 Elizabeth Grosz, *Sexual Subversions: Three French Feminists*, Allen & Unwin, Sydney, 1989, p. 111.

3 Adrienne Rich, *On Lies, Secrets and Silence: Selected Prose 1966–1978*, Virago, London, 1980, p. 250.

4 Luce Irigaray, interviewed by Diana Adlam and Couze Venn, 'Women's Exile', in *Ideology and Consciousness*, no. 1, 1977, pp. 56–76: p. 76.

5 Adrienne Rich, 'Origins and History of Consciousness (1972–4)', in *The Dream of a Common Language: Poems 1974–1977*, W W Norton & Co., New York and London, 1978, p. 7.

6 Nor does Rich collude with typically heterosexual patterns of femininity: the women she portrays are rarely passive or docile.

7 Luce Irigaray, 'When Our Lips Speak Together', translated by Carolyn Burke, in *Signs: Journal of Women in Culture and Society*, vol. 6, no. 1, 1980, pp. 66–79; p. 78 There is an intriguing similarity between these passages from Rich and Irigaray which, if it were not for the incompatibility of dates, would suggest a close influence. Alicia Ostriker tells us in her book, *Writing Like a Woman* (University of Michigan Press, Ann Arbor, 1983), that Rich was, by 1973, 'assuming an influential position in an intellectual movement which includes not only such Anglo-American writers as Millett, Greer, Daly, Piercy and Olsen, but the contemporary French feminists Hélène Cixous, Monique Wittig, Luce Irigaray and Marguerite Duras' (p. 110).

8 *Ibid.*, p. 78.

9 Elly Bulkin, 'An Interview with Adrienne Rich', in *Conditions Two*, vol. 1, no 2, October 1977, pp. 53–66: p. 57.

10 Susan Griffin, 'The Woman Who Swims in Her Tears', in *Made From This Earth: Selections from her Writings*, The Women's Press, London, 1982, p. 274.

11 Susan Griffin, 'Notes on the Writing of Poetry', *Made From This Earth*, p. 226.

12 Olga Broumas' poem 'Rumpelstiltskin' is a wonderful example of revaluation through one woman's lesbian love for another. Olga Broumas, *Beginning With O*, Yale University Press, New Haven and London, 1977, p. 64.

13 Jacques Lacan, 'From Love to the Libido', collected in *The Four Fundamental Concepts of Psychoanalysis*, ed. by Jacques-Alain Miller, trans. Alan Sheridan. Penguin, Harmondsworth, 1979, p. 199.

14 Jacques Lacan, 'The Subject and the Other: Aphanisis', *ibid.*, p. 203.

15 Jacques Lacan, 'From Love to the Libido', *ibid.*, p. 194–195.

16 Jacques Lacan, 'The Subject and the Other: Aphanisis', *ibid.*, p. 218. Lacan says: 'Hence the division of the subject: when the subject appears somewhere as meaning, he is manifested elsewhere as "fading", as disappearance.'

17 Olga Broumas, 'Innocence', in *Beginning With O*, p. 45.

18 Readers interested in following this up might look at Linda Hurcombe, *Sex and God: Varieties of Women's Religious Experience*, Routledge & Kegan Paul, New York and London, 1987. See also Charlene Spretnak, ed., *The Politics of Women's Spirituality: Essays on the Rise of Spiritual Power Within the Feminist Movement*, Anchor Press, New York, 1982.

19 How far these 'small steeples' may be seen as phallic is a difficult question. I imagine a more conical design, volcano shape, wide at the base and squat! Short steeples surely can be imagined as breast-shaped, even if rather sharp! This seems to me to be an appropriation of imagery traditionally considered as male, re-inscribing it in female terms. (What male would like his organ to be described as 'small'?) But perhaps it is also useful to place this image in the context of Cixous' account of bisexuality: 'bisexuality: that is, each one's location in self (*repérage en soi*) of the presence – variously manifest and insistent according to each person, male or female – of both sexes, non-exclusion either of the difference or of one sex, and, from this "self-permission", multiplication of the effects of the inscription of desire, over all parts of my body and the other body.' Hélène Cixous, 'The Laugh of the Medusa', in *New French Feminisms: An Anthology*, ed. Elaine Marks and Isabelle de Courtivron, Harvester Press, Brighton, 1981, p. 254. This is to argue that female specificity is not bound to traditional

ideas of 'the feminine' and nor does it exclude characteristics currently considered as masculine. Openness and receptiveness to the other means that the psyche is not exclusively female. This is to posit a female specificity that is, paradoxically, both/and rather than either/or.

20 Audre Lorde, 'Black Mother Woman', in *Chosen Poems: Old and New*, W W Norton & Co., New York and London, 1982, p. 52.

21 I see Lorde as creating 'patterns for relating across our human differences as equals' in this poem. See Audre Lorde, 'Age, Race, Class, and Sex: Women Redefining Difference', in *Sister Outsider: Essays and Speeches by Audre Lorde*, The Crossing Press, Trumansburg, 1984, p. 115.

22 Alicia Suskin Ostriker, *Stealing the Language: The Emergence of Women's Poetry in America*, The Women's Press, London, 1987, p. 188.

23 *Ibid.*, p. 186.

24 Audre Lorde, 'My Words Will be There', in *Black Women Writers: Arguments and Interviews*, ed. Mari Evans, Pluto Press, London and Sydney, 1983, p. 261.

25 For an example of this see Johari M Kunjufu, 'Ceremony', in Erlene Stetson, ed., *Black Sister: Poetry by Black American Women, 1746–1980*, University of Indiana Press, Bloomington, 1981; p. 192.

26 Audre Lorde, *Black Women Writers*, p. 264.

27 Audre Lorde, 'Recreation', in *The Black Unicorn: Poems*, W W Norton & Co., New York and London, 1978, p. 81.

28 Audre Lorde, 'Uses of the Erotic: The Erotic as Power', in *Sister Outsider*, pp. 53–59: p. 53.

29 Adrienne Rich, 'Poem XI' from 'The Twenty-One Love Poems', *The Dream of a Common Language*, p. 30.

30 Audre Lorde, 'Recreation', *The Black Unicorn*, p. 81.

31 Olga Broumas, 'Leda and Her Swan', in *Beginning with O*, p. 6.

32 Rich was researching *Of Woman Born* and reading many of the founding texts of the women's spirituality movement at this time. See especially her chapter 'The Primacy of the Mother'.

33 Vicki Noble, *Motherpeace: A Way to the Goddess through Myth, Art and Tarot*, Harper & Row, San Francisco, 1983; pp. 25, 27. However, Sally Gearheart and Susan Rennie, *A Feminist Tarot*, Persephone Press, Massachusetts, 1981, first came out in 1976 and could have been influential. Rich was later to distance herself from

more individualist manifestations of the spirituality movement in her interview with Margaret Packwood, *Spare Rib*, February 1981, p. 14.

34 Adrienne Rich, 'Floating Poem' in 'The Twenty-One Love Poems', *The Dream of a Common Language*, p. 32.

35 Elly Bulkin, 'An Interview: Audre Lorde and Adrienne Rich', in *Sister Outsider*, p. 98.

36 Audre Lorde, 'Love Poem', in *Chosen Poems – Old and New*, W W Norton & Co., New York and London, 1978, p. 77.

37 Audre Lorde, 'Dahomey', in *The Black Unicorn*, p. 11.

38 Audre Lorde, *Zami: A New Spelling of My Name*, Sheba Feminist Publishers, London, 1982, from the prologue.

DIVINE VISITATIONS:
SAPPHO'S POETRY OF LOVE
Gillian Spraggs

As the Oxford English Dictionary tells us, the primary meaning of 'Lesbian' is 'Of or pertaining to the island of Lesbos'. The secondary usages, adjectivally to describe sexual attractions or relations between women, and as a substantive, to mean what the Dictionary calls 'a female homosexual', derive from what it describes, circumspectly, as 'the alleged practice of Sappho, the poetess of Lesbos', and appeared fairly recently, during the later years of the nineteenth century, at the point when the developing European subculture of same-sex love was first beginning to engage publicly in the task of self-definition and to challenge legal and customary taboos. Unlike various similar terms which came into use at about the same time, such as 'uranian', 'intermediate', 'invert' and 'homosexual', which nowadays are either obsolete or else, in the case of the last, have fallen into some disfavour, 'lesbian' has continued to be proudly claimed and cherished. A major reason for this has undoubtedly been the association with Sappho, famous as a poet in ancient times throughout the Greek-speaking world, whose immense prestige, as well as her reputation as a lover of women, have survived the passing of her culture and the loss of most of her poetry.

In the last decades of the nineteenth century and the opening years of this one, at a time when certain French poets and novelists were courting a profitable notoriety by exploiting Sappho's reputation as a sexual exotic, and up-to-date medical men, influenced by the apologists for same-sex love, were adopting 'Lesbian' and 'Sapphist' as terms for a distinct psychological type, women in the emerging 'lesbian' subculture of America and Europe, particularly those with literary inclinations, were already identifying Sappho as an exemplary forerunner. Meanwhile, in response to these developments, which they deplored, eminent scholars of ancient Greek were covering pages with passionately expressed assertions as to the 'moral purity' and generally conventional character of the poet.[1] No one who attempts to interpret the remains of Sappho's poetry, especially for a readership that is presumed to be largely non-specialist, can neglect the enormous influence of this not so distant past, or disregard the various meanings, some of them contradictory, that cluster around her name.

The surviving poems of Sappho are few and almost entirely fragmentary. The society she lived in, the Greek city of Mytilene on Lesbos in the early sixth century BC, is largely lost to us except as it appears in the poems of Sappho and her male contemporary Alcaeus. This helps to explain the existence of very divergent images of Sappho; so little is actually known, and that little is often open to multiple interpretations. However, this does not explain why Sappho's reputation became the centre of agonised dispute; nor why her sexual preferences and practices have continued to be the subject of passionate debate into recent years.[2]

The reasons for this have much to do with prestige: first of all, with the prestige of ancient Greek culture generally, which has been such a potent influence on European institutions and ways of thought. Out of the relics of that culture very few women's voices emerge with any clarity; Sappho is virtually the only woman of whose writings substantial fragments may still be read. Then there is Sappho's personal prestige as a poet whose work was admired for many centuries throughout the Greek-speaking world, so that it survived the ruthlessly selective process of continuous written transmission until well into the Christian era. Her poems were still circulating in twelfth-century Byzantium, but by the time of the Renaissance, four centuries later, all that survived was a handful of quotations embedded in the text of other writers. A number of additional fragments, written on tattered papyri or bits of broken pot, have since been retrieved by archaeologists; but even so, out of nine books of Sappho's poems circulating in ancient times, only one complete poem is extant, along with substantial parts of eight or nine others, a few more of which perhaps the gist can be made out, a number of very short but still intelligible fragments, and others of which only odd words may be read here and there. A key factor in the disappearance of Sappho's poetry was probably the attitude of the Christian Church, which regarded her work as immoral. During the sixteenth century a tradition was circulating among scholars that the manuscripts of Sappho and several other Greek poets had been lost when the Church authorities had ordered them to be burnt.[3]

Because of the circumstances under which Sappho's poems have reached us, the process by which the reader constructs the text is thrown into peculiar prominence. Much of the text of Sappho has quite literally been reconstructed by scholars, correcting obvious errors of transcription and filling gaps with more or less informed guesses. Some, perhaps, are inspired; for at least one has been confirmed by a later archaeological discovery. Others may be quite inaccurate. This process is obviously wide open to distortion caused by personal taste or prejudice; as is the whole process of interpreting these poems, incomplete, as most of them are, and written in an obscure dialect of an ancient language in the context of a society which has left few monuments besides the poems themselves. It can be fruitful to look for parallels with other Greek texts and societies; but this may be potentially misleading as well as helpful. There are over a hundred years between the time that Sappho flourished in Mytilene and the cultural flowering of classical Athens, the society of which we have by far the clearest and most detailed picture. Nor was the Greek-speaking world at any time entirely homogenous in its social institutions, customs and attitudes.

However, perhaps these special problems of interpretation may be seen to have positive effects if they help to remind us that whatever it is that we have inherited in the surviving Sapphic corpus it is very far from offering us direct and unproblematic access to the consciousness of a woman of ancient Greece. This is all the more important because Sappho's poems have often been seen as inviting such a reading: sometimes to the point of absurdity, as when the briefest of fragments is taken as a statement of Sappho's own feelings and views. Thus one brief quoted fragment, 'I shall always be a virgin', was pressed into service earlier this century as evidence of Sappho's resistance to heterosexuality; but a papyrus find has shown that this is part of a speech put in the mouth of the virgin goddess Artemis.[4]

This poem, or at least the part of it which is extant, is a narrative, but much of the work which survives falls into the category of 'personal' lyric; Sappho writes about events and feelings which she claims, explicitly or implicitly, to have experienced herself. Nevertheless, we must not forget that her work is not auto-biography or reportage but poetry, and poetry of a far from artless kind. We know very little about the lyric tradition before Sappho and Alcaeus, but there is no doubt that such a tradition existed and helped to shape Sappho's understanding of her task as a poet and her handling of her material. Sappho's poetry may often be intimate in its subject matter and passionate in feeling; but it is also intricately wrought and intensely self-conscious.

On one level, the question of whether Sappho was a lesbian in the modern sense is simply inadmissible: a lyric poem is not a page from the writer's diary, still less a sworn statement in a court of law, and the confessions of a poetic persona can never be taken as unproblematic evidence for the behaviour of the poet. On another level, the question is unanswerable; the poetry that survives is, at certain points, open to being read as referring to physical relationships between women, but nowhere does it compel such a reading. Even if we possessed the entire corpus of Sapphic poems which circulated in ancient times, it is doubtful whether the ambiguity would be dispelled; at all events, the comments of various writers in later antiquity, who had access to a much larger body of Sappho's work than is available nowadays, and who generally interpreted the poems as a straightforward record of the poet's life, make it plain that her sexual practice was at once the subject of curious speculation and open to dispute.[5]

What may be said for certain? The world of Sappho's poems is pre-eminently a world of women, many of them mentioned by name: Atthis, Anactoria, Mnasidica, Gongyla, Gyrinno. The beauty of individual women is a frequent topic. Love, desire, longing: these and related words recur over and over again, but the context is often fragmentary or bedevilled by textual uncertainties. A handful of fragments show unmistakably that for Sappho, the erotic feeling that one woman may have for another was an appropriate theme for poetry; and to judge from the comments of various later writers, it was a theme which ran through much of her writing.[6]

To observe, then, that the subject of erotic friendships between women must have been one in which the poet herself was interested would seem to be labouring the point, were it not for the amount of scholarly ink which has been spilled in disagreement. It was also, plainly, a subject that interested others in her society. Sappho's situation was very different from that of most poets nowadays, who write in solitude poems which will be disseminated in print to readers few of whom the poet will ever meet. Sappho's poems were written as songs, for performance primarily by the poet herself in front of an audience well known to her. Fame in the wider Greek-speaking world was possible, and we know that Sappho achieved it, but in her pre-electronic age it must have depended mainly on chain transmission from performer to performer, and to some extent, perhaps, on the circulation of hand-copied manuscripts. In circumstances like these no poet will survive unless her material strikes a chord with her audience and is acceptable to the community at large. The fact that Sappho, time and again, took up her lyre to sing, among other things, about the physical attraction she felt for some of her women friends and about their attachments to each other tells us that her culture, the culture of Mytilene in the early sixth century BC, was one in which such feelings did not need to be concealed and were not regarded as freakish or exceptional, or not, at any rate, by an influential section of society. As for whether Sappho actually had sex with the women who stirred her well-publicised desires, this is something which we simply cannot know. But there can be little doubt, given the pragmatic pagan Greek attitude to sexual appetite, that her audience will have assumed, at least, that she wanted to, and would have, given the opportunity; and she herself was clearly not made anxious by the idea that they might think this.

In the most famous of Sappho's longer fragments, Fragment 31, a lover describes her responses to the proximity of a woman to whom she is powerfully attracted:

> φαίνεταί μοι κῆνος ἴσος θέοισιν
> ἔμμεν' ὤνηρ, ὄττις ἐνάντιός τοι
> ἰσδάνει καὶ πλάσιον ἆδυ φωνεί-
> σας ὑπακούει
>
> καὶ γελαίσας ἰμέροεν, τὸ δὴ 'μαν   5
> καρδίαν ἐν στήθεσιν ἐπτόαισεν,
> ὡς γὰρ ἔς σ' ἴδω βρόχε' ὥς με φώναι-
> σ' οὐδ' ἓν ἔτ' εἴκει,

ἀλλ' κὰμ μὲν γλῶσσα μ' ἔαγε, λέπτον
δ' αὔτικα χρῶι πῦρ ὑπαδεδρόμηκεν,   10
ὀππάτεσσι δ' οὐδ' ἒν ὄρημμ', ἐπιρρόμ-
βεισι δ' ἄκουαι,

κὰδ δέ μ' ἴδρως ψῦχρος ἔχει, τρόμος δὲ
παῖσαν ἄγρει, χλωροτέρα δὲ ποίας
ἔμμι, τεθνάκην δ' ὀλίγω 'πιδεύης   15
φαίνομ' ἔμ' αὔται.

He seems to me the peer of gods, that man
who sits and faces you,
close by you hearing
your sweet voice speaking,

and your sexy laugh, which just this moment makes
the heart quake in my breast: for every time
I briefly glance towards you, then I lose
all power of further speech.

My tongue is smashed; at once a film of fire
runs underneath my skin; no image shapes
before my eyes;
my ears are whining like a whirling top;

cold sweat pours down me, and in every part
shuddering grips me;
I am paler than summer grass,
and seem to myself to be at the point of death.

(Fragment 31)

The opening stanza introduces us to the three figures who inhabit
the world of the poem: 'me', 'that man' and 'you'. Word endings in
the Greek show that both the speaker and the person being
addressed are female. In the economy of the poem, the function of
'that man' is to be contrasted with the speaker. This contrast is
implied in the strongly echoing phrases at beginning and end: 'He
seems to me to be equal to the gods . . . I seem to myself to be
very nearly dead'. 'That man' is also contrasted to the speaker in
that he sits opposite the woman being addressed – a position that
suggests that he is looking directly at her – and listens attentively –
'hear' is rather a weak translation – while she speaks and laughs.
The speaker, on the other hand, is not able to look at the other

woman for more than a brief glance, and this is enough to end any capacity for listening: 'my ears are whining'.

After the first half of the fifth line, the action of the poem takes place entirely within the consciousness of the speaker. One after another, speech, sight, hearing are put out of action, while the speaker's skin is simultaneously burning and running with cold sweat, as if in a fever. Much of the imagery is intensely painful and violent: the sound of the beloved speaking and laughing literally 'terrifies' the lover's heart, her tongue 'is shattered'. By the final stanza, the lover's whole frame is shaking: 'trembling takes hold of me all over', and she is close to physical dissolution – or so it seems. Although speaker and poet are nowhere formally identified in the poem, the accumulation of intimate physical detail pushes the reader towards accepting the authenticity of the experience. It is not altogether surprising that several eminent classical scholars have been beguiled into identifying the poem's persona straight-forwardly with the person of Sappho, even to committing the absurdity of seeking to psychoanalyse her on the strength of it.[7]

But the symptoms listed in the poem are intended to serve a poet's purposes, not those of an analyst. Almost all of them are drawn from poetic convention. In the epic poems of Homer, written more than a century earlier, the characters frequently experience, at moments of strong emotion, one or another and sometimes a couple of the sensations described by Sappho, usually when they are overcome by grief, fear or physical pain. Later, the poet Archilochus (?c. 650 BC) adapted some of these signs to the description of sexual passion (*eros*). However, the way in which Sappho piles one extreme physical symptom on another, culmi-nating in the near-faint that seems to bring the lover close to death, is something new.[8]

Why does the man seem to the speaker to be 'equal to the gods'? One interpretation is that he is felt to be 'as fortunate as the gods', because he is enjoying the company of the woman, but the phrase might imply that he is 'as handsome as the gods', and there are several scholars who draw on Homeric parallels to argue that it means 'as strong as the gods': unlike the lover, he is able to face the beloved, he is not shattered by her proximity.[9] It seems more than likely that the ambiguity here is deliberate, and that Sappho meant to suggest all three, and more.

Above all else, the gods are the immortals, the deathless ones:

that is the primary reason why they are thought of as fortunate. They are also beautiful, with the ageless beauty of the ever-young; so that more than once in the surviving fragments we find Sappho comparing her friends to goddesses.[10] But the beauty of the gods can be dangerous to mortals. When the goddess Aphrodite reveals herself to her mortal lover Anchises, who has just made love to her not knowing who she is, she shines with unearthly beauty; but he hides his face in terror and begs her to deliver him, 'since no man's strength flourishes, who shares a bed with the deathless goddesses'. Simply seeing a god in his or her true form was likely to have a shattering effect.[11] Just so, the devastating presence of the woman she desires has brought the lover almost to fainting: it has nearly killed her. Only a god can look on the beauty of a revealed goddess and not risk being blasted at the sight. This is the major reason why the man seems equal to a god, and it is one of the reasons why the lover's heart quakes, and her whole body responds with signs that mean fear and pain. What she is experiencing is sexual passion, but there is also more than a suggestion of the awe and holy dread that the worshipper feels in the presence of divinity.[12]

On one level this is a tribute to the beloved, a flattering conceit; but there is more to it than that. The man, appearances to the contrary, is not a god; but there is a god present. It is hard for most of us nowadays to enter imaginatively the divinity-thronged world of the pagan Greeks, in which sexual love (*eros*) was much more than just an emotion or a physical response to a certain kind of stimulus. In a teasingly short but very expressive fragment Sappho writes:

> Ἔρος δ' ἐτίναξέ μοι
> φρένας, ὡς ἄνεμος κὰτ ὄρος δρύσιν ἐμπέτων.

> Love shook my senses,
> like a wind rushing down upon the oaks of the mountain.
>
> (Fragment 47)

Here *eros* is compared to an uncontrollable natural force, violent and physical in its effects, mysteriously descending on the lover from somewhere outside. In another fragment, the image is of some kind of creeping thing, like an insect or a reptile:

> Ἔρος δηὖτέ μ' ὁ λυσιμέλης δόνει,
> γλυκύπικρον ἀμάχανον ὄρπετον

> Once more Love stirs me up, the limb-loosener,
> a creature bitter-sweet, baffling.
>
> (Fragment 130)

In Sappho's time, 'limb-relaxing' had become a traditional epithet
to apply to love or desire, but 'bitter-sweet', which now sounds
hackneyed, is not found in earlier writers, and may have been her
own coinage. The word which I have translated as 'baffling' means
both 'irresistible' and 'incomprehensible'. One commentator has
argued strongly that the 'bitter-sweet creature' that Sappho had in
mind was a bee, which both stings and makes sweet honey. Yet
although such an image may well be buried in these lines, we are
missing the point if we do not also recognise a strong element of
deliberate ambiguity: in essence, love is a creature of no known
species, painful, delightful, enigmatic and terrifying.[13]

This mysterious force from outside, this inescapable monster,
was also experienced as a personality, Eros, the god of love, whom
Sappho once pictured,

> ἔλθοντ' ἐξ ὀράνω πορφυρίαν περθέμενον χλάμυν

> having come from heaven wearing a purple cloak.
>
> (Fragment 54)

Sappho's Eros is not the chubby child or cupidon of later art, but a
winged youth, handsome and richly dressed. He was the attendant,
and in some myths the son, of Aphrodite, the love goddess.[14]
When the lover in Fragment 31 merely glances at the object of her
desire, a divine power touches her, and she is shaken. In the contest
of wooers, the implied contrast with the man is thus made to work,
with ironic effect, to his disadvantage: for while he enjoys from
close at hand the conversation of the beloved, the very ability that
makes him seem godlike is a sign that he himself has not
experienced the divine visitation of Eros which has set its marks so
strongly on the lover.

The only poem by Sappho which is known to be complete, apart
from a few textual uncertainties, concerns itself explicitly with the
manifestation of a divinity.

> ποικιλόθρον' ἀθανάτ' Ἀφρόδιτα,
> παῖ Δίος δολόπλοκε, λίσσομαί σε,
> μή μ' ἄσαισι μηδ' ὀνίαισι δάμνα,

πότνια, θῦμον,

ἀλλὰ τυίδ' ἔλθ', αἴ ποτα κἀτέρωτα   5
τὰς ἔμας αὔδας ἀίοισα πήλοι
ἔκλυες, πάτρος δὲ δόμον λίποισα
χρύσιον ἦλθες

ἄρμ' ὑπασδεύξαισα· κάλοι δέ σ' ἆγον
ὤκεες στροῦθοι περὶ γᾶς μελαίνας   10
πύκνα δίννεντες πτέρ' ἀπ' ὠράνωἴθε–
ρος διὰ μέσσω,

αἶψα δ' ἐξίκοντο· σὺ δ', ὦ μάκαιρα,
μειδιαίσαισ' ἀθανάτωι προσώπωι
ἦρε' ὄττι δηῦτε πέπονθα κὤττι   15
δηῦτε κάλημμι

κὤττι μοι μάλιστα θέλω γένεσθαι
μαινόλαι θύμωι ὶ ίνα δηῦτε πείθω
ἄψ σ' ἄγην ἐς σὰν φιλότατα; τίς σ', ὦ
Ψάπφ', ἀδικήει;   20

καὶ γὰρ αἰ φεύγει, ταχέως διώξει,
αἰ δὲ δῶρα μὴ δέκετ', ἀλλὰ δώσει,
αἰ δὲ μὴ φίλει, ταχέως φιλήσει
κωὺκ ἐθέλοισα.

ἔλθε μοι καὶ νῦν, χαλέπαν δὲ λῦσον   25
ἐκ μερίμναν, ὄσσα δέ μοι τέλεσσαι
θῦμος ἰμέρρει, τέλεσον, σὺ δ' αὔτα
σύμμαχος ἔσσο.

Intricately adorned with flowers, deathless child of Zeus,
Aphrodite, weaver of plots:
I beg of you,
do not, my lady, wear down my spirit with heartache and
grief,

but come to me here, if ever before
you caught my distant cry,
and listened to me, and came,
leaving your father's golden house,

your chariot yoked:
sparrows, beautiful, swift, their packed wings beating,
drew you down from the sky through the middle air,
above the black earth;

suddenly they arrived;
and you, goddess, a smile on your deathless face,
asked me what ailed me this time,
and why I called on you this time,

and what was the special wish of my love-crazed soul:
'Whom shall I seduce back to your love
this time? Who is it, Sappho,
who flouts you?

No doubt of it: if she's in flight, soon she'll pursue;
if presents she will not accept, she shall give;
if she does not love, then love she shall, and soon,
even against her wish.'

Come to me now once again,
and free me from thoughts hard to bear;
what my soul longs for, fulfil;
you yourself be my comrade in battle.

(Fragment 1)

Aphrodite, the goddess of love, is summoned to come to the aid of a rejected lover, identified internally with Sappho herself, who reminds her, in considerable detail, of previous occasions when the goddess has come in person to promise redress. The evidence that the beloved is a woman rests primarily on the disputed ending of a single corrupt line, though the point has been made that Sappho would have been unlikely to depict herself as aggressively pursuing and pressing gifts on a reluctant male.[15]

At the heart of the poem is the description of the epiphany, the manifestation of the presence of the goddess. What level of reality is being represented in the elaborate description of Aphrodite's descents from heaven to visit the poet as she prays? 'A flight of fancy', says Denys Page: Sappho saw a flock of sparrows, sacred to Aphrodite, and 'superstition' led her to fantasise that their divine mistress rode invisibly behind them in her chariot. 'Religious experience', argues C M Bowra: Sappho believes that she has had a visionary encounter with Aphrodite, 'and we have no reason to doubt her word'. A literary contrivance, pronounces M L West: 'The groans of love serve as a neat symmetrical frame for that ornately pretty centrepiece'.[16] If Page and Bowra are naive in their easy identification of the poem's 'Sappho' with the poet, West seems crudely reductive in his assumption that the description of the epiphany is merely the occasion for a certain kind of poetic effect.

There can be no doubt that Sappho and her audience believed in a divine personage who had under her control all aspects of sexuality, who might be offered worship through sacrifice and prayer, who was open to appeals from worshippers for her intervention and showed favour to those who pleased her. Moreover, like other divinities, Aphrodite might manifest herself in person to chosen individuals. In the vanished age of heroes, such encounters with gods had been commonplace; now, perhaps, they were exceptional, but only the impious might doubt that such things happened.[17] The action of the poem, then, takes place not in 'fancy', but on a non-ordinary level of reality.

Sappho lived in what William Blake called an 'age of imagination', in which imagination was not contrasted sharply with reality, but was experienced as a transforming power. The epithets that are used in summoning Aphrodite have the effect of creating a mental image that will become the presence of the goddess herself; and by picturing so vividly the flight down from heaven, the lover ensures that Aphrodite is even now hastening to answer her appeal. Read like this, the poem produces its own epiphany; and while rationalists will agree with Page in calling this 'superstition', there can be no doubt that the poem has more to offer to those who are prepared to join Bowra in recognising a common, if mysterious, transcultural human experience.

The figure of Aphrodite dominates the poem: it is she who is responsible for the lover's pain, by causing her to be drawn to a woman who does not return her love, and it is she alone who can bring her deliverance. She is the power who, as earlier poets proclaimed, wears down the resistance of gods, mortals and beasts alike, and as the epithet 'weaver of plots' suggests, she is devious and insinuating in the way she goes to work.[18] The smile on her face is propitious; but it is also the smile of a 'deathless' goddess, who even as she responds to her worshipper's appeal remains

essentially untouched by the sufferings of mortals. It is a smile of
gentle mockery, too, at the antics of one whom she has touched
with her power; Aphrodite is not above taking such amusement.[19]
She imposes love as a law on all creatures, so that Sappho has her
say of the obdurate beloved, 'Who, Sappho, is doing you wrong?'
and she promises to see justice done by turning the beloved herself
into a pursuing lover 'even though she doesn't wish it'.[20] Perhaps,
as Kenneth Dover thinks, the implication is that the other woman
will turn and pursue 'Sappho'; if so, as he points out, it means that
erotic relations between women were very different from the
Greek male pattern, where a rigid distinction was generally
assumed between a dominant older lover and a subordinate
partner.[21] Perhaps, as Anne Giacomelli has suggested, 'Sappho' is
anticipating the inevitable time when the other woman will herself
experience the pains of unrequited love and she, 'Sappho', will be
avenged.[22] More than likely, the ambiguity is deliberate: one way
or another, in the course of time, the love goddess is certain to
assert her power over the soul of the beloved. In the meantime,
'Sappho's' dearest hope is plain enough: she wishes for Aphrodite
to come now, as her own ally and deliverer, and turn the beloved's
desires towards herself.

Aphrodite is a tricky and powerful goddess; like all the
immortals, she is remorseless, and she can be very cruel. But she is
also a goddess of beauty and delight, and this aspect is uppermost
in another summoning prayer by Sappho of which a substantial
fragment survives:

δεῦρύ μ' ἐς βρῆτας ἐπόνελθε ναῦον
ἄγνον, ὄππαι τοι χάριεν μὲν ἄλσος
μαλίαν, βῶμοι δὲ τεθυμιάμε-
νοι λιβανώτωι·

ἐν δ' ὕδωρ ψῦχρον κελάδει δι' ὔσδων   5
μαλίνων, βρόδοισι δὲ παῖς ὀ χῶρος
ἐσκίαστ', αἰθυσσομένων δὲ φύλλων
κῶμα κατέρρει·

ἐν δὲ λείμων ἱππόβοτος τέθαλεν
ἠρίνοισιν ἄνθεσιν, αἰ δ' ἄηται   10
μέλλιχα πνέοισιν [
[   ]

ἔνθα δὴ σὺ γ᾽ ἔλθ᾽ ὀνέλοισα Κύπρι
χρυσίαισιν ἐν κυλίκεσσιν ἄβρως
ὀμμεμείχμενον θαλίαισι νέκταρ   15
οἰνοχόεισα.

Come back to me here once more in the festival time,
to the holy temple, where stands your apple-grove of graceful
                                                          trees,
where there are altars
smoking with incense.

Here through the apple-boughs trickles the sound of cool
                                                          water,
and the whole ground is shadowed with roses;
down from the shimmering leaves
flows the sleep of enchantment.

Here is a meadow, fit to graze horses,
blooming with flowers of spring,
and sweetly the breezes are blowing . . .

Here, now, come Aphrodite:
take nectar, exquisitely mixed,
in cups made of gold
pour out for our feasting.

                                        (Fragment 2)

The loveliness and grace of the goddess are everywhere immanent
in her sacred grove. The speaker, with her friends, or perhaps with
one special friend, has come to celebrate Aphrodite and her gifts,
and she prays to the goddess to grace the feast in person, and to
pour for them nectar, the marvellous drink of the gods, which
bestows on those who receive it immortal vigour and beauty.
Lovers and party-goers, and religious celebrants also, often
experience heightened feelings of energy and awareness. Aphrodite
inflicts at will the anguish of unassuaged passion, but to those she
favours she brings delight, and the quickening of every sense.

That Sappho was, as her poems proclaim, a lover of women has
caused scandal and anxiety to many in almost every age of which
we have a record. To some of us, particularly in the West, in the
last century of the second millenium of the Christian era, it has
seemed a matter for celebration. But we are missing a good deal if

we simply seek to appropriate Sappho, as others have done in the past, to one side or another of the long-running debate about homosexuality. We must acknowledge that Sappho lives only in her poems, and that these are mutilated artefacts of a long buried culture, yielding up meanings that may not always fit easily with the taboos, preconceptions, disputes and obsessions of the culture in which we live ourselves. As part of this acknowledgement, we must recognise that in Sappho's world, love-making and the worship of the Love Goddess are sides of a single coin. Central to the experience of love as it is manifested in Sappho's lyrics are the presences of Aphrodite and her attendant Eros, and if we are seeking to respond to her poetry in full, we must open ourselves to the world of the numinous where these divinities may be encountered.

AFTERNOTE: TRANSLATION AND TEXT

In translating Sappho's poems, my aim has been to stay as close to a literal rendering as possible while producing a text which conveys at least some of the poetic qualities of the originals. The metrical system used by the Greeks works on very different principles to anything in English poetry, and no one has ever successfully naturalised it, so I have not attempted to reproduce Sappho's metres. Several short translated quotations embedded in the critical analysis will be found to differ in wording from the translations which follow the Greek texts. My intention has been to open up an awareness of some of the many different possibilities which are available to the translator, and to call attention to the point that my translations are only versions, not the actual texts under discussion. For readers with no Greek who want to read more Sappho, the best translation in modern English is that by Josephine Balmer in *Sappho: Poems and Fragments*, Brilliance Books, London, 1984. A literal prose translation, by David A Campbell, is included in his edition of Sappho in *Greek Lyric*, vol. i, Loeb Classical Library, Harvard University Press, Cambridge, Massachusetts, 1982.

The standard English edition of Sappho's poetry is that by Edgar Lobel and Denys Page in *Poetarum Lesbiorum Fragmenta*, Clarendon Press, Oxford, 1955. All references to Sappho's fragments in the text and notes of this essay follow the numbering given them in Lobel and Page, and the text of the passages I have quoted and translated substantially follows their edition. However, there are several places where I have preferred to accept alternative readings.

In Fragment 31, I have preferred the older reading of line 4, given by J M Edmonds in *Lyra Graeca*, vol. i, Loeb Classical Library, Heinemann, London, 1922, Fragment 2. Lines 9 and 16 follow Campbell's edition. Line 13 is emended in line with Page's suggestion in *Sappho and Alcaeus: An Introduction to the Study of Ancient Lesbian Poetry*, Clarendon Press, Oxford, 1955, pp. 19, 25. I have omitted the fragmentary and doubtful line 17.

For Fragment 1 I have departed from Lobel and Page only in line 19, which follows G M Kirkwood, *Early Greek Monody: The History of a Poetic Type*, Cornell Studies in Classical Philology vol. xxxvii, Cornell University Press, Ithaca, 1974, pp. 109, 246–247. In addition, I have preferred to understand *poikilothron'* as a compound with *throna*, flowers, rather than the generally accepted *thronos*, throne – which would have made the first epithet mean 'elaborately-throned'. In support of this reading, see Anne Pippin Burnett, *Three Archaic Poets: Archilochus, Alcaeus, Sappho*, Duckworth, London, 1983, p. 250 and note 53.

The text of Fragment 2 has come down in a badly scrambled state. I follow the text given by Page in *Sappho and Alcaeus*, p. 34, apart from line 1, where I have taken suggestions from M L West, 'Burning Sappho', *Maia*, vol. 22 (1970), p. 316, and lines 8, 13, 16 where I follow Kirkwood in *Early Greek Monody*, pp. 114, 250–251. In my translation I have rejected Page's proposal (on p. 39) to take *ommemeichmenon*, 'mixed', with *thaliaisi*, 'feasting', which gives very clumsy sense, and have taken it instead with 'nectar'. Fragment 141 is ample evidence that in Sappho's mind, the gods mixed their marvellous drinks with water, just as mortals mixed their wine. For reasons of accessibility and euphony I have chosen to translate 'Kypris', one of the goddess' many titles, with the more familiar 'Aphrodite'.

NOTES

1 Joan DeJean, *Fictions of Sappho, 1546–1937*, University of Chicago Press, Chicago, 1989, pp. 198–285; Frederic Silverstolpe, 'Benkert Was Not a Doctor: On the Non-medical Origin of the

Homosexual Category in the Nineteenth Century', in *Papers of the Conference 'Homosexuality, Which Homosexuality?'* (a conference in lesbian and gay studies), Free University/Schorer Foundation, Amsterdam, 1987, History Volume I, pp. 206–220; Lillian Faderman, *Surpassing the Love of Men: Romantic Friendship and Love between Women from the Renaissance to the Present*, Junction Books, London, 1982, original publication William Morrow and Co., Inc., New York, 1981, pp. 361–363, 368–370; Richard Jenkyns, *Three Classical Poets: Sappho, Catullus and Juvenal*, Duckworth, London, 1982, pp. 1–5.

2 Judith P Hallett, 'Sappho and Her Social Context: Sense and Sensuality', *Signs*, vol. iv, no. 4, Spring 1979, pp. 447–464; Eva Stehle Stigers, 'Romantic Sensuality, Poetic Sense: A Response to Hallett on Sappho', in the same issue of *Signs*, pp. 465–471; John J Winkler, 'Double Consciousness in Sappho's Lyrics', in *The Constraints of Desire: The Anthropology of Sex and Gender in Ancient Greece*, Routledge, New York, 1990, pp. 162–163, 187.

3 Petrus Alcyonius, *Medices Legatus De Exsilio*, Aldus, Venice, November 1522, sig. C3v; Joseph Scaliger, *Scaligeriana: Editio Altera*, The Hague, 1666, p. 308.

4 Arthur Weigall, *Sappho of Lesbos: Her Life and Times*, Thornton Butterworth, London, 1932, pp. 91–92, 98; compare also *Greek Lyric*, ed. David A Campbell, vol. i, Loeb Classical Library, Harvard University Press, Cambridge, Massachusetts, 1982, Sappho Fragment 44A.

5 *Greek Lyric*, Sappho testimonia 1, 2, 4, 17, 22.

6 Sappho, Fragments 1, 16, 22, 31, 94, 96; *Greek Lyric*, Sappho testimonia 18, 19, 20, 49, 50, 51.

7 George Devereux, 'The Nature of Sappho's Seizure in Fr. 31 LP as Evidence of Her Inversion', *Classical Quarterly*, new series, vol. 20 (1970), pp. 17–31; K J Dover, *Greek Homosexuality*, Vintage Books, New York, 1980 (originally published 1978), pp. 178–179 and 179, note 24.

8 Denys Page, *Sappho and Alcaeus: An Introduction to the Study of Ancient Lesbian Poetry*, Clarendon Press, Oxford, 1955, pp. 28–29 and 29, note 1; M Marcovich, 'Sappho Fr. 31: Anxiety Attack or Love Declaration?', *Classical Quarterly*, new series, vol. 22 (1972), pp. 26–27.

9 C M Bowra, *Greek Lyric Poetry from Alcman to Simonides*, second edition, revised, Clarendon Press, Oxford, 1961, pp. 187–188; Page, *Sappho and Alcaeus*, p. 21; Garry Wills, 'Sappho 31 and

Catullus 51', in *Greek, Roman and Byzantine Studies*, vol. 8 (1967), pp. 171–184; Marcovich, 'Sappho Fr. 31: Anxiety Attack or Love Declaration?', pp. 23–25; Emmet Robbins, ' "Every time I look at you . . .": Sappho Thirty-One', *Transactions of the American Philological Association*, vol. 110 (1980), p. 260 and note 22; Anne Pippin Burnett, *Three Archaic Poets: Archilochus, Alcaeus, Sappho*, Duckworth, London, 1983, p. 234, note 10.

10 Fragments 23, 96 (twice).

11 *Homeric Hymn to Aphrodite*, lines 172–175, 181–190; *Homeric Hymn to Demeter*, lines 275–283; Homer, *Iliad*, vol. 20, lines 129–131.

12 Compare Plutarch, *Moralia*, 762f–763b (*Amatorius*, 18); M J Edwards, 'Greek into Latin: A Note on Catullus and Sappho', *Latomus*, vol. 48, no. 3, July–Sept 1989, p. 595.

13 Bonnie MacLachlan, 'What's crawling in Sappho Fr. 130', *Phoenix*, vol. 43, no. 2, Summer 1989, pp. 95–99; Jenkyns, *Three Classical Poets*, pp. 59–60.

14 Fragments 22 (lines 11–12), 159, 194, 198; compare Hesiod, *Theogony*, lines 195–202.

15 DeJean, *Fictions of Sappho*, pp. 127, 306–307, 319–321; Page, *Sappho and Alcaeus*, pp. 10–11; Marcovich, 'Sappho Fr. 31: Anxiety Attack or Love Declaration?', p. 27.

16 Page, *Sappho and Alcaeus*, p. 18; Bowra, *Greek Lyric Poets*, p. 202; M L West, 'Burning Sappho', *Maia*, vol. 22 (1970), p. 310.

17 Bowra, *Greek Lyric Poets*, pp. 202–203; Robin Lane Fox, *Pagans and Christians in the Mediterranean world from the Second Century AD to the Conversion of Constantine*, Penguin, Harmondsworth, 1988, (originally published 1986), pp. 102–167.

18 Homer, *Iliad*, vol. 14, lines 198–199; *Homeric Hymn to Aphrodite*, lines 1–5, 33–39; Hesiod, *Theogony*, lines 203–206.

19 Homer, *Iliad*, vol. 24, lines 525–526; *Homeric Hymn to Aphrodite*, lines 48–52, 249–251.

20 Compare Burnett, *Three Archaic Poets*, p. 256.

21 Dover, *Greek Homosexuality*, p. 177.

22 Anne Giacomelli, 'The Justice of Aphrodite in Sappho Fr. 1', *Transactions of the American Philological Association*, vol. 110, (1980) pp. 135–142.

'SHE WAS NOT REALLY MAN AT ALL': THE LESBIAN PRACTICE AND POLITICS OF EDITH ELLIS

Chris White

Edith Ellis (1861–1916) was a lesbian, a campaigner in eugenics, a lecturer and a writer of fiction and essays. She was married to the sexologist Havelock Ellis, who, with John Addington Symonds, wrote *Sexual Inversion*.[1] After her death several collections were made of her stories, essays and lectures, which were prefaced and mediated by discussions and analyses of her character by her husband, friends and colleagues. In this essay I will begin by looking at those mediations, which are attempts to explicate and define Edith Ellis' character, in the context of her sexuality and gender presentation. I will go on to discuss her own theorisations of homosexuality, or sexual inversion, and the political implications of those theories. In conclusion I will indicate the ways in which these ideas are related to the historical formation of homosexual identity: Ellis wrote at a time when the theory of sexual inversion was being developed as a scientific defence for the toleration of homosexuals.

Her theorisation of inversion through the ideas of eugenics effectively produces a critique of her husband's account of inversion with its emphasis on the relationship between gender and sexuality. In *Sexual Inversion* Havelock Ellis draws on a variety of contemporary and historical sources, and explicitly and implicitly points to a well-developed male homosexual culture. But the women in his work appear as isolated individuals with no place in any social structure other than within traditionally male professions. Havelock Ellis views lesbians as both failed women and failed men: failed men because their instincts and physiology are basically female; failed women because they enter masculine professions and seek to adopt a masculine role in relation to other women. It is not possible, in this formulation, for a female invert to be properly feminine because that femininity would be premissed upon a specific relationship with men and patriarchy, and it is precisely this that she gives up when she enters into relationships with women. Havelock Ellis detaches femininity from inversion but does not detach femaleness. According to him, a woman can be female and an invert, that is not necessarily androgynous or hermaphroditic, but she cannot be feminine and an invert. In this way, he implicitly acknowledges the social and cultural nature of femininity.

Where Havelock Ellis connects gender identity and inversion, Edith Ellis connects, through eugenics theory, individual, spiritual perfection and the acceptable face of inversion through a vision of the perfect society. It is the connection she makes between the condition of the individual and the condition of society, each of which is seen as simultaneously influencing the other, that marks Ellis' work as much more politically radical than her husband's.

Edith Ellis' analysis of the relationship between the individual and society also has significant implications for the histories of homosexuality that have been written in the last two decades. In recent works about the history of homosexual desire and practice, most notably Michel Foucault's *History of Sexuality*,[2] there has been a change in the way homosexuality is understood. There has been a shift away from essentialist notions of identity – where the individual is in possession of an internal coherence that is inborn – to constructivist theories of identity – where the individual's internal coherence or otherwise is determined by the institutions and practices of society. This change has also been marked by an alteration in the conception of sexuality. Foucault has argued that in times past a person's sexuality was perceived as the essential truth about them; recent theoretical developments instead consider sexuality as an expression of power relations and practices. The constructivist approach has the advantage of producing a position on gender and sexuality which, rather than defining a catalogue of natural, universal and permanent characteristics of women, men, homosexuals, lesbians, instead makes those attributes social and political. Foucault's theory legitimises a history of sexuality that is truly liberated – in the sense that sexuality is conceived as being free from the containment of essentialist identities. The theory produces the homosexual as an unstable, unfixed category.

Although this change in the analysis of sexuality has the advantage of not drawing on ideas about human nature and essential truth, it still has its problems: most importantly, the relationship between the homosexual and the dominant culture is, in Foucault's theory, a one way street. According to Foucault, the dominant culture, through education, medicine, law, religion and the family, shapes and defines the practices of homosexuality and the ways in which it is thought of and about. The theory has, therefore, the consequent problem of emphasising the determination of individuals by society, effectively removing from them any potential to determine any part or practice of society and politics.

What I will attempt to show in this essay is that Edith Ellis, like many of her contemporaries engaged in similar work, developed a strategic framework in which to argue for a greater tolerance of homosexuality and lesbianism. In the context of the existence of this debate, it becomes clear that the relationship between sexual inversion and the production of a homosexual identity in the late nineteenth century has misguidedly been seen as one where an ideological institution of the state, science, attempted to produce a category of deviant that would permit the state to have a much greater control over sexual behaviour. According to that Foucauldian analysis, by producing a special group, a species which not only performed certain acts but which were seen as having been thoroughly defined by their sexuality, the state can restrict and legislate over sexual behaviour. Recent evidence suggests, on the contrary, that the so-called scientific production of the category homosexual as a congenital or pathological being in fact originated in a strategic effort by homosexual activists, including Benkert, the man who coined the term 'homosexual'.[3] This strategic effort aimed to produce a model of homosexuality which not only freed homosexuals from any culpability for their desires, but also constructed them along the lines of nineteenth-century scientific practice. Sub-groups of homosexuals and heterosexuals were identified and named by such men as Benkert, Ulrichs and Krafft-Ebing, and photographs of specimens of the different sub-groups were taken and published. Case histories were recorded, anthropological studies of the history and geographical incidence of homosexuality were performed. All of these activities represent efforts by homosexuals themselves to define homosexuality in their own interests. These activities were both shaped by dominant culture, taking the form of scientific works, while also attempting to shape that culture.

In the next section I will look at how these ideas about sexual inversion and dominant ideas about masculinity and femininity shaped the attempts by writers and friends to define Edith Ellis. All of these focus in some way on her relationships with other women, and almost more crucially, the effect on the writers' perceptions of the fact of those relationships on Edith Ellis' nature.

VERSIONS OF EDITH ELLIS

I will begin where the modern reader, the one who comes to Ellis' texts after her death, is encouraged to start, with the prefaces to her collected works by Charles Marriott and Daphne Bax. The prefaces to *Stories and Essays by Mrs Havelock Ellis*,[4] published in two volumes in 1924, present contradictory ideas about their subject. In the preface to volume one Charles Marriott wrote

> She was most herself in her enthusiasms. She had one or two women friends of more than average good looks, and she would have you observe the fact, in their presence, at first acquaintance. 'Isn't she the most beautiful thing you ever saw?' – 'Don't you love her?' which, to a slow-witted man, was a trifle embarrassing. (p. vii)

In addition to the slightly prurient quality of this passage, what is also noticeable is that his patronising tone creates an image which has shades of the schoolgirl crush for the good-looking older woman. This effectively disarms any true sexual content to Edith Ellis. There is nothing explicitly pejorative about the reference to her passion for women, only in the demand that it be acknowledged and agreed with. To describe a woman as beautiful and loved is not explicitly equated here with lesbianism. What is implied in this text is the attitude which is identified as typically Edith's, that she behaved like a man in relation to other women. This consists of appreciating women primarily or only for their physical appearance, that their appearance is the mainspring for the love of women, and that the appreciation takes place in a public arena where the woman is passive and a man is called on to agree. The male commentator produces the woman as a masculine lover of women, but for her to behave in this masculine manner is embarrassing, because she does not stop being a woman just because she behaves like a man. He identifies Edith Ellis' 'self' as residing in the expression and practice of these enthusiasms, rather than in an internal identity as a lesbian/lover of women. Edith is already safely contained by this male commentator, who assumes that the reader is male and in sympathy with the 'slow-witted' author who is initially duped and then embarrassed when forced to see Edith Ellis' lesbianism.

The other prefatory note to this same work is by Daphne Bax, and is entitled 'Johannes: A Memory'. Here Edith is referred to by a male epithet, through an act of renaming. Daphne Bax reports that Edith Ellis invited her, Daphne, to rename her. Ellis asked 'What are you going to call me?' to which Daphne replies 'Johannes! because you are the voice of one crying in the wilderness' (p. ix). Edith is here constructed as an outsider with a message of righteousness and deliverance, but there are also implications of gender ambivalence which are further borne out in her presentation of Edith Ellis that follows:

> I used to wonder whom next I should meet in her – the child longing to be petted; a passionate lover; a man-like being of immense energy; or a woman whose maternal longing fulfilled itself in deep purposes. (p. x)

This list of significant essentialist identities, organised by gender, age and relationship, is undermined by the very fact of its being a series of identities that are interchangeable. There is nothing fixed about masculine or feminine self-presentation: it is simply that, presentation, not identity. Her phrase 'a passionate lover' carries with it not only a sense of maturity, but begs a series of questions about the nature of the relationship between the two women. The text of 'Johannes: A Memory' has several sub-erotic moments: kissing each other in the hall of the Lyceum Club (p. xiv); a description of the relationship as one of 'refreshing tenderness' (p. x); the concluding remarks that 'if I could think that my "Johannes" was dead, I should despair of life' (p. xv). The whole portrait celebrates the energy and work practices of Edith, and also her character contradictions, which are seen as exciting and dynamic. In Mrs Bax's version each term is expanded into a positive image, so that Edith does not appear merely to be playing or to have no genuine character.

The same triumvirate of child, man and woman persists in other accounts of Edith's character. In the preface to her *The New Horizon in Love and Life*,[5] posthumously published in 1921, Edward Carpenter wrote 'The Woman and the Man (and indeed the Child) were closely united in her' (p. xi). Carpenter's formulation moves in the direction of producing Edith Ellis as the Man-Woman, the psychological hermaphrodite. In his auto-biography *My Life*,[6] Havelock Ellis chose this version of the same formulation:

> She was not really man at all in any degree, but always woman, boy and child, and these three, it seemed, in almost equal measure. (p. 263)

The diminution of Carpenter's 'Man' to 'boy' is indicative of Havelock Ellis' double-edged attempt to explain the origins of her lesbianism, while simultaneously defending his own position as the betrayed husband. It is no accident that he places the passionate lover next to the child. Through association, the lover appears akin to a child, childlike, childish; and childlikeness is central to Havelock's treatment of Edith's inversion. He describes her inversion as a product of her premature birth, since this resulted in her being 'in some degree undeveloped, in temperament as well as physically something of a child'.[7] The model here is one of pederasty. There is the fascination with youth in itself, combined with the anxiety about boys who are sexually potent but have not yet learnt to be disciplined in the practice of their manhood. 'Boy' may therefore become 'deviant' if the practice proves to be inappropriate. 'Deviant' may become 'boy'-like, where the deviant is morally innocent while being sexually potent. Havelock produces Edith as innocent, potent, boy-like and deviant. At such times she had all the air and spirit of an

> eager boy, even the deliberate poses and gestures of a boy, never of a man, and on one side of her, deeply woman-hearted as she was, it was more than a pose (p. 325),

while Havelock says of himself, 'I remained her "boy", "her child" ' (p. 326). 'Boy' seems to have two distinct meanings in these applications. In its application to Havelock, 'boy' signals the replacement of Edith's former straightforward wifely affection with a love that is purely maternal when Edith begins to have a lesbian relationship. In the case of Edith, where 'woman' is construed as being antithetical to a pose and as a deeper truth about her identity, 'boy' is placed on the side of the pose, an inauthentic expression of selfhood which is simultaneously integral to her inversion. Havelock Ellis produces this Edith Ellis in the way that he wanted to. The models of knowledge about lesbianism he put forward and his account of his wife's character and their marriage, emerge from the same place. A sort of voluntarist empirical observation of his wife blends with his 'scientific' studies of homosexuality in the context of a biologically determined gender and sexual identity. In *Sexual Inversion* Ellis asserts that 'the inverted woman is not usually attractive to men' (p. 98). In *My Life* he writes 'I, though I failed yet clearly to realise why, was conscious of no inevitably passionate sexual attraction for her' (p. 233). There are striking similarities between some of the descriptive phrases he applies to Edith in *My Life* and his general characterisation of inverted women in *Sexual Inversion*. Havelock Ellis tells us there that her 'restless activity and her merry ringing laugh' (*My Life*, p. 326) were features of Edith's character which revealed her lesbianism. (It is nice to think that the lesbians he knew were so cheerful!) 'The brusque, energetic movements . . . the direct speech, the inflexions of the voice' (*Sexual Inversion*, p. 96) are characteristics of the inverted woman, as are the 'masculine straightforwardness and sense of honour' (p. 96) they display.

By reproducing a letter he wrote to Edith which gives her permission to continue her relationship with Claire and which expresses his own positive feelings towards Edith's lover, he simultaneously includes himself in the relationship: Edith's lesbianism is constructed as part of a heterosexual marriage, not separate from it.

Nothing in the world or out of it will tear you away from my breastbone – unless you want to go. I am perfectly happy that you should be so close to Claire, I feel very tender to her. Give her my sweetest love.[8]

His involvement in his wife's lesbian relationships included helping her to put together a collection of poetry called *The Lover's Calendar*, published in 1912, which was a monument to Lily 'at which she could carry on a kind of worship of Lily' (*My Life*, p. 338); and giving up his studio for the day 'to enable them to picnic quietly there' (p. 325). In his presentation of the relationship between the women, they are seen as visiting an alien pseudo-countryside which is not their own territory, but Havelock Ellis' professional space. The idea of picnicking quietly not only contrasts with the loud laughing lesbians characterised above, but is leisurely and a little frivolous, especially when it is seen in the context of the women taking over Havelock's work space. In this description, then, this apparent tolerance can be seen to be combined with a narrow assertion of what lesbians are like.

Edith Ellis emerges in Havelock Ellis' construction as a mass of contradictions – all of them his – in conflict with one another, rather than as a character in possession of a set of diverse qualities which nevertheless exist in harmony with one another. These contradictions are expressed through a set of roles which are determined biologically rather than culturally. According to him, her biological make-up determines her ideas and practices of sexuality and love. The result is a version of lesbianism which combines immaturity with feminine purity, which serves to keep in place a proper femininity, where purity is always to do with immaturity, including child-like dependence and a lack of self-responsibility.

The fractured sense of self that is produced by the portraits of Edith Ellis is indicative of the problems in defining a coherent identity that is in opposition to the dominant culture. Attempts to define a coherent identity or subjectivity that is capable of either standing fully outside society or of being included within it in a positive manner form a central plank of the various treatments of the theories of sexual inversion. I will next look at Edith Ellis' uses of the theories and the political underpinnings of those usages. On the basis of this, I will in the final section of the essay return to the problem of identity, and attempt to explicate Edith Ellis' particular solution to the question of oppositional subjectivity and the related issue of how social opposition and social change are brought about by the agency of the marginalised subject.

THE POLITICS OF SEXUAL INVERSION

Edith Ellis' discussion of inversion is certainly indebted to her husband's scientific terminology, but at the same time it is much more politically directed. The political content is centred on her use of eugenics, which she employed to emphasise the place and toleration of inverts in society. Edith Ellis' insistence on the proper treatment and proper role of inverts needs to be understood in the context of the overall programme of eugenists to create the conditions for the development of what they saw as the best possible race health, and thus the best possible world. To understand what Edith Ellis is up to, it is important to realise that eugenics theory is not a single monolithic system, but is flexible and often contradictory. Frank Mort, in his book *Dangerous Sexualities*,[9] shows how the concept of eugenics was defined by its founder, Francis Galton, in the early 1880s as the 'study of those agencies under social control, which may improve or impair the racial qualities of future generations'.[10] Eugenics strategy focused on attacking environmentalist reformism in medicine, charity and philanthropy which failed to deal with the underlying causes of social suffering and degeneracy. The eugenists' aim was to reform society by purifying conditions at their source, through controlled breeding, the elimination of the 'unfit' from the breeding pool. Unfitness was determined by such factors as alcoholism, VD and feeble-mindedness. Heredity was the ultimate determining factor, over and above any environmental or cultural influence.

Eugenics has long been linked with fascism and racism, from the Nazis' attempts to bring about racial purity and Aryan supremacy through the elimination of Jews, Black people, criminals, the disabled, romanies and homosexuals; to the ideas of the National Front, succinctly expressed by John Tyndall's call for 'the greatest increase in the most intelligent and the most fit . . . to these aims . . . all ephemeral social considerations must be subordinated'.[11] Where the National Socialists and the National Front would see the state and/or the nation as being the ultimate arbiter in making this policy a social reality, the British eugenics societies of the 1880s and 1890s saw expertise – in science, medicine, ethics – as the means by which the theories of eugenics could be put into practice if the exponents of these disciplines were to support and develop the programme.

Edith Ellis' clearest statement on eugenics appears in Volume II of *Stories and Essays*,[12] in her portrait entitled 'Havelock Ellis'.

> We have not sufficient knowledge or humanity as yet, to enact laws as to who are fit or unfit to marry. What we need is deeper knowledge and an increased sense of personal responsibility toward the race. Every artist must learn technique, even the Love-Artist, and eugenics may possibly take the place scales have in teaching music. (p. 36–7)

For Edith Ellis, then, eugenics provides the elementary lessons in the process of learning responsibility and moving towards perfection. This argument also characterises her treatment of Hinton, Nietzsche and Edward Carpenter in *Three Modern Seers*,[13] where she wrote that 'all meet on the common-ground of a striving towards perfection of individual character as the chief factor in social progress' (p. 7). If her words on the fitness or unfitness of people represent the negative side of her eugenics theory, its positive side is indicated in her discussion of Edward Carpenter and his belief, as she describes it, that 'to rid life of snobbery and class prejudice tends towards the understanding of the criminal and the sufferer apart from all questions of philanthropy and expediency . . . Perhaps it is this attitude of democratic solidarity, combined with visionary mysticism, which places him in the forefront of modern teachers' (p. 213). The political implications of eugenics depend on who is classed as unfit, and this quotation seems to indicate that amongst those groups Edith Ellis deemed unfit were the rich and the aristocracy.

The politics of Ellis' version of eugenics can also be inferred through a consideration of her membership of the Fellowship of the New Life, which she joined in 1887. This was not specifically a eugenics society, but its declared object was 'the cultivation of a perfect character in each and all'.[14] On the establishment of its charter by the Fellowship, the majority of members left to form the Fabians, while the remaining members focused not on political action and analysis, but on creating the right kind of 'atmosphere' in which perfection could be achieved. The emphasis of the Fellowship was on changing individuals already in existence, rather than developing systems and structures to ensure that in the future only perfect individuals would be born. This represents a departure from eugenic theory which sought to control motherhood and reproduction. It implies that the social, as expressed in relations of class and gender, has to be changed as a priority.

It is this version of eugenics that goes some way to explain why a social radical and a lesbian would have chosen eugenics as a model through which to discuss sexual inversion and the place of inverts in society. An examination of the available alternatives might also indicate why Ellis would employ eugenic theory. Stella Browne, a feminist writing in 1916, said that 'the realities of women's sexual life have been greatly obscured by the lack of any sexual vocabulary'.[15] The vocabularies that were available included the legal constructions of the Contagious Diseases Acts, which, through the forcible examination of prostitutes for venereal diseases, made those women responsible for the 'contamination' of their clients, the stereotypes of the spinster/old maid and the discourses surrounding motherhood and marriage. In addition, there were the purity movements which were initiated by the Salvation Army in 1885. While the movements began as a reactionary onslaught on sexual behaviour, and focused on campaigning for a higher age of consent and more stringent police powers to act against brothels, they were supported by both socialists and feminists, in part as a means of preventing the daughters of the working classes becoming the victims of the vices of the rich. Primarily, however, the campaigns developed as a means of teaching the working classes moral law, that is, the moral law of the ruling class. Purity campaigns did not, therefore, provide a politically or sexually radical context in which to talk about inversion.

There was no focal point where lesbian desire and liberation could be explicitly discussed and campaigned for in Britain at the time Ellis was writing. In Germany, lesbians formed a small part of the homosexual liberation movements of the late nineteenth and early twentieth centuries. The contemporaneous British work concerned itself almost without exception solely with male inverts and male homosexual desire. Within the eugenics societies, by contrast, the concern was equally with the proper roles of men and women: the participation of both sexes was regarded as necessary for the perfect society to come about. These factors may go some way to explain why Edith Ellis argued from within the eugenics movements for the rights of inverts. She did not accept all the tenets of those movements, and seems to have used the eugenics model to her own ends.

In 'Eugenics and the Mystical Outlook',[16] she disputes the opinion of some eugenists that inverts belong to 'the same class of the neurotic or the abnormal' (p. 42), and are therefore of no benefit to the larger purpose of improving the race. She sees that the consequences of such an attitude would be to turn inverts into rebels, and thereby produce apparent justification for the belief that they are not useful to the race. She suggests instead that inverts may be turned into allies of the larger society if they are educated into aiding the improvement of the race. This, she claims, can be achieved by the practice of eugenics and by religion (a combination that she does not comment upon nor regard as extraordinary), which can go beyond the prejudices of the conventional attitude to inverts. Under the doctrines of eugenics and religion, combined with her formulations of the ideals of relationships between people, Edith Ellis sees two possible solutions based on the invert's own values and trustworthiness. In her programme, the invert will either renounce all physical relations, or 'if Fate send him [sic] a true mate in the form of another alien' (p. 65), then the invert shall create a relationship as binding and as beneficial to society as 'the bond of normal marriage' (p. 66). She views this as part of allowing the invert to 'follow his [sic] *own* best ideals' (p. 68) rather than forcing him to follow 'normal ideals'. Her accounts of the qualities of inverts and of the consequences of forcing normality upon them parallel, often in precise terms, Havelock Ellis' ideas in *Sexual Inversion*. She, like him, identifies the character of the invert and that of the genius as possibly having 'some sort of affinity' (p. 64), and sees the result of forced normality as a crippling of the invert's 'special powers of work in the eugenics fields of spiritual parenthood' (p. 69). Even though inverts might be feeble and alien, as opposed to the 'robust' normal heterosexual individuals (p. 59), they too must be given their chance to be creative; since it is the robust ones who are fitted to be the best physical parents, the invert falls into the group of those specially endowed with powers to create spiritual children, works of art.

Her investment in the issue appears clouded by her use of the generic 'he', and usage of the terms 'abnormal' and 'alien'. But her use of the word 'abnormal' cannot be seen as simply pejorative. In her story 'An Idealist' reprinted in *The Mine of Dreams*,[17] she writes about an abnormal who has a strange and intimate relationship with the dead. This man, when he is understood, is depicted as someone special and in possession of positive and unique gifts. His abnormality in itself is a good thing, but his treatment by society as an abnormal results in condemnation by the law, and an existence which is beyond language and under-standing. Only when he can explain to a sympathetic listener does his abnormality cease to be negative and become positive in itself; his abnormality is viewed by the narrator as self-sufficient and authentic, and as a result of this acceptance he does not require any further social approval. The subject matter of the story is obviously a long way from inversion, but the use of the term 'abnormal' links this text and those by her specifically about inversion. If this is her fictional construction of abnormality, a unique, special and incomprehensible possession of the individual, it may be that this is her construction of inversion as well. The sense of fitness in oneself is a powerful element in some eugenics theories. It constitutes a kind of moral autonomy which stems from physical nature, and although it is in contradiction to the theory of the socially appropriate, the morally fitting, with which it is usually coupled, the two elements are often argued together.

FITNESS AND OPPOSITION

Edith Ellis' discussion of inversion draws on the combination and contradiction of fitness in oneself and social responsibility in the context of the treatment of inversion and abnormality. I will open this final section with a discussion of Ellis' writing on Oscar Wilde, as an example of the relationship between individual fitness and social treatment of inverts.

She begins by describing Wilde as 'an exotic product of a commercial age . . . a feminine artist in the body of a man . . . a strange medley of undirected genius, misguided femininity, fascination and tragedy'.[18] The terms she uses here are problematic and need unravelling. 'Commercial' seems to infer that under capitalism, the age of philanthropy and charity, a creature may be produced who is feminine – not, I think, a positive term in Edith's vocabulary – and not socially useful or socially adjusted to the drive towards individual and therefore race perfection. Her explanation for the origin of this in Wilde does not fit with any part of the mainstream congenital theory. Both here and in *The New Horizon* lectures on eugenics, she relates a story (which may have had common currency in gossip, although I have found no other written contemporary record of it) about Speranza praying for a girl while pregnant with Oscar. His strange, mixed nature, she suggests, was a direct consequence of this prayer being 'partially granted' creating one of 'nature's satires' (p. 47) in the form of something imperfectly masculine and imperfectly feminine.

> Wilde never found out the implacable meaning of love which is self-surrender or deep suffering . . . These extracts (from *De Profundis*)[19] prove Wilde to have become a deeper man. Depth implies regeneration.[20]

Wilde's 'tragedy' may be viewed as the product of his 'misguided femininity',[21] which cannot be properly deep or masculine. The feminine, the frivolous and the socially irresponsible are all one, and are all in contradiction to the perfect direction of society.

She recognises the political purpose behind Wilde's prosecution, and the meaning behind the distinctions drawn and maintained between inverts and upstanding citizens.

> Wilde was a scapegoat for much that was in the hearts of men and women and expressed in their secret lives, . . . was brought to the tribunal for the many.[22]

She views Wilde as having been made an example to encourage others to keep their desires secret and private. The condemnation of the privatisation of desire and sexuality is entirely in accord with the eugenics programme in which every individual is responsible to the whole society, and the whole of society is determined by the perfection or otherwise of the individuals of which it consists. Again, this draws on the contradiction of the word 'fit': it combines bourgeois individualism, which is highly mobile and self-determining, with a constant reference to the social and social determination.

Edith Ellis believed that the law confines and warps individuals it cannot understand. Oscar Wilde, she argues, was a 'martyr to unscientific legislation',[23] and was *made* into a menace to the state through 'limited laws and barbaric persecution' (p. 47). In order to stop such injustice and cruelty, she appeals to 'Nature'. In other words, she resorts again to a eugenics model in order to defend inverts, and mobilises eugenics as an oppositional rhetoric. Her use of scientific-sounding language is not supported with biologistic theories of heredity, statistics or any of the usual treatment of individual and social degeneracies. Her anecdotes, for example that concerning Speranza, and her metaphors, usually those of music, seem to connect sexual explanation and political analysis through polemical devices.

> Even in abnormality, in its congenital manifestations, Nature may have a meaning as definite in her universal purpose as the discord is in music to the musician.[24]

'Discord' meant in musical terms at this time a combination of two or more notes sounded together which are unsatisfactory or foreign to prevailing harmony. The second half of the definition suggests that just because a discord is foreign it is not in itself a bad thing. Inverts form the discord against which harmony is recognised and defined, and the element of creativity which apparently goes against the grain, but, if listened to with an understanding, professional ear, adds to the harmony its own specific and unique quality. The 'disharmonies' in the character of the invert (a term later applied to Edith by Havelock) are here turned into a modernist critique which parallels atonal or discordant music with the place of the invert in society. This seems to conflict with her earlier formulation that eugenics are the musical scales of the future society. But this contrast actually helps to unravel the direction of her argument beneath these musical metaphors. Where the control of the breeding pool, the musical scales, is the most basic strand of sexological activism, the role of the invert and his/her character represents the most advanced position in sexological practice; represents that is, the new musical forms being produced by composers. In this way she produces inversion as a form that may be totally inimical to the majority of people who would not understand or appreciate it, but which, if understood and appreciated, is positive, creative, innovatory and modern.

Edith Ellis uses metaphors and anecdotes as a means of grappling with the difficulties of congenital theory and its relationship to eugenics. These may be seen to be a determined critique of or dissatisfaction with congenital theory. Congenital theory produces inverts outside the social, as isolated individuals. In its classifications and typologies it creates a set of individuals who are inherently and absolutely at odds with the dominant order of society. The political side of this construction is that society should be tolerant of inverts because they cannot help it, and that inverts should be treated in the same way as non-inverts. Ellis, through connecting inversion theory to eugenics, makes other strategic moves available to campaigners that go beyond those of the apologists for homosexuality.

In eugenics, the individual cannot be detached from the state. An oppositional identity – one which subverts or seeks to subvert dominant ideology through its very existence – is possible, but its existence will adversely affect the social. Inclusion of inverts in society is therefore much superior as a social strategy to exclusion, since it protects the organisation of the state from opposition. Inclusion also allows each individual to achieve their own perfection. Each individual's perfection is a necessary precondition for the perfection of society. Society cannot be perfect when it warps and confines its constituent parts. The political implications of this are that it is in the state's own interests that it actively sanction the acceptability of inversion and same-sex relationships. It is in the state's own interests that individual inverts actively campaign for that acceptability. Both of these things are fundamentally in the interests of both the majority of heterosexuals and the minority of homosexuals.

This has large-scale implications for the history of homosexuality. It is not the case that homosexuals and lesbians were defined and contained by inversion theory against their will or their better interests. Inversion theory was not imposed from the outside, by dominant culture. It was, instead, developed by inverts themselves and subsequently entered into dominant culture. The strategic nature of inversion theory reveals the extent to which homosexuals and lesbians were able to find or create a space for themselves that simultaneously participated in the medical, legal and scientific discourses of dominant culture. This represents a subcultural formation in so far as it indicates a group constructing an identity and culture for themselves. But it does not represent a ghettoised subculture; it is rather a strategic intervention in the society that sent Wilde to prison for two years, that punished sodomy with life imprisonment and which did not acknowledge lesbianism in law at all.

NOTES

This essay would not have been written without the close and careful attention of Elaine Hobby and Simon Shepherd. I accordingly acknowledge my great debt to them.

1 Havelock Ellis and John Addington Symonds, *Sexual Inversion*, Wilson and MacMillan, London, 1897.

2 Michel Foucault, *History of Sexuality: Volume One*, Penguin, Harmondsworth, 1979.

3 Frederic Silverstolpe, 'Benkert Was Not a Doctor: On the Non-medical Origin of the Homosexual Category in the Nineteenth Century', in *Papers of the Conference 'Homosexuality, Which Homosexuality*? (a conference in lesbian and gay studies), Free University/Schorer Foundation, Amsterdam, 1987.

4 Edith Ellis, *Stories and Essays I*, Free Spirit Press, New York, 1924.

5 Edith Ellis, *The New Horizon in Love and Life*, A & C Black, London, 1921.

6 Havelock Ellis, *My Life*, Heinemann, London, 1940.

7 Arthur Calder-Marshall, *Havelock Ellis: A Biography*, Rupert Hart-Davis, London, 1959, p. 123.

8 Vincent Brome, *Havelock Ellis, Philosopher of Sex: A Biography*, Routledge & Kegan Paul, London, 1979. The quotation is from a letter from Havelock Ellis to Edith Ellis, cited on p. 110.

9 Frank Mort, *Dangerous Sexualities: Medico-Moral Politics in England since 1830*, Routledge & Kegan Paul, London, 1987. The following paragraphs on the history of eugenics are much indebted to Dr Mort's work.

10 Francis Galton, quoted in K Pearson, *Darwinism, Medical Progress and Eugenics: The Cavendish Lecture: An Address to the Medical Profession*, University College, London, 1912, pp. 4–5.

11 John Tyndall, *Spearhead*, Nov/Dec 1968. This publication deserves no more space than this.

12 Edith Ellis, *Stories and Essays II*, Free Spirit Press, New York, 1924.

13 Edith Ellis, *Three Modern Seers: James Hinton, Frederic Nietzsche, Edward Carpenter*, Stanley Paul and Co., London, 1910.

14 Calder-Marshall, p. 119.

15 F W Stella Browne, 'The Sexual Variety and Variability among Women and their Bearing upon Social Reconstruction',

The British Society for the Study of Sex Psychology: No. 3. First read 14 October 1915, and published privately by the Society in 1917.

16 Edith Ellis, 'Eugenics and the Mystical Outlook'. This was originally one of two lectures Edith Ellis delivered to the Eugenics Education Society in 1911. It was modified and printed under this title in *The New Horizon in Love and Life*.

17 Edith Ellis, *The Mine of Dreams: Selected Short Stories*, A&C Black, London, 1925.

18 *Stories and Essays II*, p. 53.

19 Oscar Wilde, *De Profundis*: a letter from Wilde to Lord Alfred Douglas, written while Wilde was in Reading Gaol. The letter was first published in truncated form in 1905, edited by Robert Ross and published by Methuen & Co., London. The first unabridged edition was published in 1949, edited by Wilde's son, Vyvyan Holland, and published by Methuen & Co., London.

20 *Stories and Essays II*, pp. 54 and 59.

21 *Ibid*, p 53.

22 *The New Horizon*, pp. 46–47.

24 *Ibid.*, p. 47.

TOWARDS A NEW CARTOGRAPHY:
RADCLYFFE HALL, VIRGINIA WOOLF
AND THE WORKING OF
COMMON LAND
Lyndie Brimstone

Dear Jax, as always, thank you.

Radclyffe Hall, *The Well of Loneliness*, London, 1928.[1]

There is something extremely satisfying about being able to pin-point a *moment*; a name, date, person, place or event that we can positively see. A concrete fact, a shape in the midst of chaos, a fixed point in the flux of time, ours to interpret and understand. We gather *moments*, trace patterns, identify endings and beginnings, births and deaths, pre, post and neo periods, New Women, second waves, shifts of direction and momentous happenings that have altered the entire course of history! As, indeed, Virginia Woolf put it in her famous half-mocking pronouncement: 'in or around December, 1910, human character changed'.[2]

Woolf, of course, had little respect for such categorical *moments* and even less for the pompous Edwardian men who assumed stature in the light of their importance. Life cannot be mapped out flat on the page, colour coded, listed and learnt by heart, she insisted, since it just isn't lived or experienced that way. What's more, she goes on, the historical facts that dominant culture venerates are often quite arbitrary and always highly selective. In view of the history teaching requirements laid down in the new National Curriculum Woolf's criticisms are certainly as pertinent now as they were more than half a century ago. What we might briefly consider, though, are some of the less reprehensible pleasures associated with our attraction to the *moment* that she appears to overlook.

One such pleasure is undoubtedly derived from the simple fact that once a *moment* has been established it becomes public property, a common reference, opening up possibilities for a shared discourse in which anyone can participate. We don't have to agree about the meaning or value of any particular *moment*; we can praise it, rail against it, examine it from this angle and that for there it is, a kind of landmark, or milestone even, that will stay in one place long enough for us to approach it in as many different ways as we wish. We might measure, too, how far we have travelled in relation to this *moment* or explore the distance between *moments*, and in this lies another pleasure, for regardless of whether or not we like what we see, these markers on the cultural map provide reference points that help us to establish who and where we are in the overall scheme of things. We are this and not that, in agreement with some but not others, and so on. When we can embrace the *moment*, however, our satisfaction is greatly increased, for with the recognition of a valued past comes an empowering sense of 'predisposed continuity': we who are represented by that *moment* have been, are, and have every reason to expect that we will be. Just that.[3]

For those who have found little in the way of explanation, validation or direction in the record of significant *moments* produced and preserved by dominant culture, the impulse to claim, name and restore those markers that do come to light has been understandably great. So, in or around June, 1969, large numbers of culturally disinherited peoples began the self-conscious project of both filling in the spaces on the existing map and demanding territorial rights. Often through a positive (re)appropriation of what has been rejected by dominant culture, these groups would determine their own (oppositional) identities, values and beliefs and set up their own reinforcement networks. Of course, as my parody of Woolf's 'in and around' suggests, the formation of the contemporary Black, Gay and Women's Liberation Movements was not at all as precise as this and, despite the very real existence of Harlem, Greenwich Village, ghetto communities and subcultural enclaves, there never has been, nor could be the kind of complete separation implied by the map metaphor. Nevertheless, with the turn of the decade it did *feel* as though these Movements had effected an overnight revolution and occupied identifiable physical space, especially to those who found themselves situated in the border country where the cultural

boundaries overlapped. It was, after all, on this 'common-land'
that lesbian feminism was conceived and out of the experiences
that each of the 'mothers' brought with her that the lesbian
feminist was born.

Cohesion, under these conditions, has not been easy and
neither, without a clearly identifiable and shared past, a binding
tradition strong enough to hold together all the disparate bits and
pieces with which lesbian feminists variously identify, could it be.
Some had been living as lesbians long before they ever heard of
feminism while others came to lesbianism as a logical expression of
their feminist politics. Many are Jewish/Black/working class/
disabled, some have children, few, it would seem, have anything
more than a contingent interest in the kind of unified lesbian
identity promulgated by white, middle-class lesbians in the 1970s.
The value of these early endeavours has been rightfully acknowledged but, as the editorial comment in any recent lesbian
anthology will demonstrate, the question that preoccupies lesbians
in the 1990s is not so much, 'How can we reach uniform agreement
about what it means to be part of this composite group?' as, 'How
can we represent, value and use its complexity?' In other words, to
continue with the territorial metaphor, boundary marking and
colour coding won't do any more. What we need, if we are to avoid
reproducing *ad infinitum* the hierarchical and exclusionary systems
that have marginalised us, is a fresh approach to cartography and
the creation of a new, as yet barely envisaged, multi-dimensional
cultural map.

The often bitter struggles to impose, defend or negotiate
meaning and value in the 'common land' are well exemplified in
the discourses surrounding the small, but increasing number of
moments that lesbian feminists have salvaged in recent years.
These, after all, are *our* points of reference, the markers that help
us to determine who we are and where we're going. Possibly
because of its notoriety and subsequent widespread availability,
but more probably because of its threshold positioning both
historically and ideologically, one particular landmark has been
invested with such enormous significance that it appears, at times,
to have become *the* (white) lesbian *monument* and that, of course,
is Radclyffe Hall's *The Well of Loneliness*. But here we must
return to Virginia Woolf's unease, for whilst the empowerment to
be derived from our knowledge of cultural events is important

there are, as the slippage from *moment* to *monument* indicates, further dangers to be considered.

In the course of this preamble I have given examples of ways in which we commonly invest the *moment* with the qualities of a solid, material object – a concrete fact, landmark, milestone that we view, approach and, in both senses, see. As a means of getting our bearings, understanding the relationship between one pheno-menon and another and communicating our findings, this substantialisation of the moment is entirely valid. It is in our tendency to then render what could only ever be provisional, absolute, that the problem lies. Using a metaphor that is particularly apt when discussing *The Well*, Hall's earlier novel *The Unlit Lamp* (1924)[4] or, indeed, her own writings, Woolf highlights the limiting effects of this tendency. 'Life is not a series of gig-lamps systematically arranged' she says, but 'a luminous halo, a semi-transparent envelope . . .'[5] Woolf, of course, was a great one for tantalising 'half lights and profound shadows'[6] but why she should have chosen 'gig-lamps' to represent imposed order or fixity, given that these were the lights attached on both sides of the small, single-horse carriages that raced through London's crowded streets, is not altogether clear. She may have been referring to the impression created by a line of gigs waiting, perhaps, outside a theatre or a house such as Mrs Dalloway's on the night of a high-society party. What's also possible, though, is that she was punning on the slang use of the term which, according to the 1929 edition of the *Concise Oxford Dictionary*, meant spectacles, thereby lampooning once again the Edwardian author's finicky view of life. At any rate, the two ideas combined do suggest an artificially magnified and illuminated sphere creating peripheral blind spots and, reading through the many commentaries on *The Well* published in the last decade, it's not hard to see what Woolf was getting at. Certainly both book and author have been accorded a quasi-mythical status out of all proportion to their contextual significance but, even more striking, is the way *The Well* itself is so frequently described in terms suggestive of a fixed light either in or along the lesbian path. A cold, stark blinding light to those who see it as an obstacle in the course of (lesbian) feminist development; a rather romantic, solitary streetlamp to those who view it as a transformative *moment* that facilitated, rather than impeded, the establishment of an active lesbian (feminist) identity.

It is not my intention here to reduce what are often fascinating and densely theoretical arguments, but simply to suggest that much of the discourse surrounding *The Well* has had remarkably little to do with the novel itself. Indeed, at the end of August 1928, Woolf rather scathingly noted that, despite all the furore surrounding *The Well* and the rallying of artists in the 'cause of freedom of speech', no one had actually read Hall's book at that time or particularly wanted to.[7] And again, three months later, she confirmed that it wasn't really the little-read novel that was a hot issue but the idea of sex between women: 'At this moment all our thoughts centre on Sapphism . . . all London they say is agog with this.'[8] The point being that in much the same way that everyone has something to say on the more contemporary Salman Rushdie affair and the issues it has come, via the media, to represent, so it was and still is both possible and perfectly legitimate to enter into the Hall debate without reading the novel at all. *The Well*, that is to say, has been well and truly 'gig-lamped'.

Claudia Stillman Franks, Gillian Whitlock and Rebecca O'Rourke make much the same point and, by 'shifting the terrain' and approaching Hall 'from a fresh angle', each attempts to demonumentalise and revitalise this notorious lesbian *moment*.[9] It is these studies, indeed, that must be acknowledged as providing the impetus for my own re-readings. The combined idea of looking at Hall and Woolf (Whitlock) within the framework of a more flexible critical approach, 'that draws on and refers back to politics and cultural possibility, as well as to literary judgement' (O'Rourke)[10] caught my imagination, for it would seem that if the promise of a 'multi-dimensional cultural map' is ever to be realised, it is precisely this kind of laterally expansive approach that we will need to develop.

My starting point, then, is O'Rourke's questioning of the congenitalist cardboard cut-out interpretation of Hall's highly determined heroine, Stephen Gordon, and her equally astute reading of the counter commentary in *The Well* that, far from supporting the crude taxonomies established by the sexologists, 'emphasises the history and multiplicity of lesbian existence'[11]:

> the grades were so numerous and so fine that they often defied the most careful observation. The timbre of a voice, the build of an ankle, the texture of a hand, a movement, a gesture – since few were as pronounced as Stephen Gordon. (W, p. 356)

In creating a larger-than-life lesbian heroine, Hall hoped to end the 'wilfully selfish tyranny of silence evolved by a crafty old ostrich of a world for its own well being and comfort' (W, p. 121). She also makes it clear, though, that most lesbians weren't tall, narrow-hipped and athletic, didn't wear stiff collars and ties, even then, or share Stephen's preference for 'heavy silk masculine underwear' (W, p. 324). Neither, as the angst-ridden heroine notes, did they 'all live out crucified lives, denying their bodies, stultifying their brains . . . they lived natural lives – lives that to them were perfectly natural' (W, p. 302). But who were these lesbians and how were they negotiating positive lives within a hostile society? Since 'common sense' tells us there were such women we might ordinarily pass this question over. What I would like to do, though, is to pick up this seemingly minor point just to see where it might lead.

Many critics note that Hall's depiction of Valerie Seymour's (Natalie Barney's) Parisian salon is more or less positive and the hostess admirably well-balanced. Given the limited number of lesbians in a position to enjoy such privileged immunity, however, it could hardly have been this elite circle that Stephen had in mind and neither, at the opposite end of the spectrum, could it have been those without private incomes or family support whose only comfort was to be found in the exploitative and demoralising homosexual ghetto that Hall describes. Certainly it wasn't those who attempted to be open about their sexuality in conventional society for, as O'Rourke notes, 'there are no instances documented in the novel of hostility transformed by knowledge and understanding into acceptance',[12] and nor was it those, like Stephen's governess and companion, Puddle, who sublimated their desires in service. One other possibility we might explore, then, is that Hall was alluding to lesbians who were indistinguishable from heterosexual women and maintained that illusion, i.e. those who 'passed'.

For Stephen, who bears the added 'burden' of an aristocratic heritage, the 'passing' option is rejected as unthinkable and described in disparaging terms as the life a criminal might lead; one 'of perpetual subterfuge, of guarded opinions and guarded actions, of lies of omission if not of speech'. A life, in Hall's terms, both painful and dishonourable in the extreme for, not only did the lesbian who maintained 'a judicious silence' become 'an accomplice in the world's injustice', she 'deeply degraded' her own spirit and that of the lover she must publicly deny (W, pp. 244, 337). Beyond *The Well*, however, it seems that this is the kind of secret life many women positively enjoyed. Indeed, Woolf's *Orlando*, published in the same year as *The Well* and much preferred by many feminist critics, makes it all sound rather naughty and deliciously exciting. So much so, in fact, that it would appear to be very much in women's interests 'to pass', and to keep their pleasure in each other's company a closed secret. As with the book itself, lesbian desire is something to be enjoyed by those 'in the know' and dismissed as trivia by those who cannot 'read' it:

> Many were the fine tales they told and many the amusing observations they made, for it cannot be denied that when women get together – but hist – they are always careful to see that the doors are shut and that not a word of it gets into print. All they desire is – but hist again – is that not a man's step on the stair? All they desire, we were about to say, when the gentleman took the very words out of our mouths. Women have no desires, says this gentleman ... only affectations ... And since it is well known (Mr T.R. has proved it) 'that women are incapable of feeling any affection for their own sex and hold each other in great aversion', what can we suppose that women do when they seek out each other's society?
>
> As that is not a question that can engage the attention of a sensible man, let us, who enjoy the immunity of all biographers and historians from any sex whatever, *pass it over*, and merely state that Orlando professed great enjoyment in the society of her own sex.[13]

Orlando, inspired by Woolf's lover at the time, Vita Sackville-West, certainly does have a grand time experimenting with transhistorical sex/gender reversals and confusions and, if her own diary entries and letters are anything to go by, Woolf too was delightfully happy to be exploring the dark caverns of lesbian possibility. Now Woolf is quite clear that the reason why lesbianism must be kept behind closed doors is because dominant culture, as represented by Messrs S W and T R, would not accept or allow it, but there seems to be no indication that this albeit necessary 'subterfuge' hurt or bothered her over much. If anything, the secrecy would seem to be endorsed as part of the fun.

At the height of the Radclyffe Hall scandal in October 1928

Virginia Woolf gave the lectures published the following year as *A Room of One's Own*. Again she spoke of women's 'society' but so subtly that, despite her fears of being 'attacked for a feminist and hinted at for a Sapphist', it is not until recent years that the lesbian implications have been noted.[14] As a clue, though, Woolf prefaced her lecture with a clear invitation to read between the lines:

> When a subject is highly controversial, and any discussion about sex is that . . . one cannot hope to tell the truth, one can only give one's audience the opportunity to draw their own conclusions as they observe the limitations, the idiosyncracies and the prejudices of the speaker. (RO, p. 6)

Much later, after ensuring that 'there are no men present' in the audience (a device guaranteed to sharpen her listeners' attention) she introduces Chloe and Olivia working together in a laboratory (with phials of prussic acid perhaps?) and the author, Mary Carmichael, who'd like to write about this hitherto unrecorded relationship:

> For if Chloe likes Olivia and Mary Carmichael knows how to express it she will light a torch in that vast chamber where nobody has yet been. It is all half lights and profound shadows like those serpentine caves where one goes with a candle peering up and down, not knowing where one is stepping. (RO, p. 80)

Woolf explains that because the writing of this cultural secret would be not only a difficult task, requiring the creation of 'words that are hardly syllabled yet . . . some entirely new combination of [Mary Carmichael's] resources', but an almost impossible one for the woman writer 'still encumbered by that self-consciousness in the presence of "sin" which is the legacy of our sexual barbarity', the truth must wait a while (RO, pp. 80, 84). Now I don't want to underestimate the problems of adapting existing language usage to express 'unspeakable' desire, but it would seem to me that it is the 'self-consciousness' argument that is most evident in the Chloe and Olivia interlude. Woolf does make the point that irrespective of what the experts said or the general public chose to believe, women were having close relationships with each other. We note, though, that she isn't referring to 'mannish' or identifiable lesbians, like Hall and her heroine, but to 'normal' women, for she twice stresses that one of her fictional friends is married with children to go home to. Very much, indeed, like Vita Sackville-West, Violet Trefusis, Vera Brittain and Woolf herself, all seemingly 'normal' women who enjoyed lesbian attachments 'between the lines' of their respectable marriages. We might also 'observe' the way that Woolf further obfuscates a lesbian reading of this scene by introducing 'the fetters of class' (RO, p. 84), an undeveloped idea that serves only to distance lesbian subject and speaker by providing a distraction. Chloe and Olivia are not aristocratic or upper middle class, like those in Woolf's circle but, rather strangely in a 'class' context, unsupervised workers in a field not generally associated with women. Also notable, here, is the unstated fact that one of them is *not* married; like three million or so other women in England at that time, she's a spinster.

That Radclyffe Hall was also a spinster appears to have been obscured both by her notoriety as a lesbian and by our contemporary distance from the term. A brief look at spinsterhood in the 1920s, then, might shed further light on why Miss Hall felt the time had come to create an unambiguously lesbian text while Mrs Woolf most definitely did not.

The demographic, social and political forces that cohered to create an identifiable spinster class in mid nineteenth century England have been ably documented by a number of contemporary feminist historians: a marked population imbalance, the concomitant development of organised feminist campaigns, improved education and employment opportunities, and increased possibilities for independence from the family being prime factors. They have also noted that from the 1860s on the 'surplus' or 'redundant' woman problem, as it was called, caused great alarm for it was perceived, quite rightly, that unwed women could create 'mischief' and, with their demands for improved conditions, upset the whole 'natural' order of British life.[15] It was not until the opening decades of the twentieth century, however, when it became clear that increasing numbers of women were actually choosing not to get married, that the spinster caught the public and, indeed, the literary imagination as a distinct *type*:

I write of the High Priestess of society. Not of the mother of sons, but of her barren sister, the withered tree, the acidulous vessel under whose pale shadow we chill and whiten, of the Spinster I write. Because of her power and dominion. She, unobtrusive, meek, soft-footed, silent, shamefaced, bloodless and boneless, thinned to spirit, enters the secret recesses of the mind, sits at the secret springs of action, and moulds and fashions our emasculate society. She is our social nemesis.[16]

The capitalised Spinster was a danger to society; a 'sexually deficient and disappointed' woman, according to Stella Browne in 1912, 'impervious to facts and logic and deeply ignorant about life'.[17] Not an image that many women would wish to be identified with and an uncomfortable one indeed for intelligent and sexually active lesbians, like Hall.

Interestingly enough it was also in 1912, when attacks like these were a regular feature in 'free-thinking' humanist magazines, that the marriage rate began to rise for the first time in over half a century and in 1912, too, that Virginia Stephen, already 30, finally agreed to marry a man for whom she had no sexual feeling, Leonard Woolf. I don't want to make too much of this or to imply a direct causal relationship between society's increasing hostility towards single women and Woolf's decision to change her status. However, in the same way that Radclyffe Hall, for all the protection of her inherited wealth, literary status and acquired social standing, could not have remained completely impervious to the contempt in which unmarried women were held neither, it would be reasonable to assume, could Virigina Woolf. Indeed, both writers reflect the spinster debate in their fiction.

In 1924 Hall published *The Unlit Lamp* and the following year Woolf published *Mrs Dalloway*.[18] By 1920 a number of medical, sociological and psychoanalytic theories had filtered through into the public arena and in particular those put forward by Havelock Ellis, Edward Carpenter and Sigmund Freud. Again not many people outside of medical and intellectual circles would have actually read their works but, via magazine articles and novels, their quite diverse and even contradictory ideas were acquiring common currency and coalescing in most peculiar ways. The spinster, it seems, was the perfect carrier for them all for she, a social no-thing in herself, could be sexless, hermaphroditic, homosexual, man-hating, timid, tyrannical, pitiful and powerful all at the same time. Her problem, according to even the most sympathetic commentators, was sexual frustration, and some were even prepared to entertain the idea that it might not, in every case, be thwarted heterosexuality that was at the withered root of it all:

No one who has observed the repressed inverted impulse flaring into sex-antagonism, or masked as the devotion of daughter or cousin, or the solicitude of teacher or nurse, or perverted into the cheap malignant cant of conventional moral indignation, can deny its force.[19]

Even though Stella Browne, speaking here in 1923, suggests that these 'repressed inverted impulses' might be better expressed, it is hardly likely, given the prevailing attitude towards homosexuality, that this line of argument would have done anything to improve the status of the spinster, whatever her sexual proclivities. Indeed, because of the widespread belief, articulated in the 1921 Parliamentary Debates and again throughout the trial of *The Well* in 1928, that lesbianism was a vice that could be learned by any woman, the spinster became an even more frightening figure capable of corrupting any female she came into contact with and most especially those, given Freud's theories, who were still in their formative years.[20] It was also at this time, then, that the spinster teacher came to the fore of the debate, not because this was the occupation that most unmarried women pursued, for it will be remembered that by the turn of the century the clerical professions had also opened up to women, but because of the influence she was assumed to have over the pupils in whom she would almost certainly take a perverted interest. A view more recently reflected in Section 28 of the Local Government Act 1988.[21]

It would be impossible to give an adequate account here of the many lines of attack used to deter middle-class women from seeking any kind of physical, emotional or intellectual satisfaction that might detract from the primacy of heterosexual sex and, in an extremely eugenics conscious post-war climate, motherhood. Neither can I begin to discuss the spirited defence that many spinsters put up for they were, in fact, anything but 'bloodless and boneless' and, with university educations behind them, many were perfectly capable of analysing exactly what was happening and answering back. Suffice it to say that the spinster came to represent a nation in decline, the literal embodiment of all dominant culture's worst fears. Even pleas on behalf of unmarried daughters bound to ageing mothers can be understood in this way for the only ones to suggest that some women might be quite happy remaining outside of marriage were the spinsters themselves. With this general background in mind, then, there are several strands that I would like to pick up in relation to *The Unlit Lamp* and *Mrs Dalloway*.

Hall and Woolf were both in their early forties when they published these novels and both take as their subject an unfulfilled mother:

> There was an emptiness about the heart of life . . . the room was an attic; the bed narrow; and lying there reading, for she slept badly, she could not dispel a virginity preserved through childbirth which clung to her like a sheet (Clarissa Dalloway in MD, p. 29)

> What a life – and this was marriage! . . . I can't face the thought . . . of you being maltreated by a man, the thought that it might happen to you as it happened to me. (Mary Ogden in UL, pp. 26, 128)

with an intelligent daughter aware of the new professional opportunities opening up for women, and a well-educated orphan governess who is seen as a corrupting influence and a threat:

> Kilman her enemy . . . how she hated her – hot, hypocritical, corrupt; with all that power; Elizabeth's seducer; the woman who had crept in to steal and defile (MD, p. 155)

> Mrs Ogden said that [Miss Rodney] was a thief . . . who had stolen her child from her . . . [an] unsexed blue-stocking (UL, pp. 166, 221)

Both authors include lesbian possibilities and are critical of the limited roles available to women within conventional society.

Hall's is without doubt the simpler tale. Joan Ogden is the elder of two daughters and, as if Hall really believed that the firstborn should be sons, she is endowed with many of the same socially ascribed masculine characteristics as Stephen Gordon. She has 'a rather gruff voice' (W, p. 142; UL, p. 13), is tall and 'lanky as a boy' (UL, p. 11; W, p. 57), looks 'all wrong' in a dress (UL, p. 209), and insists on cropping her hair well in advance of fashion. We note, too, that both Puddle and Elizabeth Rodney describe their pupils as 'colts' (W, p. 243; UL, p. 36) and that all four of these

women are credited with exceptional intelligence and correspondingly flat 'unfeminine bosom[s]' (UL, p. 200). It was, of course,
Havelock Ellis who made this spurious, though arguably well-
intentioned connection between reduced 'feminine' characteristics
and 'above average [i.e. masculine] intellect'[22] and it is his
sentiments the sophisticated and well-read Valerie Seymour
echoes when she urges the 'blocked' lesbian writer not to give up
since 'the sooner the world came to realise that fine brains very
frequently went with inversion, the sooner it would have to lift its
ban' (W, p. 413). For most of the talented lesbian artists in *The
Well*, however, the cost is too high and their potential never
realised.

Indeed the primary stress throughout *The Well* and *The Unlit
Lamp* is on waste: wasted lives, brains and bodies that atrophy
because there's no place for them in the accepted social order. The
emphasis on hands, then, always significant markers in the lesbian
text, is worth noting. Beatrice Lesway, another Cambridge woman
with 'the brain of a masterful man', appears only as a cameo
portrait in *The Unlit Lamp*, an example to Joan of how life could be
if she took the 'lesbian way' and moved to London with Elizabeth.
With only two pages in which to capture all this means, Hall
includes a description of her hands and shapely nails, softened and
manicured with 'immense care' but never stained or polished (UL,
p. 200). Attention is also drawn to Joan's strong, capable hands
but it's Elizabeth Rodney's that are most telling here for in the
context of wasted lives they become symbols of sacrificed potential.
In a brave attempt to help a woman on fire her 'fine long hands' get
badly burnt and will remain 'hideously seamed and puckered with
large, discoloured scars' for the rest of her life (UL, pp. 19, 109).
Not, however, as a testament to her courage but as a reminder of
her failure, for Elizabeth was no more able to save the burning
woman than she was to save Joan from slow death in Seabourne.
The 'lamp' remains unlit and Elizabeth finally opts for marriage to
a man she has never loved, while Joan grows prematurely old in
the care of her demanding mother. Her mind, once sharp and
enquiring, becomes 'littered with little things', her body, once fine
and strong, becomes a burdensome 'mass of small ailments; real or
imaginary', and all will to struggle is lost (UL, pp. 268, 299).

Year after year, from January to December, she plays the part of
daughter, companion, hospital nurse, housekeeper, accountant,

amanuensis, and general factotum and slave, with no thanks, no wages, no holidays, and nothing to look forward to but a release for which she cannot pray. (*The Times* 19 April 1914)[23]

Though it is most unlikely that the writer of this article about wasted womanhood would have condoned the lesbian alternative that Joan might have chosen, it is nevertheless this strand of the spinster debate that Hall articulates in *The Unlit Lamp* via Richard Benson: 'How long is it to go on,' he cried, 'this preying of the weak on the strong, the old on the young; this hideous unnatural injustice that tradition sanctifies' (UL, p. 300). To her credit, Hall does suggest that dependent elderly women, who get nought out of marriage but their daughters, are also victims of a system that affords minimal choice. Richard, however, focuses on Joan's plight and makes it clear that society's contempt for her as a pathetic old maid is misplaced. Like his brother Lawrence, who waits years for Elizabeth to marry him, and like Martin Hallam in *The Well* who proposes to Stephen and then, years later, woos Mary Llewellyn, her lover, Richard also serves to disprove the medically endorsed myth that women become lesbian because they're unattractive to men. Both Joan and Stephen reject what would, in heterosexual terms, be very acceptable proposals, while Elizabeth is described as a beautiful woman, more akin to Lawrence's lesbian teacher in *The Rainbow* (1915) than to the 'withered tree' model that Hall was later to employ in *The Well*, Lawrence in *The Fox* (1923) and Woolf in *Mrs Dalloway*.

In fact, the withering terms that Mrs Dalloway uses to describe her feelings for her daughter's governess, Doris Kilman, could almost have been lifted directly out of *The Freewoman* article quoted earlier. It could, of course, be that Woolf was deliberately employing a popular model that readers would recognise, a suggestion that is further supported by Clarissa Dalloway's awareness that she is not being altogether fair. Her husband, Richard, after all, isn't in the least bit threatened by Miss Kilman, despite her rather obvious emasculatory name, and Clarissa herself admits that a trifle more generosity wouldn't be amiss. Doris Kilman has no family support and, for all her commendable academic abilities, had lost her chance of a decent career during the First World War. Unlike Mrs Dalloway, that is to say, who was prepared to conceal a great deal in order to protect her social position, the German-born teacher had remained loyal to her girlhood memories of happiness and refused to lie, refused to say 'all Germans were villains', even if it meant losing her job (MD, p. 110). The fact is, as Clarissa concludes, 'it was not her one hated' at all:

> but the *idea* of her, which undoubtedly had gathered in to itself a great deal that was not Miss Kilman; had become one of those *spectres* with which one battles in the night; one of those *spectres* who stand astride us and suck up half our life-blood, dominators and tyrants; for no doubt with another throw of the dice, had the black been uppermost and not the white, she would have loved Miss Kilman! But not in this world. No. (MD, p. 13, emphasis added)

So in which world *might* it have been possible to love Miss Kilman? One, most certainly, that didn't hold spinsters in such open contempt, one also, perhaps, that paid them enough to live decently and buy better clothes: 'so insensitive was she, dressed in a green mackintosh coat. Year in year out she wore that coat' (MD, p. 12). Certainly one that could accept women's desires for each other, for the possibility of these relationships Clarissa 'could dimly perceive'. She had, after all, known lesbian love in her own youth and even now 'could not resist sometimes yielding to the charm of a woman' as she supposes a man might (MD, p. 30). But again she 'had a scruple picked up Heaven knows where', one, like the ideas that had gathered around Miss Kilman, that had become so much a part of common thought that she felt it must have been 'sent by Nature (who is invariably wise)' (MD, p. 30). The world in which Mrs Dalloway cannot love Miss Kilman is a conventional, upper middle-class world and Clarissa's scruples, as Woolf's capitalisation of the noun and parenthetical comment indicate, are not to do with nature at all. It is the world that Clarissa chose when she left passion behind to become Mrs Richard Dalloway, 'invisible; unseen; unknown . . . not even Clarissa any more', but a successful society hostess with no independent identity and minimal self-respect: 'Oh if she could have lived her life over again!' she would have been tall, dark, strong, assertive . . . (MD, p. 11).

  Longings like this suggest that the reasons why Mrs Dalloway can't love Doris Kilman have little to do with the middle-aged spinster herself and a very great deal to do with the 'brutal monster' of culturally repressed desire that 'rasps' throughout the novel and lies at the (Freudian) 'root' of Clarissa's malaise (MD, p. 13). Whether it's Peter's new heterosexual love or the lesbian love which she suspects between her daughter and Miss Kilman makes no difference. It's all 'horrible' and 'degrading' to Mrs Dalloway, a 'monster' that sucks people under and threatens to disrupt the 'whole panoply of content' she has constructed around her (MD, pp. 13, 41, 113). In fact, 'the cruellest things in the world,' thought Mrs Dalloway, 'seeing them clumsy, hot, domineering, hypocritical, eavesdropping, jealous, infinitely cruel and unscrupulous', were 'love and religion' (MD, p. 112). Yet when Clarissa, after considerable resistance, allows herself to recall how it actually felt to be in love with a woman '(and what was this except being in love)' (MD, p. 33), the brute is nowhere to be seen. When Sally kissed her:

> she felt that she had been given a present, wrapped up, and told not to look at it . . . something infinitely precious, wrapped up, which, as they walked (up and down, up and down), she uncovered, or the radiance burnt through, the revelation, the religious feeling! (MD, p. 33)

Nothing monstrous in this association between 'love and religion', at least not till Peter interrupts: 'It was like running one's face against a granite wall in the darkness! It was shocking . . . horrible!' (MD, p. 33). Like the woman writer in Woolf's 'Professions for Women', Clarissa had been exploring 'the pools, the depths, the dark places where the largest fish slumber' and, about to catch, to uncover, to realise something, she was violently 'roused from her dream'.[24] The explanation Woolf gives in her essay serves equally well here. She 'had thought of something, something about the body, about the passions which was unfitting for her as a woman to say' and men, as Peter's presence reminds her, 'would be shocked'.[25] Clarissa quickly returns to the safety of shallow, superficial waters, and opts for a companionate marriage to a man for whom she has no sexual feeling, Richard Dalloway.

In both *The Unlit Lamp* and *Mrs Dalloway* the options available to most women are presented as life-threateningly few. Unlike the later hero(ine)s, Stephen Gordon and Orlando, neither Joan nor Clarissa have independent means and, being further inhibited by their acquiescence to traditional values, they suffer the physical consequences of their different confinements. Hall does indicate that as early as 1912 a number of working women were managing to jump the 'granite wall' and survive, but only the indomitable army general's daughter, Lady Bruton (brute one) and her Kilman-type companion, Milly Brush, manage to do so in *Mrs Dalloway*. Others who cannot or will not accept the boundaries of social acceptability are shown to take a very grave risk indeed. Doris Kilman, after all, is reduced to a pathetic object of ridicule, materially and emotionally starving to death, while Septimus Warren Smith, the young homosexual 'who found himself unable to pass' (MD, p. 15), is quite literally 'condemned to death' by the guardians of the wall and, per se, by Nature – Drs Holmes and Bradshaw (MD, p. 86).

They 'make life intolerable, men like that', says Clarissa, well aware that she might also have been subjected to their probings, gone mad or killed herself had she not controlled her desires by scheming, pilfering (MD, p. 164) and projecting her fears on to others:

> Odd it was, as Miss Kilman stood there . . . how, second by second, the idea of her diminished, how hatred, (which was for the ideas, not people) crumbled, how she lost her malignity, her size, became second by second merely Miss Kilman, in a mackintosh. (MD, p. 112)

Unhappy, frustrated, ugly and angry Doris Kilman may be but, as this passage makes clear, there is little to support the widely accepted Lawrentian condemnation of her:

> Fanatics and ideologues like Miss Kilman . . . commit the crime of 'forcing' the soul, where forcing has the meaning of forcible entry into a locked house, of rape, and of making a growing thing bloom out of its proper season.[26]

Elizabeth, who finally takes her pink-frocked feminine place by her father's side, has no more been corrupted or raped by her governess than Joan or Stephen were by theirs, although the concentration on Doris Kilman's hand would suggest a vague, but hardly 'forced', sexual awareness in Elizabeth's eventual rejection of her (MD, pp. 117–8).

I would argue, then, that Woolf not only employed the

prevailing stereotype of the Spinster, but that she placed it within the bourgeoise context that both created and feared it so as to suggest the purposes it served. Time and again she indicates that the Miss Kilmans that dominant culture despised were products of respectable people's imaginations, *spectres* that they conjured up to carry everything their enclosed world could not contain, *brutes* and *monsters* that they could fight the good fight against, not flesh-and-blood women called Doris (or Joan or Puddle). This is not, however, as the sample from Rose's not untypical study demonstrates, the generally accepted reading of this canonical text. Indeed, had it been so, *Mrs Dalloway* might never have found its way into the canon in the first place. So how do we manage to justify such disparate interpretations?

There are two possibilities that I'd like to offer here. The first is that mine is nothing more than the fanciful product of a mind so long practiced in the art of appropriation that it can make a lesbian text out of just about anything. An aptitude that Woolf's subtlety and apparent ambivalence at very least facilitates. The second, more likely though not unrelated, possibility is that Woolf, like Hall, was well aware of the perceptual screens that protect dominant culture from seeing anything that might threaten 'its own well being and comfort' (W, p. 121) and so took advantage of the 'peripheral blindspots' to explore her lesbian theme. Woolf, of course, had no way of knowing just how many generations of readers would have an investment in preserving both Mrs Dalloway's 'panoply of content' and the concomitant image of the 'singularly repulsive . . . masculine woman . . . embittered by what she does not have'[27] that allowed her this 'safety and comparative freedom', but a survey of critical responses to Miss Kilman (who is often denied a first name altogether) certainly confirms that we are further away from the kind of world in which Clarissa Dalloway might have loved her than Woolf, in 1925, imagined.

Although she was to employ remarkably similar images of lesbian eroticism in the posthumously published 'Moments of Being: *Slater's Pins Have No Points*',[28] *Mrs Dalloway* remains not only the most lesbian specific piece of writing Woolf ever published, but the most sexually explicit of the four novels considered here. Hall might allude to nights of passion but she was never to attempt anything as graphic as Woolf's 'match burning in a crocus', or as sensuous as the extraordinarily long sentence that describes Clarissa's 'falling in love with women':

a tinge like a blush which one tried to check and then, as it spread, one yielded to its expansion, and rushed to the furthest verge and there quivered and felt the world come closer, swollen with some astonishing significance, some pressure of rapture, which split its thin skin and gushed and poured with an extraordinary alleviation over the cracks and sores. (MD, p. 30)

By 1928 Woolf had grown rather more cautious. Being involved in a lesbian relationship herself at that time may, of course, have made her more acutely aware of the dangers of exposure and influenced the degree of risk she was prepared to take, but it is also worth restating Woolf's argument that any attempt to write openly about lesbianism would be so hampered by the awareness of dominant culture's disapproval that it couldn't realistically be done (RO, p. 84). Better the half-lights, better the closed doors, better the 'semi-transparent envelope' of Orlandian fantasy, she suggests, than the distorting 'gig-lamps' that a more direct approach would inevitably invite. At the same time, though, and in response to the same increasingly (hetero)sex-insistent social climate, Radclyffe Hall made the opposite decision and, in the writing of *The Well*, quite deliberately created an artificially illuminated and magnified lesbian sphere that couldn't be ignored. Better the confrontation, better the open argument than half-lies, half-lives and doors closed on potential. The 'serpentine caves' that Woolf 'peers up and down' in and celebrates, then, are degrading 'holes and corners' in Hall's terms (W, pp. 274, 275), and the shadowy nature of lesbian existence that allows Woolf to play with *Orlando*, a desolate 'no-man's land' lacking form, order and future. Was one more right than the other?

To return to the map, I began this exploration at the site of *The Well*, a valuable *monument* but one that has acquired such colossal proportions that people can line up either side of it without seeing each other any more. As I stepped back, one small stone drew my attention because it seemed to me that it didn't quite fit in with the others, had come from a different quarry if you like, or been shaped by a different (significant) hand. I wandered off, then, in search of others like it and found a good many, some distance away, in Woolf. Putting the two together clearly invited comparison and the implicit question, which I have chosen to make explicit here: 'Was one more right than the other?' At that point my unstated bias was towards Hall. I felt protective towards the committed lesbian, the one who was prepared to confront the 'wilfully selfish tyranny' of dominant culture and set an example for future lesbians refusing to be accomplices 'in the world's injustice'; the one who isn't revered and taught. As I moved into the related spinster discourse I fully expected to endorse this valorisation of Hall by drawing attention to the different ways that she and Woolf responded to social pressure but I was on far from level ground and, in accordance with our culturally ingrained habit of hierarchical thinking, I found myself belittling Mrs Woolf in order to elevate Miss Hall, compensating, in part, for the many times lesbians experience this kind of 'thinking' (or lack of thought) in reverse. This is not to invalidate the observations made in the course of this amble, but to acknowledge that they are weighted by my own position as an 'out' lesbian in contemporary society. As I then re-read *Mrs Dalloway* against the background of the spinster discourse my antagonism was modified through the appreciation of an ostensibly heterosexual woman's pain and the admission of her own distorting bias ('it was not her one hated . . . but the idea of her, which undoubtedly had gathered into itself a great deal that was not . . .'). Social pressures, as both Hall and Woolf demonstrate, take many forms and in the end, the very idea of evaluating their choices became untenable. What purpose, in any case, would it serve? As it is, there are too many variables, too many odd stones, each raising further questions and initiating wider, more interesting searches. Would Hall, for example, have taken such a principled stand had she not had an independent fortune and devoted partner to back her? Might Woolf have gone further in her attempts to write about women's desires if Hall hadn't taken the limelight so dramatically? Why was the 'mannish lesbian' so reticent about sex in her writing and the 'feminine frigide' so lyrical and exciting? How did Hall acquire the arrogance to speak on behalf of all lesbians and why didn't Woolf, amongst others, try to correct the impression she gave? Would either of them have made the same choices if they had had parents or children to consider, if they had been Black, or poor, or born fifty years later?

Stone by stone, then, monuments come down, 'angles' get more difficult to establish, biases become harder to support, and the much needed multi-dimensional cultural map begins to take shape. Yes Hall and Woolf shared common land but they were situated very differently. Rather than attempting to equate or otherwise evaluate the personal and contingent choices they made, then, we might take a broader look at the framework of cultural possibility that informed their decisions. We would note, for example, that no two of the dozen or so diversely situated women named in the course of this study respond to lesbianism in the same way and remind ourselves that the texts Hall and Woolf left us are not tablets of stone but partial records of a complex process that didn't start or finish with, or adequately represent either of them. At the same time, rather than seeking to assess the influence Hall and Woolf have had on future generations of women defining their relationship to lesbianism, we might pay more attention to the cultural possibilities and limitations that inform our readings and make these more explicit in our arguments. We'll still have preferences, of course, still find agreement with some but not others, and still take strategic positions but on far more open, less predetermined terrain. If we are to develop the more flexible critical approach that O'Rourke and others have called for, we may even have to accept that whilst a lesbian appropriation of the monumentalist tradition is not without its satisfactions, it is also a limiting and exclusionary tradition offering only an illusion of security.

NOTES

1 Radclyffe Hall, *The Well of Loneliness* (1928), Virago, London, 1982. All future references will appear in the body of the text (W, p.-).

2 Virginia Woolf, 'Mr Bennett and Mrs Brown' (1924) in Virginia Woolf, *Collected Essays 1*, Chatto & Windus, London, 1967, pp. 319–337. For a more comprehensive discussion see Rachel Bowlby, *Virginia Woolf: Feminist Destinations*, Basil Blackwell, Oxford, 1988, particularly pp. 1–6.

3 Raymond Williams, *Marxism and Literature*, Oxford University Press, Oxford, 1977, p. 116.

4 Radclyffe Hall, *The Unlit Lamp* (1924), Virago, London, 1981. All future references will appear in the body of the text (UL, p. -).

5 Virginia Woolf, 'Modern Fiction' in Virginia Woolf, *The Common Reader* (1925), Penguin, Harmondsworth, 1938, p. 149.

6 Virginia Woolf, *A Room of One's Own* (1929), Granada

Publishing, London, 1981, p. 80. All future references will appear in the body of the text (RO, p. -).

7 Nigel Nicolson and Joanne Trautmann, (eds.), *The Letters of Virginia Woolf Vol. 3*, Harcourt Brace Jovanovich, New York, 1977, p. 520.

8 Woolf, *Letters*, p. 555.

9 Claudia Stillman Franks, *Beyond the Well of Loneliness: The Fiction of Radclyffe Hall*, Avebury, England, 1982, p. 98. Gillian Whitlock, ' "Everything Is Out of Place": Radclyffe Hall and The Lesbian Literary Tradition' in *Feminist Studies 13*, no. 3 (Fall 1987), pp. 555–582: p. 560. Rebecca O'Rourke, *Reflecting on The Well of Loneliness*, Routledge, London, 1989.

10 O'Rourke, p. 143.

11 *Ibid.*, p. 10.

12 *Ibid.*, p. 47.

13 Virginia Woolf, *Orlando* (1928), Penguin, Harmondsworth, 1963, pp. 154–155, emphasis added.

14 Virginia Woolf, *A Writer's Diary* (1953), Triad Panther, St Albans, 1978, p. 146.

15 See Sheila Jeffreys, *The Spinster and her Enemies: Feminism and Sexuality 1880–1930*, Pandora, London, 1985, particularly pp. 86–101; and Lillian Faderman, *Surpassing the Love of Men: Romantic Friendship and Love Between Women from the Renaissance to the Present*, The Women's Press, London, 1985, particularly pp. 178–189.

16 *The Freewoman*, 23 November 1911, quoted in Jeffreys, p. 95.

17 *The Freewoman*, 7 March 1912, quoted in Jeffreys, p. 97.

18 Virginia Woolf, *Mrs Dalloway* (1925), Granada Publishing, London, 1976. All future references will appear in the body of the text (MD, p. -).

19 Stella Browne, 'Studies in Feminine Inversion', in *Journal of Sexology and Psychoanalysis*, 1923, p. 51, quoted in Jeffreys, pp. 118–119.

20 See Vera Brittain, *Radclyffe Hall: A Case of Obscenity?*, Femina Books, London, 1968, pp. 47–51; *Parliamentary Debates 1921* discussed in Jeffreys, pp. 113–115; and Jeffrey Weeks, *Coming Out: Homosexual Politics in Britain*, Quartet Books, London, 1977, pp. 106–107.

21 See Madeleine Colvin, *Section 28: A Practical Guide to the Law and its Implications*, National Council for Civil Liberties, London, 1989; and Alison Oram, ' "Embittered, Sexless or

Homosexual'': Attacks on Spinster Teachers 1918—1939', in The Lesbian History Group, (eds.), *Not a Passing Phase: Reclaiming Lesbians in History 1840–1985*, The Women's Press, London, 1989.

22 Havelock Ellis, *Psychology of Sex*, Emerson Books Inc., New York, 1936, p. 246.

23 Quoted in Zoë Fairbairns' 1980 Introduction to *The Unlit Lamp*, pp. 5–6.

24 Virginia Woolf, 'Professions for Women' (1931), in Virginia Woolf, *Women and Writing*, The Women's Press, London, 1979, p. 61.

25 *Ibid*.

26 Phyllis Rose, *Woman of Letters: A Life of Virginia Woolf*, Routledge & Kegan Paul, London, 1978, p. 134; compare D H Lawrence, *The Rainbow* (1915), Penguin, Harmondsworth, 1978, p. 357.

27 Rose, pp. 147, 149.

28 Virginia Woolf, 'Moments of Being: *Slater's Pins Have No Points*', in Virginia Woolf, *A Haunted House* (1944), Granada Publishing, London, 1982, pp. 102–109.

2

Lesbians Reading

KATHERINE MANSFIELD'S PEAR TREE
Gillian Hanscombe

A LESBIAN READING?

Sometimes being a lesbian reader is rather like being one of the favoured few in the cinemas of the 1950s who were given red and green specs so they could see the breathtaking perspectives of the new 3–D movies. Audiences viewing without the specs saw only the usual thing; and sometimes not even all of that. But with the specs, all was revealed.

Some time ago I was working on Modernism and reading the women writers of the period 1900–1940. I wasn't aware of my lesbian specs, having worn them all my life; and in any case, my training in the heteropatriarchy had made perfectly clear that Lesbianism was irrelevant to Literature. The irrelevance of lesbianism in writers was covered by the doctrines of true criticism remaining unsullied by biographical pollutants (since we professed Art über Alles); whereas the irrelevance of lesbianism in the content of literature was covered by its 'non-universality'. Even had the matter been broached by a few rowdy women lacking both taste and decorum, simple logic might suffice: was it not obvious that there had been lesbian writers who never put lesbians in their books or poems; and was it not obvious that non-lesbian writers had occasionally used lesbian characters or themes as they might use anything under the sun?

Further, women writers themselves were inheritors of the heteropatriarchal tradition and therefore ambivalent about the struggle inherent in trying to reach a perspective that was woman-centred, or, even harder, lesbian-centred, since to say that a woman-centred perspective might be different from the traditional male-centred one was, according to humanism, tantamount to saying that a woman's perspective was not universal. In addition, to introduce elements of a lesbian perspective would carry the extra peril of abnormality. On the other hand, since the women writers were women, rather than men, the fact of their being women had inevitably to enter into the perspective they offered if they were to write authentically. If it were possible, that is, to excise their women's perspective, they would inevitably produce copies of men's work. They would find themselves writing other people's (i.e. men's) fiction or verse.

Nevertheless, I couldn't help noticing things. If they shared nothing else, women writers did seem to share a knowledge of lesbianism. Many lived straightforwardly as lesbians and encoded their work (Gertrude Stein, for example). Others worked and socialised among lesbians (Mina Loy, for example). Still others – a significant number of them – repeated in their lives triangular, bisexual patterns, where conventional heterosexual partnerships were underscored or paralleled by passionate relationships with women. H D, Dorothy Richardson, Virginia Woolf, Katherine Mansfield – Modernist writers whose work was accepted within the heteropatriarchal canon as Literature (and not mere women's work) – all these women knew more about lesbianism than they could have read in books. All of them married men; all of them loved women.

Was it really possible – or likely – that lesbianism had nothing to do with the making of literature? No wonder biography was shunned: what might it reveal? No wonder everyone pointed to Lawrence's story 'The Fox'. Lesbian experience was obviously just a part (a tiny part) of human experience; and of no special significance. Anyone could write about it – if they chose. But it wasn't part of the literary tradition; and it quite clearly had nothing to do with sensibility . . .

It was during my reading of Katherine Mansfield's story 'Bliss' that I noticed my lesbian specs for the first time. Traditional criticism told me that this was a story about an unawakened and immature woman who discovers, during the course of a dinner party she's holding, that her husband is conducting an adulterous affair with one of the guests. But what I was reading was a story about how to have a lesbian relationship without having it. Yes, adultery was going on; but that was a symptom of the real story, not its main point. The story was about the surge of feelings between women who did not know 'what to do with' them (Mansfield repeats the phrase more than once in the text).

'Bliss' isn't a story about lesbians; but it is a story about lesbianism. It's a story where a woman writer shows and explores (as no man could) her ambivalence and bafflement about the arousal of passion and sexual excitement in a woman who has been trained to believe that these feelings could not possibly have another woman as their object. But like any artist, this writer is impelled towards the truth. What is the truth about human bliss? Must the flow between women always be made marginal and ironical by the intrusion of the male? Or is the intrusion just that: an intrusion? We can see how Mansfield dealt with these questions by considering some texts underpinning 'Bliss', as well as by considering the text of the story itself.

DEFLECTIONS AND INVERSIONS: THE CONTEXTUAL DOCUMENTS AND THEIR CONTRIBUTION TO THE ICONOGRAPHY OF 'BLISS'

Reading 'Bliss' accurately involves understanding how and when it was written; how its central image of the pear tree was constructed and what meaning it bears. This involves, in turn, reading relevant journal entries and letters, where Mansfield's preoccupations with taboo passions lie embedded. Incest and lesbianism are dreaded, tormenting, preoccupying; and provide the skeletal structure upon which 'Bliss' is appended.

I don't mean to suggest that there is a simple equivalence between 'art' and 'life': that the imagistic structure of 'Bliss' has no integrity of its own; or that Mansfield's literary skills are somehow out of control. What does seem to me to be the case, on the other hand, is the absurdity of the sleight of hand prevalent in some schools of criticism which claims that the human dilemmas of the artist as individual have no significant bearing on the literary process. Even traditional images have multiple meanings, so that it is necessary to look at the structures of a writer's imagination in order to understand more accurately the specific way in which a particular image is used in a particular context. The age-old myths are used over and over, but each myth is re-created and re-interpreted by the individual writer. I accept, that is, that literature is one manifestation of the workings of the unconscious, both collective and individual; and that there is a continuum between the preoccupations, fantasies, conflicts, dreams, inner imaging and all other forms of psychic irresolution that make up mental life, and the formal themes, images, structures and perspective that characterise literary work.

More specifically, I accept, too, that the chief tenets of psychoanalytic theory – loosely interpreted – can clarify the nature and direction of the creative energies released and controlled in works of literature. In 'Bliss', quite particularly, the repression of sexual desire and a consequent confusion and conflict, are played out within the ordered aesthetic parameters of the story. And part of the playing out involves the projection of inchoate (i.e. repressed) desire on to the image of the pear tree which carried, for Mansfield, a personal significance.

Illicit sexual desire is the theme of 'Bliss'. But the irony implicit in the story's title is only fully revealed when one excavates other texts of Mansfield's that are also preoccupied with this theme. What seems to me clear is that the writer as artist conflated in her story the repressed energies of two culturally forbidden desires: those of incest and of lesbianism. The story is ostensibly about adultery; it is ostensibly about Bertha's realisation that her husband Harry is having an affair with Pearl Fulton. Adultery, of course, may be illicit, but it is not forbidden; and it may, therefore, act as a 'safety valve' or acceptable distraction if what is really at stake are far more unspeakable desires.

The story's two central characters, Bertha and Miss Fulton, are ambivalent about what they feel and what to 'do with' their feelings. So is their creator. The text itself makes this much clear. Mansfield has brought to fruition a story about fruit that may not ripen. How she does so is particularly fascinating for a lesbian reader, whose specs allow her to see what others may miss.

In space and time, alongside a story or poem, indeed any text, is the analogue of the writer's writing of it, a phenomenon which held particular and self-conscious significance for those who lived and wrote in the aesthetic environment of Modernism and its nodding acquaintance with the theories of psychoanalysis, quantum mechanics and other 'subjectivisms'. In Mansfield's case, this free flow between inner and external realities, between subjective and objective, was heightened by powerful lyric resources. She didn't write long, naturalistic novels; nor, in any other writing did she exhibit any commitment to notions of objective reality. Her stories are similar to lyric poems in their use of images and of 'associational' logic.

The central image in her story 'Bliss' is a pear tree. It grows in the natural world (and yet betokens 'unnatural' passions); it blossoms (but does not fruit); it is slender like a poplar (not round as a pear tree should be . . .). The pear tree appears as an expression of (forbidden?) love between Mansfield and her brother Leslie in an entry Mansfield made in her *Journal*.[1] Its 'unnaturalness' extends to cover her intense feelings for her friend, Ida Baker, with whom she was obsessed during the writing of the story (shown in letters written at the time and extracted below). On Mansfield's insistence, Ida Baker had long before agreed to take the name 'Lesley' (for Mansfield's beloved brother), together with the name 'Moore', her own mother's maiden name. So she became Lesley Moore, otherwise known as LM.[2]

Indeed, for Mansfield, everyone had many selves; and this perception underscored her conviction that human relationships are continually subject to shifts of tone, emphasis, affect and meaning. She seems to have felt that such a subjection was not due only to the pressures of external environment; it resulted from the randomness with which different selves may collide. The personal dynamic dramatising this perception was her experience of the Murry/Mansfield/Lesley Moore triangle,[3] her relationships with these two 'significant others' providing themes and meanings explored many times over in her fiction.

The relationship with Murry has remained as well known as it was when it took place, not least because of his publishing of her letters to him. (It's interesting to note, however, that he didn't publish his letters to her, though it seems unlikely that she would have destroyed them.) Her relationship with LM, on the contrary, was documented only by her letters to Murry until LM published her own recollections, together with a handful of Mansfield's letters to her, in 1971. The emphasis, unbalanced as it is, is hardly unusual, given the readings of women's lives provided by conventional scholarship, where a woman writer's heterosexual connections are assumed to be all-consuming, while her lesbian ones are either elided or marginalised.

Mansfield's first Leslie was equally significant and almost as troubling. Ida was named for him; but Murry, too (together with explicit sexuality) could be conflated with him. In one *Journal* entry she records:

> when I lay in bed, I felt suddenly passionate. I wanted J. to embrace me. But as I turned to speak to him or to kiss him I saw my brother lying fast asleep, and I got cold. This happens nearly always.[4]

In such taboo longings lies the origin of the image of the pear tree, presented most clearly in a *Journal* entry addressed to her brother after his death and fashioned as a dialogue.

In 1915, the much-loved brother came to England to train for the army. LM was on an extended visit home to Rhodesia. During their reunion, Mansfield and her brother shared memories of their childhood in New Zealand, memories set off by the sight of the pear tree in the garden of the St John's Wood house in Acacia Road where Mansfield and Murry were living.

The conversation Mansfield records took place shortly before Leslie Beauchamp left for the front. He was killed almost immediately, on 7 October 1915, an event so traumatic for Mansfield that she dedicated herself to the task of recording their shared past. Her *Journal* entry is simply dated 'October', but it seems to have been written after she had heard of her brother's death. It's early autumn, since the Michaelmas daisies are in bloom and the pear tree is in fruit. The pear tree is 'slender', 'rather like a poplar'; and one of its fruits – 'a little round pear' – falls to the ground 'hard as a stone', suggesting that it isn't yet ripe. Unlike the single Acacia Road fruit, the New Zealand pears were plentiful, scattered far and wide. The dialogue deliberately obscures which character is brother or sister, as if to emphasise their like minds, until the final two exchanges.

There are echoes of the Eden myth of innocence, though the figures are children. And though no serpent enters, promising knowledge, there is a tree and it bears fruit. The Eden myth, and the image of the garden generally, are emblematic in literature of the Judaeo-Christian tradition of the 'Fall': the conflation of sin with sexuality and the consequent loss of innocence. Here, particularly, unsexualised love is both innocent and blissful; and, being unsexualised, allows the shared nostalgia of the adult sister and brother to claim a territory which is somehow gender free. However, the claim suggests, in turn, its own 'negative capability', so that the pressure to emphasise freedom from the pollutant of sexuality becomes a pressure to conceal the forbidden eroticism of incest.

The pears remembered from childhood are idealised, enhanced by the glow of memory and the serenity of the mood: they are 'bright, canary yellow'. Brother and sister sat together as children on the garden seat, devouring pears. At this point, the emotions are made explicit: their happiness was extraordinarily *'deep'* (Mansfield's italics indicate the unconscious source from which the feelings arise); and it was hidden. They share a 'secret'. But the the secret is below the surface – *'deep'*. What was it? It must have been the 'family feeling', is the conclusion.

The uninhibited intensity and sensuousness with which the pears are described, together with the italicised *'deep'*, however, point to a pun embedded in the phrase. 'Family feeling' connotes the affection and loyalty shared by kin; but here it carries, too, the echo of the 'family way', a 'secret' about which the two characters must remain unaware. Their identification is clearly stated – 'we were almost like one child' – an identification traditionally characteristic of romantic passion.[5] But in this instance, since the passion is 'unnatural' – and therefore taboo – it is deflected on to the pears, the fruit, the offspring, of the natural order, a deflection which makes the pears stand in apposition to the real 'forbidden fruit'. Instinctively aware of this, the two can sigh for the garden of their happiness.

To the extent that the pears fail to deflect all the passion of brother and sister, they are vulnerable:

'Do you remember that some of the pears we found used to have little teeth marks in them?'
'Yes.'
'Who bit them?'
'It was always a mystery.'

The 'mystery', like the 'secret', must not be discovered. Thus far, the conversation has taken place between dusk and moonlight. Now the Acacia Road pear tree shines under the round moon, the ivy 'glitters like metal', the 'air smells chill . . . heavy . . . very cold'. What is important is the coldness of the contrast; it interposes between them an adult dread, so that their comfort resides in the hope that they can 'go back together' and 'find everything'. Now in the adult world of the moon their characters unconsciously differentiate. He asks for her hand, another implicit, and unconscious, pun, which resonates with a further, underlying pun: the sounds of the words 'pear' and 'pair' are, after all, indistinguishable. She, responding, addresses him as 'darling'. He is confident he'll come back; and his confidence is 'as certain as this pear'. The 'pear' stands out sharply from its context, since despite the conviction of the claim, pears are not 'certain': they either rot, or are devoured. Again there is an instinctive awareness of what lies behind the comparison; the conviction is 'mysterious'. There is a 'strange' wind and the now old moon shines on the two characters, rather than on the pear tree. She shivers from cold, he puts his arm around her and kisses her, thus signalling his realisation of what the pear prefigures: 'Good-bye, darling'. They must part and be parted. The consummation of romantic passion is death.

Textual comparisons between this journal entry and the story 'Bliss' align clearly enough the significance of the pear tree in each case. In addition, moreover, Ida Baker specifically says that Mansfield described 'the radiance of the pear tree in the little garden' at Acacia Road, 'the same pear tree that she put into her story "Bliss" '.[6]

One point of thematic correspondence between the journal entry and 'Bliss' is that just as brother and sister are undifferentiated – are, as it were, one child – so, too, are Bertha and Miss Fulton, in that both are women and do not constitute for each other, the 'other' of the heterosexual tradition. For Mansfield, the significance of Eden is that a companion is identified with her, rather than differentiated from her. Another characteristic of Eden is not so much that it is asexual – the descriptions of the experience of the two children and of Bertha and Miss Fulton are highly sensual and almost sexual – but that in it there is no consciousness of sexuality. A third characteristic is that it does not contain either God or the serpent: the two children are self-sufficient. Another way of putting this is to say that a world of childhood innocence is not shattered by the prescriptiveness of the adult world of experience. Sexual feelings are unconscious and, in a sense, natural.

In such a vision, the Fall would then entail: a) a differentiation from the 'other' (the introduction of the male); b) sexuality made explicit; and c) an acknowledgement of the children's lack of self-sufficiency and their consequent vulnerability. It is ironical, therefore, that in Mansfield's story explicit sexuality is linked with Harry, the adulterous husband, since it is his intervention that dramatises the ending of bliss. It could even be argued that Harry is the serpent responsible for the Fall. That explicit sexual significance can only be attributed to Harry is in keeping with the logic of this version of the myth, since in this version, explicit sexuality is incompatible with the paradisal state. In the adult world of experience the feeling of bliss can recur (in the story, between Bertha and Miss Fulton), but though it can be embodied in the vision of the pear tree seen through a window, it cannot, by its very nature, be made explicit or acted out.

Mansfield wrote 'Bliss' during the early months of 1918, when she was convalescing in Bandol in southern France. LM was attending her. Their relationship was under great strain; Mansfield was obsessed with LM and the violent feelings her presence engendered. Much of the obsession focused on food, that traditional repository for unconscious sexual fears and fantasies much written about by psychoanalysts and other theorists: Mansfield was tormented by LM's failures as a cook; by her consumption of food; by her references to food; and – significantly – by terrors that LM wanted to destroy her, to eat her alive, to devour her.

During these months, however, Mansfield didn't work only at writing fiction; she also wrote a large number of letters to Murry. It's important to realise that the context in which both stories and letters were written was one in which several situations reached their crux: instead of Murry being threatened by tuberculosis, Mansfield was now the victim – forced, therefore, to seek the more clement climate of southern France, though now that her divorce from Bowden had been granted, she and Murry planned to marry at the beginning of April. The Great War was at its height and official permission to travel to France was necessary. Mansfield obtained it; but LM was refused permission to accompany her. Mansfield set out alone for France, leaving London on 7 January 1918. In addition, she was extremely short of money.

On 24 January, soon after her arrival, she wrote to Murry that she was called to the town hall about permission for someone to visit her:

'You are not expecting a gentleman to follow you to France?'
'Non, Monsieur.' Then, of course, I saw it all! It was BAKER.

The letter continues, protesting that she really doesn't want LM
with her:

> She has been an angel to me but in our new life she has not a
> great part – and she realises that. It would be very painful.[7]

Two days later, deeper dread emerges:

> Our letters crossed again about LM. I heard from her today, but
> I too felt callous, cool, and retired into my shell. She *is* a ghoul in
> a way. She does blossom out and become a brick *only* when the
> other person is more or less delivered up to her. That's what I
> can't stomach. That's why I don't want her here. As long as I am
> to be massaged she's an angel, for then *c'est elle qui mange*; if I
> am not in the humour, out pours 'Mr Webb and I' and 'Why
> don't men . . .' etc. etc. She's all hungry fury, then, beating
> against my shores and trying to break down my defences. That's
> why I used to get so furious at the studio, for there she ate me
> before my eyes and I really *revolted.*[8]

Despite wanting to be alone and independent, however, she
couldn't function well alone. On 3 February she wrote to Murry
about the night terrors she suffered.[9] Part of the fear was her
inability to cope with being alone, even though that was the
condition she sought in order to work:

> The worst of R E A L insomnia is one spends a great part of the
> day wondering if one is going to bring it off the coming night.
> Can I stand another last night?[10]

The problems of coping alone, though, were in no way alleviated
by news of LM's imminent arrival:

> A MOST MYSTERIOUS TELEGRAM which SO horrifies and
> bewilders me that I don't dare to let myself think of it. I
> must wait. It says: 'Am coming leave this afternoon Baker'!!!
> Of course I thought immediately of you. Something had

happened . . . God wouldn't let it happen, and even if he did you would never leave it to that great monster to tell me.[11]

This reaction seems clearly to have contributed to the impetus to write 'Bliss', to write 'another *big* story'.[12]

Mansfield's illness, LM's impulsion to help and Murry's distance pointed up only too clearly why both LM and Murry were inadequate substitutes for the original Leslie. In the ideal world of the pear tree, Mansfield was not alone; neither she nor her brother were in need of help and the dynamic of their relationship was that of equals. Murry's distance from her allowed her to maintain a view of him as a companion and playmate, but of course precluded his presence. LM's presence and willingness to help pointed to Mansfield's need for help. The bliss felt in the companionship of the original Leslie is possible for Mansfield's character Bertha because Bertha does not need Miss Fulton any more than Miss Fulton needs her. They are indeed equal and identified with one another in relation to the pear tree.

As soon as LM had arrived and established herself, Mansfield's obsession with food began. She transferred her revulsion at LM's eating habits to a psychological dread of LM devouring her. Many letters to Murry at this time show this transference to be a persistent theme during the whole period at Bandol:

. . . but I really DO feel that if she could she'd EAT me.[13]

Send me a letter and I'll wear it over my heart and try and keep these big grown-up *mangeurs* away. You should see LM under their directions alimenting herself *avec le potage*. No, my gorge rises.[14]

LM was a constant presence during the writing of 'Bliss'; the grossness Mansfield accuses her of is evident in the character Harry; and the sentimentality she recoils from in LM is evident in the character Bertha. And yet these heightened emotional tensions weren't all. During this time, Mansfield suffered her first experience of spitting blood, an event she found appalling and terrifying,[15] and which made her even more dependent on LM and even more hostile: to Murry she wrote that she had the doctor and the 'Slave' and that it was good that LM had come, even though it seemed to her that LM had 'in some mysterious way ... *done it*.'[16] She detests LM's 'powerful broody henniness' and claims, wildly:

> I even go so far as to feel that she has pecked her way into my lung to justify her coming.[17]

Her hostility reached such a pitch that Mansfield compared the relationship to a stormy marriage, identifying herself with Lawrence, who felt devoured by Frieda:

> It is impossible to describe to you my curious hatred and antagonism to her – gross, trivial, dead to all that is alive for me, ignorant and *false* ... I felt exactly as L. must have felt with F. – exactly. You remember the feeling L. had (before he was so mad) that F. wanted to destroy him; I have – oh, just that!!![18]

On 28 February, the completing of 'Bliss' gave emotional release in more ways than one, since it was, in a sense, a story about herself, LM and Murry.[19] Not long after their return to London in April, Mansfield wrote to LM with an affection hardly credible after the hostility of Bandol and showing the extraordinary reach of her ambivalence towards her friend:

> Does it gleam to you, too ... those hours on the boat ... I was so happy – were you? ... I would like to turn to you and say 'Oh Jones, we are quite all right, you know'.[20]

Four years later, in the summer of 1922, Mansfield was more explicit:

> ... the old feeling is coming back – an ache, a longing – a feeling that I can't be satisfied unless I know you are *near*. Not on my account; not because I need you – but because in my horrid, odious, intolerable way, I love you and am yours ever KM.[21]

> But try and believe and keep on believing without signs from me that I do love you and want you for my wife.[22]

It's clear that during the writing of 'Bliss', Mansfield was in an acute state of crisis; her separation from Murry, her deep ambivalence and repressed feelings towards her friend, LM, and her sense of fear, isolation and loneliness, culminating in the first concrete symptom of consumption – all contributed to the concentration of her creative energy.

BLISS: OR, HOW TO HAVE A LESBIAN RELATION-SHIP WITHOUT HAVING IT

In the working out of its imagery, 'Bliss' explores significant elements of Mansfield's central relationships. There is the pear tree of the childhood shared with Leslie, together with its associations of mystical eroticism; and there is the food imagery associated with her ambivalent dread of, and dependence on, LM. 'Bliss' deals with the dichotomy between romantic and erotic passion; and with the dangers of unknowing. According to tradition, romantic passion is a state of intense desire which must remain sexually unconsummated or which is consummated only in death. In 'Bliss', it must not only remain unconsummated, but must not even be expressed. Erotic passion, on the other hand, is generally understood as explicit sexual desire whose goal and satisfaction is sexual congress. What is dangerous about Bertha's state of unknowing is that unawareness of sexual desire conceals a threat that taboo passions may erupt to explode the existing order; but even if the threat never materialises, unawareness inevitably leads to confusion and indecision.

Most of the critical attention given to 'Bliss' has assumed that the unfaithfulness of the husband and his illicit sexuality are Mansfield's chief concerns; but when careful attention is paid to her handling of the story's elements, it makes more sense to see the relationship between the two women characters as the focus of the writer's fascination.

Mansfield was 29 when she wrote 'Bliss': the central character, Bertha Young, is 30, though the 'Young' of her name puns upon her immaturity and lack of awareness. The story's opening tone is curiously fused: the interior monologue of 'she still had moments like this when she wanted to run instead of walk' shifts to authorial ironic detachment in 'What can you do if you are thirty and ... you are overcome, suddenly, by a feeling of bliss – absolute bliss!', where Mansfield deliberately suggests that such an overloaded enthusiasm is inappropriate. Bertha's inner voice is girlish and impetuous: 'How idiotic civilisation is! Why be given a body if you have to keep it shut up in a case like a rare, rare fiddle?'[23] Bertha wants to express her bliss with her body, in spite of having (we learn later) borne a child without experiencing sexual awakening.

At the opening of the story, the source and focus of Bertha's bliss is not located. Her inexperience prevents her from communicating directly (that is, consciously); so that when she arrives at her house she asks if the fruit has come and goes upstairs to arrange it. She bought the grapes 'to tone in with the new dining-room carpet': the fruit is ornamental, not functional. After arranging it, Bertha stands back 'to get the effect', which she finds 'most curious'. The dark table 'seemed to melt into the dusky light and the glass dish and the blue bowl to float in the air', all of which is very disturbing and makes her feel she must be 'hysterical'.

In the next section of the story, Bertha tries to play with her child, but is frustrated by the nurse, who clearly knows more about the child's routine than does Bertha. Her frustration is expressed in the same image as it was earlier: 'Why have a baby if it has to be kept – not in a case like a rare, rare fiddle – but in another woman's arms?' This time her bliss is slightly more focused as she realises her affection for the child, but again she has no way of expressing the feeling: 'all her feeling of bliss came back again, and again she didn't know how to express it – what to do with it'. This is the keystone of the story: Bertha's unknowing of 'what to do with' her feelings.

The following section reveals Bertha talking to her husband Harry, on the telephone; but again she finds she has 'nothing to say' and again she concludes that 'civilisation' is 'idiotic'. These incidents taken together suggest that the basis of Bertha's hysterical reactions is that her feelings have no object and therefore cannot find expression.

Next, the narrative carefully sketches in the dynamics that will operate in the central scene of the story, the dinner party to take place later in the evening. The guests are the Norman Knights (who are anything but gallant), Eddie Warren and Pearl Fulton. Mansfield precisely counterpoints her own irony against the semi-aware intellectual pronouncements of Bertha's pretentious inner monologue; and she did so deliberately, writing to Murry:

> What I *meant* . . . was Bertha, not being an artist, was yet artist manquée enough to realise that those words and expressions were not and couldn't be hers. They were, as it were, *quoted* by

her, borrowed with . . . an eyebrow . . . yet she'd none of her own.[24]

The Norman Knights are a 'sound couple': he is going to start a theatre and she is 'awfully keen on interior decoration' (how awfully, we learn later). Eddie Warren is a poet. But Pearl Fulton is Bertha's 'find'; she is 'beautiful . . . strange' and Bertha has 'fallen in love with her'. Previously we've seen how Bertha's failure to express herself has caused her frustration; now, by contrast, there is something in Miss Fulton – 'a certain point' – which prohibits expression: '. . . but the certain point was there, and beyond that she would not go'.

Bertha has asked Harry if there was anything beyond that point and he's said not and that she was 'cold'. (The irony of this assessment comes later, when we learn of Harry's infidelity with Pearl Fulton; that what lies beyond her 'certain point' is her sexuality.) Bertha's passion has an erotic goal, but she is unaware of it. To press this point, Mansfield shows Bertha hugging a cushion to herself 'passionately, passionately'; but it's no substitute and can't 'put out the fire in her bosom'.

Immediately Bertha notices the 'tall, slender pear tree' in the garden which, significantly, is in 'fullest, richest bloom', thus promising fruit. (Blossom was a metaphor shared by Mansfield and LM, who recalled how they'd discussed the failures in their relationship:

This inadequacy was the real cause which Katherine and I looked for *later*, in trying to understand why our friendship had never flowered, and why so many buds on the tree had remained closed . . . the full flower . . . was there for my plucking.[25])

Promise, indeed, is more important than fruition, since Bertha's fruit is ornamental (and Katherine's pears were transitory and uncertain). Bertha's bliss is centred on promise, not on fulfilment. The pear tree is 'perfect', set against the sky. But against this image is set another: down below in the garden, a black cat pursues a grey cat. Their 'intent' and 'quick' chase gives Bertha a 'curious shiver' (curious because she is unaware that the object of passion is consummation; curious, too, because the 'animal' drive exhibited by the cats sets up a resonance in her in which her own undis-covered – and undisclosed – sexuality begins to assert itself). After this disturbance, however, 'she seemed to see on her eyelids the lovely pear tree with its wide open blossoms as a symbol of her own life', a life promising fruition but as yet having not achieved it. For the dinner party she dresses herself in green and white – the colours of the pear tree – only noticing the identification with the pear tree afterwards: 'It wasn't intentional. She had thought of this scheme hours before she stood at the drawing-room window'.

The brittle, materialist, pseudo-intellectual milieu of the dinner party is symbolised by food images in the dialogue: apart from the opening picture of Bertha arranging the fruit, we're presented both with Bertha's child at her meal and with the Norman Knights' anecdotes (she explains how a man 'simply ate' her with his eyes and her husband expands this into 'the cream of it was . . .'). Mrs Norman Knight's dress looks as if it is made from 'scraped banana skins'; her ear-rings are like 'little dangling nuts' and she wants to decorate a room in a 'fried-fish scheme', with the chair-backs shaped like frying pans and 'lovely chip potatoes embroidered all over the curtains'. There are references to plays called *Love in False Teeth* and *Stomach Trouble*. Eddie Warren admires a poem called 'Table d'Hôte' which begins 'Why Must It Always Be Tomato Soup'. Mr Warren finds this 'deeply true' because tomato soup is so 'dreadfully eternal'. Harry enjoys his dinner:

> It was part of his – well, not his nature, exactly, and certainly not his pose – his – something or other – to talk about food and to glory in his 'shameless passion for the white flesh of the lobster' and 'the green of pistachio ices – green and cold like the eyelids of Egyptian dancers'.

Bertha can't quite get hold of the truth that Harry's 'something or other' – his sensuality – is fundamental to his character, since she hasn't experienced it fully for herself.

Miss Fulton is a complete contrast. She is minimally responsive to food, merely stirring at her soup and turning a tangerine in her slender fingers. Just as it's not difficult to locate Mansfield's revulsion from food (and its sinister corollary, for her, of being eaten alive, devoured) in her obsession with LM, it's easy to see Mansfield's identification with the slender Miss Fulton, whose sensuality is concealed beneath a fastidious mask. Food represents materiality, itself under condemnation; and it stands, too, for the male interpretation and expression of sensuality, about which both the author, and her women characters, are ambivalent.

Related to the fruit motif is the castration motif, which traditionally understood underlines the need for fruition and suggests the corruption that can result if the natural order is rejected. A woman under discussion cut off her hair, as well as seeming 'to have taken a dreadfully good snip off her legs and arms and her neck and her poor little nose as well'. Another girl 'was violated by a beggar without a nose in a lit-tle wood . . .'.

Yet the heterosexual innuendo running through the story has little meaning for Bertha. Her feelings are less fixed; less concretised; they are under the provenance of the moon: traditionally romantic and traditionally sterile. Yet Mansfield shows here how unconvinced she is about the accepted notion that non-heterosexist sensuality is sterile. Bertha and Miss Fulton, despite the insistence of Harry and his world, do not have to share his version of the natural order; do not have to possess and devour.

Harry's needs, Eddie Warren's preoccupations, male sensuality in general – these are identified with the chase of the cats in the garden. Pearl Fulton, by contrast, is identified with the moon. She has 'pale blonde hair', is dressed 'all in silver', has a 'cool arm' and a 'cool voice'; the pear tree under the moon will become 'silver as Miss Fulton' who has 'moonbeam fingers'. Harry's description of Pearl Fulton as 'cold' is doubly ironic: since to him she's anything but cold, his remark to his wife is deliberately deceitful. And yet it's precisely Miss Fulton's 'coldness' that makes Bertha blaze:

> What was there in the touch of that cool arm that could fan – fan – start blazing – blazing – the fire of bliss that Bertha did not know what to do with?

So far it's clear that impulsive Bertha, who has borne a child, has not been sexually awakened, whereas the unmarried, childless, 'cold' Miss Fulton may have been. It's clear, too, that neither of the women shares the materiality of the others, whereas Harry does. Harry's sensuality is of a different order from Miss Fulton's. Further, we learn from Bertha that Harry has a 'passion for fighting – for seeking in everything that came up against him another test of his power and of his courage . . . there were moments when he rushed into battle where no battle was . . .'. This disposition to rise to the challenge of threat contributes an important dynamic to the interplay between Harry and the two women.

Bertha is convinced that Miss Fulton feels precisely as she does and waits for a 'sign' that this is so. (The emphasis of the quotation marks establishes the secrecy of the feeling, as does Bertha's reflection on its exclusivity:

> . . . I believe this does happen very, very rarely between women. Never between men.)

As anticipated, Miss Fulton does give a 'sign'; she asks Bertha if she has a garden. Bertha instinctively recognises the implications in the question because it is 'exquisite' in its aptness. What Miss Fulton means is something like 'Have you a location for your sensuality?'. Instantly Bertha opens the curtains. But neither woman looks at the garden; they look at the pear tree, which seems animated: like Miss Fulton, it is under the moon; and seems to quiver 'like the flame of a candle', a flame associated with Bertha's own blaze. The tree seems 'almost to touch' the rim of the moon (the important word is 'almost', since the conjunction of the two is romantic and therefore incomplete). The two women stand together in the 'unearthly' light: unearthly because it comes from the moon, but equally because it is non-material. In this union *neither* knows 'what they were to do . . . with all this blissful treasure that burned in their bosoms'. And perhaps because they do not know what to do with it, it drops from them 'in silver flowers' – flowers for which there will be no metamorphosis into fruit.

Patriarchal critics find the story's central symbolism confused at this point, arguing, typically, that although the pear tree represents Bertha, it is also as a phallic symbol that it attracts the two women. As such, it ought to be identifiable with Harry, who divides his attentions and his masculinity between them. Given the evidence both of the text itself and of its hidden antecedents, this seems clearly a misreading, as if the story were conceived along similar lines to Lawrence's anti-lesbian story, 'The Fox'. The slenderness of Mansfield's pear tree is certainly phallic; but in a phallocentric culture, an unconscious response to a phallic image will simply represent a response to sexuality, not merely to maleness. In addition, the pear tree bears blossom: a female symbol. For Mansfield, the tree represents taboo passion: whether between brother and sister, or between woman and woman, such passion must be prevented from achieving fruition and such passion must never be expressed. In Mansfield's account of her conversation with her brother, it was clear that their sharing of the pears was symbolic of the deflection of their feelings into an acceptable mode. Precisely the same psychological shift occurs in 'Bliss'. Since Bertha does not know 'what to do with' her feelings (but they are so strong that she must do something), she deflects them into an acceptable mode, not subject to taboo: 'For the first time in her life Bertha Young desired her husband'. It is entirely consistent that she should be suspicious of this shift: 'Was this what that feeling of bliss had been leading up to? But then, then –'.

Lawrentian or other patriarchal readings of 'Bliss' distort the poise of the narrative because of the inappropriateness of male preoccupations. Within patriarchy, the male is the catalyst, the primal force and the pursuer, from whom the female longs to receive the gift of fulfilment. In Mansfield's feminist world, women long to express themselves and find fulfilment in doing so. Ten years earlier Mansfield had written in her *Journal*:

> It is the hopelessly insipid doctrine that love is the only thing in the world, taught, hammered into women, from generation to generation, that hampers us so cruelly.[26]

Further, a patriarchal reading requires the view that the authorial tone remains continuously one of ironic detachment, thus rendering Bertha's sensitivity to the pear tree – as well as her conviction that Miss Fulton's feeling is the same as her own – deluding and unfounded (or 'hysterical'). This entails, too, that Miss Fulton's responses to Bertha be seen as deliberately mocking and provocative. But in a feminist world, it's clear that just as Bertha is forced by the operation of taboos to deflect her passion into an acceptable mode, so Harry senses the collusion of the two women and is motivated to fight it, since he always takes on 'everything that came up against him'. This provides a frame in which we can see freshly the violence with which he turns Miss Fulton towards him in the final scene (Mansfield gives no support to any notion that she responds to him with equal violence). The pear tree, in a feminist world, represents the power of taboo desires.

It's only after this identifying of her bliss as awakened sexuality that Bertha has eyes to see with and can recognise the sexual dynamic passing between Miss Fulton and her husband. Mansfield achieves this perception with great finesse and delicacy: Bertha sees the two in an attitude, 'Miss Fulton with her back turned to him and her head bent', and Harry holding her coat. Then Harry turns her 'violently to him'. Bertha actually hears nothing; but she sees Harry's lips say 'I adore you' and she sees, too, the sensuality of his quivering nostrils (previously it was the pear tree that 'quivered') and his lips 'curled back in a hideous grin'. He whispers 'tomorrow' and with her 'eyelids' Miss Fulton says yes. Miss Fulton never moves her lips, nor does she move towards him. It is to Bertha that she gives her 'slender fingers' and to whom she speaks, recognising the impossibility of what has passed between them by murmuring 'Your lovely pear tree!' And Eddie the poet follows her 'like the black cat following the grey cat', emphasising the chase allowed to the male. For the first time, Bertha's world poses her an urgent question: 'What is to happen now?' But the pear tree has lost its animism (it no longer quivers, but is still) and its power to subsume her feeling. It passes inscrutably back to the natural world.

The psychological traits exhibited by the characters are fascinating in themselves, but acquire added significance when considered in relation to the Murry/Mansfield/LM triangle so preoccupying in Mansfield's consciousness during the composition of 'Bliss'. In the life triangle, it is LM who has Bertha's sentimental and naive tendencies; and it is LM who threatens the conventional heterosexuality of the planned Murry/Mansfield marriage. It is also LM who exhibits a solid materiality in her interest in food and who is imputed by Mansfield to want to devour her, though these traits are displayed in the story by Harry. Only Miss Fulton, Mansfield explained, was entirely invented,[27] though it's easy to see her as an idealised self-portrait: cool, reserved, romantic, passionate, slender and fastidious[28] – all qualities Mansfield admired and which were remarked to be characteristic of her. Like Mansfield, Miss Fulton can evoke erotic responses from either gender. Like Mansfield, Miss Fulton's consummated relationship is heterosexual; but the repressed yearning of taboo lesbian passion is as central to Bertha's bliss as it was to Mansfield's tormented relationship with LM. It's Harry who is given LM's possessive traits and Bertha who has Murry's ineffectualness. The sensuality passing between Harry and Miss Fulton is challenged by Bertha's passion for Miss Fulton, to which threat Harry responds by violently asserting his claim to Miss Fulton.

In the life triangle, the sensuality shared between Mansfield and Murry is threatened by LM's devotion to Mansfield, together with Mansfield's often unacknowledged response. In 'Bliss' Mansfield shows how romantic passion may be felt between women, as in her life she was sometimes able to acknowledge to her beloved 'Jones':

> Now my *idea* is that we should spend the foreign months together, you and I . . . I'm only talking in the dark – trying to keep you – yes, I will own to that, and trying to make things easy, happy, good, delightful. For we *must* be happy. No failures. No makeshifts. Blissful happiness. Anything else is somehow disgusting . . . But I know any form of life for Jack, you and me is impossible and wrong.[29]

> I want you if you can come to me. But *like this*. We should have to deceive Jack. J. can never realise what I have to do . . . Jack can *never* understand. That is obvious . . . It's not wrong to do this. It is right. I have been wanting to for a long time. I feel I cannot live without you.[30]

Lastly it's worth noting that the relationship between LM and Murry was truly domestic. She organised and ran his house for him on several occasions; and after Mansfield's death, helped him to sort out her papers. No passion of any kind passed between them. They shared a love for Mansfield, just as what makes Bertha desire her husband is her desire for Pearl Fulton. The reverberations of Mansfield's life triangle infuse the thematic content of 'Bliss', showing how the richness of her unconscious life produced the fabric with which she could weave stories.

If the basic myth of the pear tree in Mansfield's childhood garden is seen to be the underlying myth of 'Bliss', then the diverse elements in the story fit together. Seen merely in terms of acceptable heterosexuality, the relationship between the women becomes extraneous. Seen in conventional lesbian terms, the revelation that Harry and Miss Fulton are having an affair seems gratuitous. Seen, however, in terms of the underlying myth which dictates that lesbian desire must not be made explicit, the logic of the story becomes inevitable. 'Bliss' is one tale from Literature in which heterosexual adultery is by no means triumphant; indeed, its proper and logical function, according to the structure of the story, is to shatter the vision of bliss embodied in the pear tree. It is, for a lesbian reader, all too common an unhappy ending. The provenance of patriarchy, overwhelming in its symbolism, energised by its own aggrandisement, arrogant in the confidence of its interventions, almost obliterates the possibility of bliss between women. Almost. But not entirely. The stories have been written, and go on being written; the lives are lived, however precariously. She who has ears to hear, let her hear; she who has eyes to read, let her read.

NOTES

1 *Journal of Katherine Mansfield*, ed. J Middleton Murry, definitive edition, Constable, London, 1962, pp. 83–85.

2 See *Katherine Mansfield: The Memories of LM*, Michael Joseph, London, 1971, p. 21.

3 Most of Mansfield's standard critics have commented on her use of autobiographical materials. And the triangle had precedents: a *Journal* entry for 1907 (p. 8) refers to a lesbian passion for 'Edie', as well as a relationship with 'Caesar'. Similarly, in 1911 (pp. 45 and 47) she wrote about responses to both William Orton and his mistress Lais.

4 *Journal*, p. 95.

5 In the *Journal*, following the extract, Mansfield addresses her dead brother: 'Other people are near, but they are not close to me. To you only do I belong.... I give Jack my "surplus" love, but to you I hold and to you I give my deepest love. Jack is no more than ... anybody might be.' (Final ellipsis Mansfield's.)

6 *Memories*, p. 95.

7 *Letters of Katherine Mansfield to John Middleton Murry*, ed. Murry, Constable, London, 1951, p. 133, dated Thursday (24 January 1918).

8 *Letters*, p. 136, Saturday (26 January 1918).

9 *Ibid.*, p. 150, Sunday Night (3 February 1918).

10 *Ibid.*, p. 152, Monday Night (4 February 1918).

11 *Ibid.*, pp. 159–60, Sunday (10 February 1918).

12 *Ibid.*, p. 162, Monday 8 p.m. (11 February 1918).

13 *Ibid.*, p. 169, Saturday (16 February 1918).

14 *Ibid.*, p. 200, Wednesday (6 March 1918).

15 See *Journal*, p. 129; *Memories*, p. 108; *Letters*, p. 173.

16 *Letters*, p. 174, Tuesday (19 February 1918).

17 *Ibid.*, p. 177, Wednesday Night (20 February 1918).

18 *Ibid.*, p. 181, Saturday Night (23 February 1918); and again in letters written on Monday (25 February) and on Wednesday (27 February).

19 In a letter to Murry she calls it 'our' story: *Letters*, p. 210, dated Wednesday (13 March 1918).

20 *Memories*, p. 112.

21 *Memories*, p. 197, dated 29 V 22.

22 *Memories*, p. 203, dated 14 VI 22.

23 The image occurs twice, the second time negatively. It's worth noting that a fiddle is often described as being 'pear-shaped'.

24 *Letters*, p. 211, dated Thursday (14 March 1918).

25 *Memories*, p. 96.

26 *Journal*, p. 37.

27 *Letters*, p. 281, dated Thursday (28 February 1918). 'Miss Fulton is "my own invention" – oh, you'll see for yourself.'

28 Mansfield was sometimes described as the only silent one among talkative artists at gatherings. And LM quotes from a letter dated 18 IV 18 and addressed to 'Jones': 'But you see I am ever so gay – with long beams coming from my fingers and sparks flying from my toes as I walk.' *Memories*, p. 114.

29 *Memories*, p. 186, dated 15 III 22.

30 *Memories*, pp. 200–201, dated 'before 9 VI 22'. It's interesting to note LM's own gloss: '. . . she was to write me a letter in which she said that to her friendship was as sacred and binding a relationship as marriage. In the important things of life our values were always the same.'

THE CHINESE GARDEN:
A CAUTIONARY TALE
Gabriele Griffin

Rosemary Manning's autobiographical novel,[1] *The Chinese Garden*[2] details life at a girls' boarding school, Bampfield. The school is ruled by four female teachers headed by one 'Chief' who appears to have (had) a sexual involvement with at least two of the others. Having served in the war the women, their appearance stereotyped through Eton crops, heavy tweeds and men's suits, run the school as 'an amalgam of Sparta, Rugby and Cheltenham Ladies' College' (p. 63). At Bampfield femininity and all it connotes is discouraged, and the pupils are 'brought up as public school boys' (p. 65). The discovery that two of the girls, Margaret and Rena, are having a sexual relationship, leads to the accusation that Rachel, the heroine of the novel, was complicit in their affair. Rachel denies this, her 'innocence' is accepted, but her hitherto unquestioning allegiance to Bampfield – and what it stands for – is destroyed.

Initially Rachel's attitude to Bampfield is 'very much that of a lover' (p. 24). The school provides her with the structures and boundaries which are absent in her home context (p. 93) and without which she feels adrift. Her 'innate puritanism' (p. 21), which makes her embrace the regime at Bampfield, is associated with Rachel's 'loathing of home, and disgust with her parents' version of wedded life, together with the deeper though virtually unrecognised disgust which accompanied her dawning knowledge of sexual love' (p. 100). Her rejection of a heterosexual existence as exemplified by her parents' life takes the form of a resistance to all sexual knowledge, and a fervent embrace of those activities, intellectual and physical, which take her out of her private self. The school supports this attitude through its emphasis on the use and ability of the will to overcome the self:

> ... it was our task to strengthen and train our wills in the limited field of school reverses and discomforts, that we might face and overcome the struggles of adult life, the world, the flesh, and the devil. To this end generous opportunities for self-denial and endurance were provided by Bampfield. (p. 67)

Rachel, unlike her friend Bisto, initially does not appear to suffer as a result of this regime because, as indicated above, its strictures coincide with her own inclination to suppress her self.

Rachel's acceptance of the structures provided by the school, structures that deny not only her femininity ('the feminine was in any case at a discount' p. 31) but, more than that, her femaleness (the Bampfield ideal being 'to turn us into English gentlemen' p. 63), is paralleled by her choice of literary pursuits. She imitates rather than originates, producing parodies of her teachers and translations of Virgil. She delights in form and structure, writing poetry and a play, *Clytemnestra*, on a theme taken from Greek mythology 'about the horrors of marriage' (p. 100). Her writing thus tends towards the adaptation of pre-existent, other-generated structures and ideas. On the one hand, this is, of course, part of what one might consider a 'natural' maturation process but it is also expressive of Rachel's reluctance to engage with her self.

Significantly, the texts which she reads, in the main poetry, are mostly written by men. Romantic poets such as Blake, Keats, Coleridge, Shelley and Byron are referred to, but then, too, e e cummings, T S Eliot, and Clemence Dane. An avid reader of poetry concerned with doubt, crises of identity, religious sentiment and the imagination, Rachel herself experiences, in a sense, a crisis of identity, especially of sexual identity, but the world which her reading offers to her is not one which can help her find her self – the texts written by/for men to which she is drawn and which she attempts to imitate, provide a corridor of distorting mirrors in which the self becomes impossible to perceive and what is portrayed is other. Thus the quotations from Rachel's reading which form part of *The Chinese Garden* do not serve to reveal that which Rachel avoids, are not used to disrupt, but, rather, to conceal.[3] Form and content of the novel coincide perfectly at this point where Rachel's reluctance to confront her self and her awakening sexual knowledge is mirrored by the text's lending a voice to a literary tradition which cannot speak directly of women's (sexual) selves.

As *The Chinese Garden* is told predominantly from the adolescent Rachel's point of view only the literature she engages with is accessed and made available – in excerpts – to the reader. This literature, as pointed out above, comes out of a male/ mainstream tradition of 'high' culture. It delights (because that tradition, in part, defines itself in terms of the complexity and subtlety of its representation) in the use of symbol and metaphor. A pronounced use of such devices indicates a particular attitude towards meaning in that metaphor and symbol are associated with the notion of substitution (a word/phrase for another which is not named but implied) and thus with the destabilisation of meaning. Not only does the deciphering of these devices depend on the reader's knowledge of what is being substituted for what (thus pointing to the potentially elitist/excluding nature of symbolic/ metaphorical language); such usage foregrounds polysemy (multi-plicity of meaning) *per se*. The resultant possibility of multiple readings allows for the selection of particular meanings, the privileging, for instance, of what you want to know over what you do not want to engage with. It can thus foster a politics of evasion. This coincides, of course, precisely with Rachel's needs at the beginning of *The Chinese Garden*.

Concomitant with Rachel's embrace of the male/mainstream tradition of literature is her refusal to read texts that might prove disruptive, specifically Radclyffe Hall's *The Well of Loneliness*[4] which her friend Margaret urges her to read. Rachel has come across a review of the book:

> It seemed an important book, but I could not quite see why. My technical knowledge of sex was too meagre to enable me to relate what little I knew to the reviewer's account of the novel. (pp. 110–11)

Elsewhere in the novel, however, Rachel is characterised as adventurous and curious, an avid reader. Her reluctance to read

The Well might therefore be considered a function of the fact that it is *Margaret* who recommends the book, Margaret who is 'enigmatic' to Rachel, and conversations with whom Rachel finds increasingly difficult.

Rachel recognises that her own relationship with Bampfield is different from Margaret's. This is especially evident in the area of transgression. Both girls indulge in 'violations' of the school rules but Rachel's transgressive moves are ones essentially condoned by the authorities (i.e. the teachers) to whom, fundamentally, she submits. Part of the skilfulness with which the head deals with the girls lies in her ability to allow for a certain amount of calculated rebelliousness (see pp. 115–16, p. 132). Thus transgressions such as staying out late or missing classes can be acted out in a context that is 'safe' both in terms of the head knowing exactly what is going on, and in terms of the girls knowing that they remain within secure boundaries even as they rebel.

The establishment of a 'safe' transgressive zone is, of course, enabling as well as disabling for the transgressor. Allowing licensed rebellion is one way of promoting individual growth without risk but it constitutes, simultaneously, a form of control which limits the freedom to explore to exactly those areas demarcated by the authorities. True opposition is thus driven underground.

As Rachel's transgressions are all of a nature ultimately condoned by the head she offers no true opposition to the regime at Bampfield. This is not the case with Margaret, however, of whom Rachel says,

> For her, the rules existed only to be broken. She was openly contemptuous of them. A born rebel, she would have been obliged to invent the regime if it had not existed, merely in order to kick against it. (p. 39)

Margaret does not simply possess a rebellious nature – her rejection of the Bampfield regime is born out of her need to defend the self she has discovered while being there, a self that has to be lived in secret as its transgressiveness is not merely one of breaking the Bampfield rules but of defying the expectations of a heterosexist society. Margaret, unlike Rachel, is 'sexually awakened' – and a lesbian.

Rachel's and Margaret's differences are signalled by their

different reading matter. While the former aligns herself with a male-dominated tradition of writing, the latter, through her recommendation of *The Well*, is associated with another tradition of writing, that of women writing about women and their relationships with each other.[5] But as *The Chinese Garden* is told from Rachel's perspective, her refusal to engage with this other literary tradition means that it remains unquoted, unheard. Echoes from this 'underground', however, mirrors such as Mary Wollstonecraft's *Mary*[6] and H D's poetry,[7] are there, available to those familiar with that tradition.

Witness the representation of Margaret's relationship with Rena whose main attraction for Margaret is her beauty. Comparing her to Cleopatra (p. 97), Margaret even goes so far as to say that she would be prepared to commit suicide for 'someone really worth while', this being immediately afterwards defined as 'someone really beautiful' (p. 112). Significantly, Margaret's comparison of Rena with Cleopatra takes place in the context of a conversation with Rachel in which Margaret chides the latter for seemingly having failed to acquire 'the Greek attitude to physical beauty' in her study of classics, to which Rachel replies, 'I'm not studying Greek, . . . It's Latin.' (p. 97). This alignment, on Margaret's part, of herself with a Greek attitude towards beauty, and Rachel's denial of such 'Greekness' in herself,[8] is reminiscent of another conversation in another text, H D's poem 'I Said' (1919),[9] where an 'I' berates another for the latter's failure of uncompromising, overt engagement in this life and, instead, contemplating death. The 'I' tries to suggest, as Margaret does to Rachel, that they are similar, but the 'you' replies, 'I am no Greek' (p. 322). It is possible to read this poem as an analogy to Margaret's attempt to draw Rachel, who she thinks 'might understand' (and it is never made clear in the novel whether Margaret thinks that Rachel, too, is lesbian or whether she thinks that Rachel is simply more open-minded than the others, pupils and teachers, at Bampfield), into an open dialogue about lesbianism and, more specifically, her relationship with Rena.

While H D's poetry, though pertinent to *The Chinese Garden*, is not mentioned, Clemence Dane's poetry is known and her plays referred to. But the one text of hers bearing a direct relation to life at Bampfield, her novel *Regiment of Women*[10] which describes the betrayal of a pupil by a lesbian teacher who encourages the girl's affections in the interests of furthering her academic/intellectual development, then drops the girl when she fails to make good, a move which drives that pupil to (successful) suicide, is not alluded to. Yet Rachel too is driven to a suicide attempt by a teacher's betrayal of her confidence.

The one text out of the literary tradition of women writing about women's relationships with each other mentioned in *The Chinese Garden, The Well,* is resisted by Rachel. The question arises, what would Rachel have found if she had read *The Well* as recommended by Margaret, and what does the contemporary reader of *The Chinese Garden* find when comparing these two texts?

Rachel, and the reader of *The Chinese Garden,* would, in the first instance, have found likenesses which may seem surprising, given that there is a gap of over 30 years between the publication of the two novels. Parallels exist between the characters of Rachel and Stephen Gordon: both are loners who respond well to tradition, authority and hierarchy. In fact, what Jane Rule in *Lesbian Images*[11] says of Radclyffe Hall,

> She worshipped the very institutions which oppressed her, the Church and the patriarchy, which have taught women there are only two choices, inferiority or perversion. (p. 61)

is equally true of Stephen and of Rachel. There are further similarities between these two characters: both are portrayed as liking nature and the outdoors, enjoying physical activity, using literature as a 'weapon' against the world. They both write. They have dominant masculine personalities exercised in relation to another, younger female who is dependent upon them and who is neglected for the sake of writing.

Certain dissimilarities, however, align Stephen Gordon with Margaret rather than with Rachel. In fact, one could argue that the character of Stephen is split into two in *The Chinese Garden* with Rachel representing the 'sensible' aspects of Stephen and Margaret the 'sensual' ones. Margaret, like Stephen and unlike Rachel, is sexually awakened and active, in love with a feminine woman, Rena, as Stephen is first with Angela, then with Mary. Both Margaret and Stephen actually love, with great passion and emotion, responding to physical beauty (Mary's attractiveness being characterised in part by her being attractive to men while Margaret, of course, likens Rena to Cleopatra), whereas the word 'love' is, in some respects, pointedly absent from Rachel's vocabulary. It seems to come almost as a surprise to her that Margaret and Rena *loved*:

> 'I don't understand,' said Rachel. 'Why don't you explain to me? They must have felt love for each other, surely?'
> At the moment, it was this that hammered at her mind . . . 'They *must* have loved each other. Couldn't they have been forgiven? Why was it such a crime?' (p. 164)

Rachel, at 16, exists in a world of sexual and emotional isolation. Her relationship with a younger pupil, Bisto, is, from her side, not only devoid of sexual interest but almost entirely devoid of emotional input. What keeps Rachel on this side of immorality in her dealings with Bisto is her conscience, her sense of obligation and duty towards one who loves her clearly and unquestioningly. But there is no real commitment on her side. Indeed, Rachel does not develop her emotional and sexual self within *The Chinese Garden*.

Margaret and Stephen Gordon suffer greatly from their loves which they have to live in secret and for which they are castigated by society. Ultimately they lose their relationships. There is a surprising degree of overlap as far as the representation of lesbian relationships is concerned between *The Chinese Garden* and *The Well*, an overlap seemingly derived from an acceptance on Hall's and Manning's part of Havelock Ellis' theory of inversion. In 'Inverts and Experts: Radclyffe Hall and the Lesbian Identity',[12] Sonja Ruehl indicates the extent to which the representation of lesbianism in *The Well* is based upon Ellis' theory. The 'true invert', according to this theory, is a 'masculine', active woman, whose object of desire, passive and feminine, is not necessarily a 'true' invert herself; her beauty of figure attracts the invert who, as one aspect of herself, carries the image of sterility. This sterility is compensated for by excellence in other areas, especially superiority at the level of the social and the intellectual. If one compares this with the representation of lesbianism in *The Chinese Garden* one can see that, more than 30 years after the publication of *The Well*, Manning in dealing with lesbianism is still relying on the model set by Ellis, and thence by Hall.

The Well, however, differs from *The Chinese Garden* in addressing the issue of lesbianism *directly*, and in seeking to offer an explanation of lesbianism, designed to fend off accusations of 'unnaturalness' and 'disease' by suggesting congenital defect. This, so the well-rehearsed argument goes, 'absolves the sufferer' from any responsibility for her 'condition'; rather, an object of ridicule and disdain, she is to be pitied, even by those supposedly like herself. Witness Stephen's response to the women she encounters on the lesbian bar scene in Paris (*The Well,* chapters 47–48), described as they are in lurid terms as exhibiting 'all degrees of despondency, all grades of mental and physical ill-being' (p. 393). Interestingly, and perhaps tellingly enough, Sidney Abbott and Barbara Love's *Sappho was a Right-On Woman*,[13] a book intended to present 'a liberated view of lesbianism', has a dedication which might well serve to immortalise the very women Stephen meets in the Paris bars more than 40 years before. It reads, 'To those who have suffered for their sexual preference, most especially to Sandy, who committed suicide, to Cam, who died of alcoholism, and to Lydia, who was murdered; and to all who are working to create a future for Lesbians'. Nothing much, it seems, has changed for lesbians.

In *The Chinese Garden* Margaret and Rena suffer for their sexual preference by being separated and expelled from the school. No attempt is made to provide a direct explanation for lesbianism. Instead, sexual contact between women *per se* is regarded as a given, neither condoned nor condemned. One could argue that the novel, as far as lesbianism is concerned, operates the same attitude of evasion Rachel is seen to adopt within the text. Narrative strategy and content coincide. The furthest *The Chinese Garden* goes in its representation of sexuality and lesbian relations, and even this is a matter of inference or interpretation rather than statement from within the novel, is to draw first a parallel between female genitals and the parkscape surrounding the school, then one between exploring these surroundings and masturbation/ intercourse. Ultimately the novel, by placing Margaret and Rena into the Chinese garden (foreign, yet known territory), seems to suggest that sexual relations between women are natural and, as an extension of self-pleasuring, constitute a form of pleasuring self in other. In other words, it represents lesbian relationships as a form of female narcissism. The following passages serve to illustrate the points just made. Rachel's exploration of the park surrounding the school might symbolise the exploration of her body:

Girls are not adventurous nor are they explorers like boys and few of us strayed from the paths in the gardens or penetrated the overgrown shrubberies along the stream. Nor was I any more adventurous than the rest, but a habit of solitude due to a year of lameness, and the overwhelming desire to know intimately the whole of my domain, led me to explore it inch by inch, though a natural fear of the unknown led me sometimes to take companions with me on my more daring explorations. I found that they seldom wanted to return to these secret places, often difficult to access. I returned alone. (pp. 55–6)

Rachel's first encounter with the Chinese garden at night is described through a vocabulary of sexual possession, mixing fear and desire:

The shrubbery of the Chinese garden loomed larger, and her physical terror at its black density increased with every step, but to counteract it there grew within her a stubborn determination to meet its challenge and a romantic conviction that the garden was hers only if she could win it through this night ordeal . . . Its [the garden's] bravado, its romanticism, its secrecy, were pared away, leaving in their place something so intimate, so powerful in its impact, that her final emergence upon the edge of the dark lake, with its silent pagoda and waiting willows, was like an embrace. (pp. 104–105)

Even post-coital exhaustion sets in:

When Rachel left the garden, she was too exhausted to combat the single, primitive panic of trees and darkness. (p. 105)[14]

The Chinese Garden employs nature symbolism of a conventional kind; the association of garden and knowledge (sexual and otherwise) is familiar from the Bible onwards, at least. Resorting to symbolism in order to detail female sexuality – traditionally, as all sexuality, a taboo subject in Western society – constitutes a means of dealing indirectly with this subject. It could be argued that an 'accusation of indirection' is inappropriate here in as much as its validity rests on unverifiable assumptions based on interpretations. But this, precisely, is one point I wish to make; namely, that literary texts of a particular kind, the literature of 'high culture' especially, through its use of symbol and metaphor which one might also term 'the degree of its indirection' (i.e. the extent to which the language employed obscures the issues raised), refines what it has to say – particularly on taboo subjects – so that this becomes a matter of interpretation and can therefore be avoided, or refines it even beyond that to the point of evaporation. Alison Hennegan in her introduction to the Virago version of *The Well* points out that

> Many people learned for the first time that sexual relations between women were possible. Those who turned to the book in prurient anticipation or even in a spirit of honest enquiry, however, often retired baffled: '. . . and that night they were not divided' is all Radclyffe Hall has to say about the actual consummation of her heroine's first affair. (p. viii)

A similar reticence informs *The Chinese Garden*, in tune with Rachel's ignorance. The head of the school 'told us that Margaret and Rena had been discovered in some situation with which, it appeared, we were expected to be familiar, since it was not explained to us' (p. 158). The other girls, according to Rachel, do not know what to make of this. What else, what other than this lack of vocabulary, can be expected in a context where educational institutions silence women's voices talking about women's relationships with women?

> We must have been like a group of savages holding a conference over their first sight of an aeroplane, and suffered from a similar, stultifying lack of vocabulary. (p. 158)

Ultimately, Rachel learns that 'the two girls had been found naked in bed together' (p. 158).

> This was quite sufficient for me. Though still ignorant of the exact nature of the vice, my fairly extensive reading had taught me that more than one person to a bed generally spelt wickedness. (pp. 158–9)

'This was quite sufficient for me', Rachel says. She does not want, it seems, to know any more. Her understanding is, in fact, no understanding at all. Her resistance to sexual knowledge still informs her responses.

Margaret had recommended *The Well* as 'marvellous' (p. 150) to Rachel. Why she thinks it 'marvellous' is never explained. One presumes that she likes it because it pleads the lesbian's cause and portrays its protagonist in sympathetic terms, revealing her as independent and spirited, a passionate, intense lover willing to defy the world. One could, of course, like Margaret of *The Well*, simply say of *The Chinese Garden* that it is marvellous and leave it at that. But this would amount to adopting a politics of evasion with regard to the way in which lesbian relationships are represented in *The Chinese Garden*, and, indeed, in *The Well*, akin to these novels' failure to address intra-textually the problems concerning lesbian relationships raised within them.

There is, first and foremost, the problematic of the power structures operating in lesbian relationships which, in both texts, are grounded in an implied replication of heterosexual relationships of courtly love in the lesbian relationship (complete, in the case of *The Well*, with duel between Stephen and Martin for the thus duly commodified Mary). Equality between partners is not indicated in either text. As Stephen cannot communicate with Mary about 'deep and meaningful' things such as literature (what they do together is buy clothes, eat and entertain), so Rachel and Margaret turn to each other (or, in Rachel's case, to the teachers) rather than to their lovers for intellectual companionship. Thus the notion of the supposed intellectual inferiority of the feminine/dependent woman is carried forward, and gender stereotyping of the worst kind prevails.

A second issue raised in both novels concerns the impossibility of gaining a socially sanctioned legitimacy for the lesbian relationship.[15] What haunts Stephen in *The Well* is her first female lover's question, 'Could you marry me?' Marriage is given the status of an ultimate haven, paradise regained, and it is in part Stephen's not being able to marry Mary (whereas Martin can) which makes her relinquish her lover to Martin. Margaret picks up on this theme in *The Chinese Garden* when she asks Rachel:

> Why is everybody so dead set on *marriage*? Don't you think we ought to be free to live our own lives without society interfering with us? (p. 112)

Margaret understands, because she has *read* about it, full well why society promotes 'ordinary marriage' as she calls it:

> It's only got one purpose – the procreation of children. I read the marriage service the other day, and I know all about it. And I don't want children. (p. 111)

It is precisely because of the conflation, or should one say *through* the conflation of romantic love and the biologically-based procreative function (Adrienne Rich's famous article 'Compulsory Heterosexuality and Lesbian Existence'[16] is pertinent here) that marriage as an institution is valorised within a patrilineal society. As such, and especially in a context where no alternative, socially accepted mode of procreation is possible, it militates against any union based on romantic love but devoid of the possibility of procreation. Homosexual relationships therefore become a focus for attack particularly in an era such as the postwar period when 'ideologies of family life, newly significant after the disruption of the war, sought to re-situate women firmly back within the traditional roles of wifedom and motherhood' (Alison Light, 'Writing Fictions').[17] The resultant emphasis on the nuclear family had, as its correlate, the stigmatising of homosexuals because they are considered a threat to this formation (Sheila Jeffreys, *Anticlimax*).[18] The issue of the legitimisation of homosexual relationships remains, of course, unsolved. There is still in Britain no such thing as an ungendered 'common-law partner' with all the rights that this would imply for the persons involved in a homosexual relationship.

A third problem raised in *The Chinese Garden* is women's treatment of each other. The fact that the teachers at Bampfield, themselves lesbians, do not support the lesbian girls in their care is what, in Rachel's eyes, makes the place corrupt. Chief's treatment of Margaret and Rena, separating them and expelling them from the school, provides yet another reason why Rachel might resist sexual knowledge throughout the novel. For, if Margaret's and Rena's fate is what you can expect if you are a lesbian and this becomes public knowledge, why should you hasten to bring about your own victimisation? The end of the novel suggests that Rachel's understanding of this taints her attitude towards lesbianism, symbolised here by the Chinese garden, for a long time after the events. The 'radiance, the purity, the perfection which the

Chinese garden had symbolised' for her are destroyed; only much later, when she realises that she 'would never again take the Bampfield direction' (p. 173), i.e. resist and suppress her lesbian self, does Bampfield turn to ashes for her, 'and the Chinese garden [arise] again, like the phoenix' (p. 173).

Rachel's attitude towards the teachers is condemnatory, and because *The Chinese Garden* presents itself predominantly from the viewpoint of Rachel as school girl, it does not deal with, or try to explain, the women teachers' problematic situation which leads them to be corrupt. Their difficulties are spelt out, rather, in a different text dealing with similar issues, Lillian Hellman's play *The Children's Hour*[19] in which a pupil in a girls' boarding school maliciously accuses her two female teachers of having a sexual friendship. The two teachers have, in fact, a longstanding, close relationship but it is devoid of any sexual element. The pupil's accusations lead the women gradually to realise that they do love each other but they also, in tune with society at large, regard lesbianism as a disease, an abominable aberration. As a result of this attitude towards lesbianism, shared by the teachers and the community in which they live, and because of the teachers' persecution by the society of which they are members, one of them commits suicide. Before this happens they have already been castigated by society through having their livelihood, the school, taken away from them in the wake of their defamation. At the same time all possibility of their being other than victims in this situation is removed as a consequence of the publicity their case receives.

What this play makes clear, and what is implied in *The Chinese Garden*, is that women's economic dependence on members of a heterosexist society for their livelihood puts them in a position where they can easily be manipulated to deny their (sexual) selves in favour of securing their financial as well as their social survival. Such was, indeed, the case with Rosemary Manning herself who, as she details in the second introduction of her first volume of autobiography, *A Time and a Time*[20] as a headmistress kept her lesbianism a secret until well after she had retired and could no longer be threatened in her financial livelihood. In the recent controversy concerning Clause 28, women teachers who are gay and spoke out in public against the Clause at venues such as teachers' trade union meetings frequently pointed out the fact that their livelihood might be threatened by their taking a public stance on the issue, and by publicly proclaiming their homosexuality.[21] This threat, understandably, is one that can turn women into gate-keepers for the values and attitudes propagated by a hetero-sexist society. It is compounded by the fact that the teaching of female children has traditionally been the task of women.[22] Indeed, for a long time teaching was one of the few professions open to educated middle-class women – more than that, until relatively recently, it was open to *unmarried* women only. In other words, one could suggest that women were/are used to initiate girl children into the values of our heterosexist society, which demands from those teachers who are lesbian, through the possibility of depriving them of their livelihood, that their 'teaching' reflect the norms set by a patriarchal society. This means that lesbian teachers have to deny their sexual selves (Manning discusses how oppressed she felt by the secrecy she was forced into by her situation in *A Time and a Time*). Furthermore, this situation demands that at critical moments, such as occurs in *The Chinese Garden* when an institution is made aware of lesbian relations either among teachers or pupils, these relationships be ruthlessly suppressed, thus forcing the teachers into a double betrayal, of their selves as well as of the pupils. The possibility for such occurrences is obviously somewhat greater in a boarding school than in a day school context where pupils do not live together in quite the same way. None the less, in both types of institutions women find themselves in a position where, for the sake of economic survival, they betray each other if homosexuality surfaces. It is one of the saddest triumphs of patriarchy to have established situations where women, together on a day-to-day basis for the purposes of education, are taught that they cannot trust each other or have intimate friendships. Obeying even the absent patriarchal voice, out of whatever fear, allowing it to rule friendships beween women, is surely one of the most damning aspects of a heterosexist society such as the one we live in. Antonia White's *Frost in May*[23] offers one example of the deliberate destruction of inter-female friendships in an all-female setting, worse almost than Mr Brocklehurst's Lowood School in *Jane Eyre*[24] where, at least, teachers like Miss Temple offer some secret consolation, and a certain amount of resistance to the oppressive regime set up by a man.

Suggesting an explanation for the behaviour of the teachers at Bampfield does not constitute an attempt to excuse them. Rachel's innocence, considered in purely logocentric terms (she does not know *the word* for what happened between Margaret and Rena), is in part, as indicated above, a function of her conforming nature as opposed to a possibly rebellious stance she might have taken. But her resistance to sexual knowledge and 'complicity' with Margaret is all too understandable in the light of the points made above. It still means, as she later realises, that the school 'checked, diverted and all but destroyed the elements which I later discerned as best in me' (p. 116).

The Chinese Garden is not a text which celebrates lesbian existence but, rather, one which illustrates the problems that beset the lives of lesbians. It has many of the characteristics of the lesbian novel of development as discussed in Bonnie Zimmerman's 'Exiting from Patriarchy: The Lesbian Novel of Development',[25] but as a text it does not exit from the main/male-stream tradition of novel writing. On the contrary, what is particularly striking about *The Chinese Garden* is the extent to which it foregrounds itself as a literary construct of the 'high culture' variety. Its craftedness is revealed through the alternating use of a first and third person narrator, distinguishing between the adolescent 'unknowing' Rachel, and the mature one, looking back on the events that took place at Bampfield. The symbolism in the novel is carefully worked out and maintained throughout the text. There are direct references to other literary texts. Each chapter is prefaced by a quotation from another text, all but two of which (by an author unknown, and Alice Meynell) are by 'great men' duly canonised, or from the Bible. Thoughtfully, for those who missed out in their education on classical or modern languages, Rilke appears in translation, and Virgil in the original with a translation added. In terms of style and narrative strategy *The Chinese Garden* thus situates itself within a main/male-stream tradition of literary representation. What this tradition, through the use of symbol and metaphor, offers, and in this respect it is perfectly in tune with the school regime the text describes, is a 'safe' transgressive zone in which contentious issues can be raised without being made explicit. This is what one might say it also shares with certain writers of that other tradition, that of women writing about their relationships with each other, like H D who makes use of a symbolic/metaphorical style to present 'the love that dare not speak its name'.

One stylistic manifestation of this balancing act between

revealing and concealing is the use of the Chinese garden as the central symbol in this text. Geographically at the core of the school's grounds and hidden from view, the garden is associated with decay, corruption and sensuality, attributes that are applied both by Rachel to the teachers whom she condemns for their moral failure, and by the teachers to pupils involved in lesbian relationships. Decay, corruption and sensuality are commonplaces, if one is to believe Edward Saïd,[26] of the Orientalist's attitude towards anything eastern. *The Chinese Garden* thus projects an alignment between the Orientalist's view of the Orient, Rachel's view of the school and the teachers' view of the lesbian pupils. Such a parallel implicitly raises questions concerning the appropriateness of these views. Saïd suggests that the Orient is 'a sort of surrogate and even underground self' (p. 3) of European culture, that Orientalism is 'a kind of Western projection onto and will to govern over the Orient' (p. 95) in which knowledge of the Orient, even if merely a matter of projection, becomes the source of power and domination of that 'Other' (p. 1). He demonstrates, and this is crucial for *The Chinese Garden*, that 'the Orient studied was a textual universe'; this textual universe gave rise to the acquisition of a 'second-order knowledge' about the Orient constituting 'Europe's collective daydream of the Orient' (p. 52). What is described as a day-dream here becomes a nightmare in *The Chinese Garden* where textual knowledge, as in the case of the Orientalists, becomes the basis for assessing – and misjudging – 'reality'. In both instances we have, as Saïd describes it, 'a rather complex dialectic of reinforcement by which the experiences of readers in reality are determined by what they have read' (p. 94).

The equation of the Chinese garden (and its associations with Orientalism in western culture) with knowledge about lesbian relationships indicates the parallel between the differential status of Orient/West and heterosexual/homosexual in western consciousness. As such it could be read as a critique of heterosexist attitudes towards homosexuality. At the same time, Manning in her choice of symbol perpetuates textually derived prejudices about a multiplicity of other cultures and in so doing feeds into a longstanding male-authored western tradition of denigrating the Orient as a means of self-affirmation.

The effect of Manning's style of writing and choice of central symbol as far as *The Chinese Garden* is concerned, is to re-present those conditions of lesbian existence that have marred their lives for what seems to be for ever. The novel presents as a status quo a situation where lesbians, in so far as they live out their preference for other women, are driven underground, silenced, castigated by society, betrayed by other women. The absence of an analysis of the social, political, and economic conditions which influence the lives of lesbians means that any critique of those conditions is at best implicit. There is a certain amount of direct attack in *The Chinese Garden* but that attack is directed wholly against the lesbian teachers at Bampfield, specifically against one teacher, Georgie Murrill, who betrays the secret of the Chinese garden:

> I am not going to shed tears because I spent my schooldays in a place where many of the staff were morally corrupt, the physical standards those of Dartmoor, the religion perverted and the games mistress a sadist. It looks like a formidable list, but children will always be subjected to something . . . But I find it necessary to place on record that Georgie Murrill, the least valuable in personality, the most trivial in mind, procured my affection and exploited it for her own ends . . . I think it is for the Georgie Murrills of this world that the millstones are reserved. (pp. 76–7)

This direct and specific attack, the value judgments of which are somewhat astonishing, is the result of the absence of analysis pointed to above, a failure to understand that Georgie Murrill, too, is a victim. In the introduction to *A Time and a Time* Rosemary Manning says that she began to write *The Chinese Garden* when she 'was nearly forty', and in her second volume of autobiography, *A Corridor of Mirrors*, she ends the chapter on *The Chinese Garden* by saying that with the help of the Margaret figure in the novel she might perhaps have been able to deal with the events at the school.

> Perhaps through *her* agency – she was far maturer than I was – I might have come to terms with the episode, from which I only freed myself when I wrote *The Chinese Garden* in my forties. And did I free myself even then? (p. 63)

One is drawn to suggest that the answer to this question is 'no', and to propose that the inability of Manning to 'free' herself from the experience is in part a function of her having fettered herself to a tradition, in terms of thinking and cultural representation, that belongs to a history which denies women their voices when they talk about their relationships with each other. One gets no sense in *The Chinese Garden* of a real understanding of the socio-political and economic conditions that fashion the lives of the lesbians in that novel. Of course it is possible simply to say that that is what one would expect in a novel told predominantly from the perspective of an adolescent schoolgirl. But then it is also important to take notice of the fact that Manning as a mature woman *chose* to write from that perspective – she could have used a different voice.

As the text stands it is certainly not one to promote homosexuality. It is a *cautionary* rather than an *exemplary* tale; the stereotyping of the teachers and the heartbreak of Margaret and Rena do not offer very powerful incentives to follow suit. The image of the lesbian presented is that of the isolated invert with exceptional talent, ready to defy the world and likely to be martyred for it. That particular image, at least in part, seems very dated now. But then *The Chinese Garden* does not explore the nature of lesbian relationships in any great detail. What the reader 'learns' on that score has to be inferred from hints and fleeting references, things observed in passing, such as how the teachers relate to each other (pp. 45–6). It is thus difficult to get a clear idea of the nature of even the specific lesbian relationships dealt with in the novel.

More relevant to life in the 1980s and 1990s is what seems to me to be the main concern of *The Chinese Garden*, namely, the relationship between the lesbian and society at large. The reader is offered a representation of lesbian existence as one of struggle, of living a life of secrecy perpetually under threat not merely from heterosexual women and men but also from other lesbians. Where *The Well* gave some indication of the potential fulfilment a woman might find in a relationship with another woman, *The Chinese Garden* concentrates on the problems involved in maintaining a lesbian relationship in the face of a hostile all-powerful world. It seems to suggest that no matter what the lesbian relationship is like, it is likely to be disrupted, possibly terminated, by the antipathetic environment in which it has to exist. While such a vision might appeal to a reader with a romantic desire for heroism and a flair for defiance it must be disheartening to the more timid individual unwilling to engage in struggle.

There also remains the problem of Rachel – what is one to make of a protagonist who identifies with the structures that oppress her to the point where she, even if inadvertently, destroys the relationship of two other women? Her subscription to the symbolic distances her from those around her and leads to an isolation based on the resistance to sexual knowledge which is intensified by her final assertion of innocence. The knowledge she acquires through this move, one which she herself sees as corrupting because she finally recognises that in proclaiming her innocence she has condoned the double standards of Bampfield, is one that she has also tried to resist. It teaches her that she has to make a choice between acquiescence and revolt, that her mode of acting has amounted to acquiescence, and that such acceptance affects not only herself but others. Yet it is also true that if she had pleaded 'guilty', i.e. said that she had known about Margaret's and Rena's affair, she would have been thrown out of the school, disgraced. The choice, finally, appears to be between a morally corrupt social integration and a morally intact social isolation.

If one does not read *The Chinese Garden* in terms of a romantic identification with the notion of the lonely individual engaged in a struggle against the prejudices of society then, it strikes me, one ends up with an attitude of dissociation, with what Jean E Kennard in 'Ourself behind Ourself: A Theory for Lesbian Readers'[27] calls 'polar reading' where 'the reader redefines herself in opposition to the text' (p. 168). For *The Chinese Garden* offers much to reject.

NOTES

1 In *A Corridor of Mirrors* (The Women's Press, London, 1987) Manning says about *The Chinese Garden*, 'It was autobiographical, the most truthful book I have ever written about myself' (p. 55).

2 Rosemary Manning, *The Chinese Garden* (1962), Brilliance Books, London, 1984.

3 In 'The Difference of View' (in Mary Jacobus, ed., *Women Writing and Writing about Women*, Croom Helm, London, 1979, pp. 10–21) Jacobus describes how Virginia Woolf used quotations in *A Room of One's Own* to say what she herself felt unable to; in other words, used quotations to reveal rather than conceal.

4 Radclyffe Hall, *The Well of Loneliness* (1928), Virago, London, 1982.

5 Martha Vicinus picks up on this tradition in its narrow sense in terms of girls' boarding school fictions in 'Distance and Desire: English Boarding-school Friendships' (in Estelle B Freedman et al., eds., *The Lesbian Issue: Essays from SIGNS*, University of Chicago Press, Chicago, 1982, pp. 43–65).

6 Mary Wollstonecraft, *Mary and the Wrongs of Woman* (1788), Oxford University Press, Oxford, 1983.

7 H D (Hilda Doolittle), *Collected Poems 1912–44* (1925), Carcanet, Manchester, 1984.

8 For a brief introduction to the association of 'Greekness' with lesbianism, propagated by the poetry of Sappho, see chapter 1 of Jeannette H Foster's *Sex Variant Women in Literature* (1956), Naiad Press, Tallahassee, USA, 1985.

9 I am indebted to Diana Collecott for this reading of 'I Said' (Collected Poems, pp. 322–325) about which poem I heard her give a paper at the 1987 HETE conference at the University of Canterbury, Kent. See also Diana Collecott, 'What Is Not Said: A Study in Textual Inversion', Textual Practice Vol. 4, no. 2 (Summer 1990), pp. 236–258.

10 Clemence Dane, *Regiment of Women* (1917), Heinemann, London, 1966.

11 Jane Rule, *Lesbian Images* (1975), The Crossing Press, Trumansburg, New York, 1982.

12 Sonja Ruehl, 'Inverts and Experts: Radclyffe Hall and the Lesbian Identity', in Judith Newton and Deborah Rosenfelt, eds., *Feminist Criticism and Social Change*, Methuen, London, 1985, pp. 165–180.

13 Sidney Abbott and Barbara Love, *Sappho was a Right-On Woman: A Liberated View of Lesbianism* (1972), Stein and Day, New York, 1985.

14 A similar representation of the relationship between a female protagonist and the natural environment can be found in Mary Wollstonecraft's *Mary*, pp. 9–10.

15 This problem is also explored in other lesbian novels. In Wollstonecraft's *Mary*, for example, the heroine looks forward to her death and the opportunity of going to heaven '*where there is neither marrying*, nor giving in marriage' (p. 68). In Jane Rule's *Memory Board* (Pandora, London, 1987) one of the protagonists has to invoke her professional status (pp. 95–99) as a doctor to legitimise her reunion with her partner.

16 Adrienne Rich, 'Compulsory Heterosexuality and Lesbian

Existence', in Ann Snitow, Christine Stansell and Sharon Thompson, eds., *Desire: The Politics of Sexuality*, Virago, London, 1984, pp. 212–214.

17 Alison Light, 'Writing Fictions: Femininity and the 1950s', in Jean Radford, ed., *The Progress of Romance: The Politics of Popular Fiction*, Routledge, London, 1986, p. 141.

18 Sheila Jeffreys, *Anticlimax: A Feminist Perspective on the Sexual Revolution*, The Women's Press, London, 1990, pp. 50–57.

19 Lillian Hellman, *The Children's Hour* (1934), in *Six Plays by Lillian Hellman*, Vintage Books, New York, 1979.

20 Rosemary Manning, *A Time and a Time: An Autobiography* (1971), Marion Boyars, London, 1986.

21 See, for instance, an article in The *Guardian* (5 April 1988, p. 2) entitled 'Lesbian Teacher's Plea to NUT Wins Ovation'.

22 For a further discussion of this subject see Rosemary Deem, *Women and Schooling*, Routledge, London, 1978.

23 Antonia White, *Frost in May* (1933), Virago, London, 1978.

24 Charlotte Brontë, *Jane Eyre* (1847), Penguin, Harmondsworth, 1977.

25 Bonnie Zimmerman, 'Exiting from Patriarchy: The Lesbian Novel of Development', in Elizabeth Abel, Marianne Hirsch and Elizabeth Langland, eds., *The Voyage In*, University of New England Press, Hanover, 1983, pp. 244–257.

26 Edward W Saïd, *Orientalism* (1978), Penguin, Harmondsworth, 1985.

27 Jean E Kennard, 'Ourself Behind Ourself: A Theory of Lesbian Readers', in *The Lesbian Issue*, pp. 153–168.

ANAMIKA
Giti Thadani

INTRODUCTION 1

A plastic snake encircling her neck, a crescent moon and third eye painted on her forehead, emerges a woman with a black bowl in her hand; the ascetic personification of Kali. The site is a typically urban market-place. A demand for money is made in full arrogance by the ascetic Kali. A demand that inverts the paradigm of the theatre of begging, which instead of invoking disgust and contempt creates fear. The middle-class memsahib hastily closes her car window, protecting herself with the fragile medium of glass. Fascinated by this enactment of rare archetypal theatre, I, the spectator, walk up to pay my dues to the cosmic actress. The dues are met with disdain and the answer, 'These are not the old times'.

This experience perhaps reflects and raises some of the many problematics inherent with this project. What are the semantics and politics embodied in different divinities and cosmogonies? What are their different articulations and interpretations in dominant collective representations? How do these differ from different subjective positions? What would constitute the different modalities of these relationships with the different divinities? Finally, what different kinds of historiographies are possible? What are the dynamics that shape them? And what are the different temporal frameworks within which they are constituted?

> Theologically, however, the concept of a dominance of a female
> divinity is in some ways a godsend – or perhaps a goddesssend.
> The passionate worship required of God by the 'bhakti'
> movement that developed simultaneously with the emergence of
> the Goddess often led the worshipper to imagine him or herself
> in an erotic relation with the divine. To do this in a country like
> India (a country that has never acknowledged the existence of
> homosexuality) is to establish an erotic bond with an Other.[1]

What would however constitute the erotic articulation in the case of this Kali? What would be the politics of the self that is contained in this articulation, where there is no bond of Other between the devotee and the divinity? What would be the politics of sexuality embodied in a conception of the self where the divine is enacted at the human, anthropomorphic level?

The complex hermeneutics of this particular hermetic expression can only be understood when it is juxtaposed to the dominant and antithetical representations based on rigid gender constructions which privilege only exchanges with the gender 'other' and reduce all conceptualisations of the 'self' either to obscurity or to be subsumed within the gaze of the gender 'other'. This privileged conception of the gender 'other' is what I propose to name as the ideological working of normative heterosexuality.

In effect, this stipulates that the ideology of heterosexuality is not merely limited to a sexual relationship between the opposite genders, but is in fact a very complex signifying system operating at various levels; be they sexual, cultural, sociological, cosmological, psychical, psychological, etc. It is in the deconstruction of this system and the creation of other referential signifying patterns that it becomes possible to enumerate and elaborate other subjective positions, alternate conceptions of gender and different forms of exchange as in the above stated example.

O'Flaherty's text which claims an 'objective' scholarly voice, in effect projects the semantic framework of the modern heterosexual discourse, which sees any other form of sexuality deviant from that of the classical heterosexual to be a product of 'western decadence'. This discourse, which is meant to establish or recreate an 'objective' past, is, on the contrary, a complex present statement on sexuality, with the underlying sub-text that there is no semantics of subliminal sexuality that is not based on the principle of the gender 'other'. The other forms are simply rendered into absence by the privileging of the gender 'other'. Different articulations of the self and other existing within categories of the same sex are again rendered obscure. The above discourse also implies that only in occidental thinking have there been 'homosexual' conceptualisations, as if one were dealing with monolithic conceptions of India and the 'occident'.

Further, the above text implies that women can never create a bond with a *feminine* divinity. Women therefore must necessarily worship only a *male* god.

This is obviously refuted in the practice of the wandering Kali. Although this self-chosen form of subjective semantics would 'normally' be consigned to the domain of megalomaniacal madness, in actuality its mode of signification embodies a completely different temporal framework. The choice of 'modern' materials, in the form of a plastic snake or paint, is in fact a radical act of using the 'present' to render present a subjugated 'past absence'. The statement, 'This is not the ancient times' is extremely revealing, in that it indicates on the one hand a loss of a certain space, yet on the other is a radical assertion of a feminine continuum and *demands* recognition. Hence the dissatisfaction with the insufficient payment of dues. For clearly the gaze of recognition is to be met with adequate material retribution. The cosmic demands its material price.

The choice of the cosmic figure of Kali is in itself a statement, for it locates the cosmography from the perspective of the periphery that the woman outside patriarchy inhabits. Kali becomes the living articulation of the expression of both feminine exile from the patriarchal social, as well as re-establishing the continuum of a feminine archetypal experience that resists the codification of the dominant gaze. No cosmography has an absolute meaning. It is always embedded in a context of other motifs, symbols, etc. And depending on the techniques of signification, the same cosmography would engender different conceptual patterns and modes of perspectivisation. Thus Kali from one perspective of the male devotee would represent the erotic death mother, the fearsome other of patriarchy. Again here the cosmography would exist only in relation to the gender 'other'.

However, from the perspective of the hermetic woman, Kali is not postulated as an exterior other, but as a subliminal self created out of her own desire. Desire of the self becomes the primary expression of the conflation of the self and the divine. There is no psychological other, but a form of divine fusion emerging from a critical consciousness of the chosen cosmic figure and the self-defined self. Thus the self chosen cosmogony, where the divine is enacted by oneself in the same gender economy, breaks away from the submissive nature of the devotee vis à vis the deity and the retention of the divinity at a distance. It also becomes free from any form of symbolical super-imposition as it creates its own references.

Cosmography: An Elaboration within the Framework of Hinduism

The difference between a monotheistic religion and a polytheistic culture is that in the latter the sacred or the divine is not an absolute, singular super-structure imposed from above, but an abstraction of the cosmos capable of manifesting itself in various anthropomorphic and theriomorphic forms. Instead of a single godhead imposed from above, the individual is faced with selecting her or his particular constellation. A choice is not merely made for one divinity, but perhaps an entire constellation. Yet these choices are not necessarily free from either political considerations or ideological categories. A worshipper of Shiv may have a great deal of problems with a worshipper of Kali, etc. Correspondingly, depending on different social structures, different divinities are selected and the modalities of their 'worship' often circumscribed.

This is clear in present Hinduism, which in its attempt to be a religion rather than a complex collection of different cosmographic traditions, denies their earlier specificities and histories. It instead tries to present a uniform and homogenised view with a definite mono-identity. Needless to say, this recent construction aligns itself with the earlier androcentric, heterosexist and phallocentric traditions. This is apparent in the resurrection of Ram and Sita as gender ideals.

Thus, this study is a historiographical attempt both to deconstruct the normative patriarchal traditions, as well as resurrect the elaborate gynefocal traditions. It also proposes to describe the conflictual shifting relations between the two, and the shifts in the paradigms of kinship and sexuality. Of course, this study does not in the least propose to be all exhaustive, but concerns itself simply with providing new insights into this domain by the process of creating new semantic montages of the above traditions. Neither does it concern itself either with the establishing of new 'truths' or with new normative discourses, but is concerned with articulating, inscribing, narrativising, theorising languages of feminine sexuality, cosmogonies, philosophies, that have either been obscured, kept hidden away, appropriated, mutilated or consigned to silence and oblivion.

INTRODUCTION 2

The following text takes on the form of an elaboration and journeying of different thematics and motifs. The themes and motifs interlink with each other, and create their own points of references, providing their own conceptual tools. In other words they do not seek epistemological or any other form of validation from the 'outside'. In other words, the explication of the conceptual tools lies in the implicitness of the various texts.

Thus the term 'conceptual cipher' owes its basis to a textual strategy in the original Sanskrit text, where certain words are repeated in different compound structures. The principle of repetition and the aspect of existing in differentiated forms makes these words the keys to the unfolding of the polysemy of the text. This is particularly important as the texts are in the form of citations, with no explicative readings or interpretations.

The commentaries to these texts (Sayan²) often, too, explicate the texts by providing new associations or motifs. Thus the original word *hiruk* is interlinked to *antarhita*. In other words, one of the basic principles of the commentary is not explaining the texts, but foregrounding the motifs in the citations through the association with other motifs/images; e.g. the double *yonis* associated with the mother/non-mother.

Selectivity becomes another key principle as well as the choice of which motifs to develop and in which modes. In acknowledging my own forms of selectivity, I render explicit the frame that they seek to create. This to me becomes the cognitional conflation of my own subliminal self with its generic archetypal inscription. In other words, the choice of the theme of the 'dissolution of the heterosexual pact' is in itself the act of foregrounding the theme of the impossible union of the cosmic feminine and the mortal male. It is elaborated differently through the nomination of the above theme as the dissolution of the heterosexual pact.

The added nomination becomes the inter-link and the situation of the above theme into the recent context of the politics of sexuality. Thus, my own nominations as a modern commentator foreground a certain thematic through the above nominative frame, but do not reduce one to the other.

The same principle is contained in the writing style, which becomes the intersection of the earlier Sanskrit texts and that of a new English. A new English that is a passage space, a new linguistic form that breaks away from its traditional colonialist heritage which sought to reduce the 'other' to itself. Thus the dominant philosophy of translation of any other cultural space was not the enactment of a meeting point, or the enlarging of its own space but the reduction of the difference of the other into its own limitations. Thus the translation of a dual Sanskrit form as *dyava* is reduced to a singular *male* form, as English has no generic dual grammatical form, or generic *feminine* form. The different nuances of the politics of the above is usually either not analysed or homogenised.

A major problematic in writing in English is the constant effort of breaking through the narrow subject-predicate format and the lack of gender differentiation. This has often meant that the rich politics of gender philosophy is completely obscured or simply ignored. In some cases it is blatant, as for instance in the explanation of the feminisation of various words/names as that of either a homogenised neuter or the spouse of the male god. In the case of a concept the shift of meaning is hardly ever accounted for. Thus the term Maya is generally translated as delusion, though this meaning is valid only in certain philosophical contexts (i.e. the Upanishadic), and completely incongruent with the *saktic* usages.

My translations are based on etymological and lexicographic readings, and do not aim at fixing meaning or a truth. Instead of the usually accepted Sanskrit transliteration, I have simplified it into a more accessible form, which entails no accents. Although this does not bring out the phonological differentiations, it is a lot less off-putting for the lay reader, and does not detract from the gender politics. What brought into question is the ideology of any fixed truth or meaning. This questioning is inherent, too, in the style of presentation, where the citations are seen to have their own intrinsic significance/s and the commentaries are kept as basic as possible. My interpretative voice is distinct from that of the citations, and does not seek to use the other voices in establishing my thesis. On the other hand, the commentary works at establishing a thread between the citations from different texts and time periods.

The commentative voice is not passive or active. It works with and through the citations. The choice of working with citations instead of with complete texts is to enunciate a process of associative meaning. This also means that each citation is not seen as dependent on the text as a unified whole, but creates its own possibilities of references. In fact, a number of the texts are a collection of often contrary cosmographies, and are not based on one underlying principle. It must also be kept in mind that a number of texts were transmitted orally and documented often in various versions much later. Subsequently the modern transcription and printing, too, has created its own variations. Further, a number of texts were secret – meant only for the initiated. In their written form, a number of words were deliberately left out. This coded aspect meant one meaning for the uninitiated general public and another for the initiated.

The allusive and coded aspect in fact provides for a richness in reading and has its own form of eros and aesthetics. My own elliptical style is in harmony with the above, for to over explain is often to kill the citations and the motifs, and thus deny the possibility of the subjective journeying of the reader. The citations and motifs have their own logic, and repeat themselves as a musical melody.

The repetition of motifs, citations, has another logic, that of constantly providing new insights and frameworks of perception. Meaning and interpretation are dynamic processes, as is the act of reading. Neither act is either passive or active but works in a triadic space which is integrative, open-ended and infinite.

ANAMIKA

wovon man nicht sprechen kann,	aber schweigen ist
darüber muß man schweigen.	wohnort der Opfer.
(Ludwig Wittgenstein)[3]	(Nelly Sachs)[4]

dvidha chakre pumasam tam jivam cha paramam tatha
tridha chakar cha atmanam svechchhya prakriti svayam[5]

Bound in the wheel of two paths he, the man and *jiv* are primary; the three path, wheel and essence, self desire (f), *prakriti* (f), the self.

Perhaps nowhere as in the above citation is the declaration of gender so concisely and synoptically demarcated, thus bringing forth entire cosmological, numerological, philosophic and erotic kaleidoscopes.

The juxtaposition of the three, vis à vis the two, functions as a leitmotif, which links signifiers and symbols of different registers: linguistic, metaphysical, sexual, psychical, psychological, temporal, etc.

Instead of the dualistic division between language and silence, the triad becomes another frame to contemplate the passage from the space of silence to language.

In a dualistic system the third point must be either sacrificed or concealed, it must on no account be revealed, as the beyond (*para*) is outside the language of duality. In other words, there is no interspace capable of integration, only the alienation of two polar extremes. From the viewpoint of Wittgenstein, a philosophical language based on the rationality of duality arrives at a point of silence when it approaches the zero space of its cleavaged other as its language stops and comes to a standstill. This space is to be contemplated in the language of silence. Silence is seen as a space to be dwelt upon.

For Nelly Sachs, however, the fact that duality tabooises this space, reduces it to the extremities of the gas chambers, means that its simplistic acceptance is tantamount to the acceptance of the law of the sacrifice, the executioner and the victim.

In, however, moving into a triadic space, the third point is no longer either the space of the void apart, the exotic, the beyond (*para*) as death, but is the point of integration, giving each individual point its individuation but at the same time linking it as well. There are no longer the dualities of silence versus language, but a multiplicity and infinity of forms to frame the undifferentiated, zero space.

This undifferentiated space is the feminine principle in the above citation.

> Bound in the wheel of two paths, he, the man and *jiv* are primary;
> the three path, wheel and essence, self desire (f), *prakriti* (f), the self.

The first line postulates a subject-object relationship, implicated not through the agency of the verb, but through the locative structure of the word *chakre*, and the objective case structure of man, he and *jivam* (referring to materiality). This implies that man and materiality are bound within the wheel-circle. Thus, this is being characterised as duality. The second line contrasts the locative and objective with that of a primarily nominative case structure, in the change of the word *chakre* to *chakar*. (There is also a conceptual shift here, for the word *chakre* is conjugated from the word *chakr(a)*, as opposed to the nominative, *chakar*. *Chakar* appears to be the older usage, and can be traced to the *Rig Ved*.[6] Ironically, it is the term *chakr(a)* that is prevalent. The word *chakar* does not even appear in the major dictionaries.)

In other words, two philosophies of grammar are juxtaposed: the dualistic and the triadic frames. In the dualistic frame, the man and the *jiv* are bound up in the wheel, hence they exist as objects of the wheel. In the triadic there is no aspect of the wheel hierarchising the other elements, which exist in an independent, nominational form, as an articulation of the generic feminine self.

Through the feminine desire of the self, the act of nomination becomes an iconic act, enunciating the process of self-reflection, which becomes the material basis of creation and all its infinite forms.

> She, the sum of all the infinite forms, etc.
> the first, carrier/generatrice through the self form spread through the luminous intellect.

At one time, Shiva perceived her own self-reflection, then the reflection became Maya, thus the abstract (*shiv*), to know:

(to know) the meaning of the creation, contemplate the bearing
– generative form

(to know) the first *nath*, thus *manasa*, contemplate in extreme –
the self-form
(to know) the meaning of creation, contemplate the first
abstract – self-generative

(she) enacting the inverted eros (*viprit rati* [f]) in the mode of the
great void (*maha shuny*[a]),
the three part serpent-foetus, the six circles, then the cave of the
lotus.

for centuries (existed) the inverted eros,
the goddess amidst the inverted eros becomes the one point of
the *pura*.

then one beautiful woman emerging from the great oceanal Kali
the beautiful form of the woman, the carrier of the first part

she of the mental energy (*manasi sakti*) emerging from the first
beyond (*parat-para*),
nominated *mahakali*, the contemplation of the form of the
beautiful woman.[7]

The motif of reflection effectuates a play, a play of creation, a play
of form. As each form is merely a part of the initial zero (*shuny*[a])
which is the undifferentiated expanse (f), it seeks in essence its
eventual fusion with this initial zero without which the One cannot
exist.

A different concept of time is indicated. The nomination as an
endless series of motifs, descriptions, frames, images is always in
movement, or always has the possibility of movement, only its
movement is not bound in a hierarchical play between subject and
object, there is no creator, no actor, no willed ego, no object to be
controlled, manipulated, but constellations of energy, of descriptions of the movement from the generic formless to form, from the
0 to 1 to infinity.

The nostalgia for or return of this passage-state is what is
characterised as the desire of the feminine self, realisable by the
inverted erotic act, which is no other than a lesbian fusional play,
free from the parameters of masculine objectification and normative
heterosexual progeny and mortality.

The Concealment of the Third Point and the Construction of Heterosexuality and Death

the daughter of *tvasht(a)*, upon the action of bearing-transporting, is the principle of the universe existing,
the mother of *yam* (the god of death), surrounded by the death principle, she the great woman, illumination lost

she, the immortal concealed from the mortals, a dual stream of light created
then occurred two copulations, two twins (of) *saranyuh* (RV, 10.17.1–2)

Saranyuh – wind, cloud, water, spring
Saranyuh = (*sri*) to flow + (*anyuch*) quick fleeted

In the myth of Shiva, light as reflection becomes the revelation and creation of the first woman. However, in the above Rig Vedic myth, the illuminating-bearing principle as *Saranyuh* must be concealed from the mortals. Subsequently a shadow double is created for the mortal world, resulting in the carrying forth of twins.

This means that the principle of revelation as reflection is now meant to be concealed, and becomes the dark shadow, as it is no longer embedded in the economy of consciousness. This concealment becomes the creation of the patriarchal unconscious, symbolised through the immortal woman. The shift from an economy based on the reflection-revelation of the dark-expansive *urva* or *shuny(a)*, to that of its concealment, becomes the basis of a series of taboos and the normativising of sexuality. Instead of the fusion of the part with the whole through the medium of the sexual libidinal fire, the whole is to be kept apart from the part, thus creating the opposition of mortality/immortality.

The Dissolution of the Heterosexual Pact or the Impossible Union between the Immortal Woman and Mortal Male

Urvashi = (*uru/urva*) expansive, spread out, voluminous + (*ash*) to attain/arrive at.
Urvashi is also named (*brihat*) expansive and (*adiva*) twilight, which are nominations again of Usha.

Whereas Urvashi is an *apsara*, a divine water goddess, Pururvas is a mortal and the son of the goddess Ida. No male parentage exists.

The juxtaposition of the oppositions of feminine immortality and masculine mortality is an underlying expression of the tension generated by the patriarchal ideology in this particular variant.

Pururvas: Alas, O wife, stay O terrible/fearful (*ghore*) woman, firm in your intentions. Let us both accede to my mixed words. If they remain unsaid, there will be no pleasure/fruit for distant days.

Urvashi: What should I do with your words? I have crossed over to/like the foremost/first of the Ushas. Pururvas, renewed is the house beyond. Here I am as difficult to grasp as the wind.

Pururvas: An arrow to prosperity, as an arrow flung that wins a hundredfold cattle. There is no pleasure in the non semenic/heroic-virile act (*avir krtau*); no *ura* and the end to *dhunya*.

She, the Ushas giving virility, vigorous long life to the father-in-law, yet when hurt is beyond grasp. Be satisfied (imperative) in the house of blind desire, night and day pierced (*shnitha*) by the penis.

Urvashi: Thrice a day did you pierce me with your penis, unwilling that I was. Pururvas, I acceded to your desire, your semen (*vir*) in me; then were you king of my body.

They (f), the blazing swarm, joined in affection, the heart's eye/the clear reflection in the pool deep; red ointments flowed, prospering cows; the endless order in accordance to cows.

As he was born there sat the goddesses, the growing rivers, self-absorbing (f); then were you raised for battle against the *dasyus* and the *devas*.

Pururvas: Having abandoned the immortal elixir (*asu*), and as mortal wanting to reside sexually in the immortal women, they rebounded from me as does a coiled snake or mares touching the chariot.

Urvashi: When the dead liquor (*asu mart*) lusts after the elixir of immortality, why does it not satiate our desires, accede to us? Why does it not make its body beautiful or play like mares nipping each other?

Pururvas: Flashing like falling lightning (*davidyod*), bringing me the craved waters (*apya kamani*) – from the waters was born a noble lad. May Urvashi grant long life.

Urvashi: You were germinated through the cows and the earth; thus in me did you constitute your vitality.

But you, transgressor, did not listen to me that day. Why now do you speak like an innocent?

Pururvas: When will the son that is born, yearn after his father? Upon knowing, he will shed flowing tears. Who would dare to separate the married pair while the ancestral fire burns in the house of the father in law?

Urvashi: In that case let him shed tears, he will not be injured meditating on my auspicious form; to you is the message – I am beyond for you. To the house here I am unobtainable, you fool.

Pururvas: The lover throws himself uncovered (*anavrit*), going to the furthest distance (*paravatam*), to the first (*paramam*), to lie down in the lap of Nirrti and be eaten by raging wolves.

Urvashi: Pururvas, no you are not to die, not to fall or be eaten by hyena-wolves.

Outside Voice: There is no friendship with women, their hearts are the hearts of hyenas.

Urvashi: When I, assuming another form, wandered among the mortals for the nights of four years, eating one drop of rain water once a day; satiated with that do I wander now.

Pururvas: I wish to submit to the atmosphere-filling, red, celestially transformed, shining Urvashi. May the gifts of good acts be yours; stay and do not turn/revert (*vartasva*); my heart burns.

Outside Voice: Thus speak the gods to you, son of Ida; now you will be bound to death, your offspring will offer sacrifices to the gods as you will rejoice in *svarga*. (*RV* X.95)

Although comprising barely 18 *riks* (citations) and possessing a skeletal narrative structuration based on the main event of Urvashi's exit from the ideological framework of heterosexuality, this text is dense in various forms of symbolic meaning, centred particularly on the usage of certain cipher words and nominational strategies, which the existing translations have hitherto not taken into account.

In the first line itself, Pururvas nominates Urvashi as 'wife', yet fearful/terrible (*ghore*) and as '*manasa*'. In existing translations, the nomination *manasa* has either not been translated, or otherwise translated as wife or woman. This is a clear phenomenon of the linguistic heterosexual gaze, which superimposes a non-contextual connotation or meaning on the original framework of signifiers. If one goes back to the etymological root and non-gendered form, one finds the basic meaning of *manasa* is mind/intellect. In fact, it is the later well-known masculinised form Manu, from the same root *manas*, that becomes symbolic of the first man. It is this that probably led to the association of *manasa* as wife, although *manasa* appears much earlier.

From Pururvas' perspective, the sequential transformation of nominations, starting from *jaye* (woman or alluded meaning of wife), to that of *manasa*, and then ultimately climaxing in *ghore*, indicates the changing perception in the image of Urvashi, from that of mere woman or 'wife', to that of *manasa* as an independent signifier of the feminine register devoid of masculine parameters. The line eventually culminates in the adjectival nomination of *ghore*: terrible/fearful.

The word *ghore*, in climaxing the above line, does not connote an adjectival usage independent from the user/speaker, but is in direct relationship to the projection and perception of Pururvas' image of Urvashi, which upon becoming independent from his gaze takes on 'fearful' attributes. Whereas the verbal construction of Pururvas' text is based on that of the imperative mode, dependent thus on being validated by the other, Urvashi's text is a subjective articulation. This is emphasised in her initial phrase, 'What shall I do with your words?'

The break with Pururvas' significatory code symbolises the crossing over to the first of the Ushas. This alludes to a symbolic shift, both of kinship patterns and cosmogenic perceptions. Here it becomes relevant to compare and contrast the rape of Usha with the above lines of Urvashi.

This heroic and masculine (*paumsyam*) deed did you commit Indra, holder of the *chakr(a)* (wheel) when the women plotted harm (*duharanya*) and you did kill the daughter of light, indeed the luminosity of light, the daughter, the great to be regarded as great, Usha, did you crush; the water-*usha*, the living breath-mother-wagon (*anah*) fluidity smashed, the terrified Usha did the bull (Indra) pierce (*shnitha*). Thus the breath-wagon (*anah*) lay smashed on the banks of the Vipas as she fled to the furthest distance (*paravatah*). (RV, 4.30.8–11)

Urvashi: What should I do with your words? I have crossed over

to/like the first of the Ushas. Pururvas, renewed is the house
beyond (*para*). Here (*ihi*) I am as difficult to grasp as the wind.

Here, what is of particular significance is the inversion of the
spatial paradigm of (*paravatah*) the beyond. The beyond is no
longer the space that has been thrust away, but that which is the
ever-renewable house beyond (*punar astam para ihi*). From
Pururvas' spatial perspective (here [*ihi*]), the beyond (*para*)
becomes impossible to grasp or attain.

Again here in the juxtaposed discourse of Urvashi and Pururvas,
one has conflicting and opposing perceptions. From the patriarchal
– Pururvas' – point of view, there is an apparent affirmation of the
masculine identity of virility, of victory, of imperative desire
governed by the piercing action of the penis and the selective
appropriation of the Ushas. The Ushas are supposed to bring
wealth and nourishment to the patriarchal fold, and must
therefore be satisfied by male desire. From the feminine –
Urvashi's – point of view, the act of lordship is established only by
the undesired penetrative act of rape, which is counterposed to the
images of the blazing feminine swarm joined in affection, the
radiance of the clear reflection in the waters and the peaceful,
grazing cows symbolising the pastoral river valley agricultural
cultures, in contrast to the nomadic warlike invader symbolised in
the cosmic opposition Usha/Indra. Thus the following table of
oppositions emerges:

Pururvas	*Urvashi*
1 discourse based on imperative tone	discourse based on subjective tone
2 notion of Ushas as the appropriated life giving feminine energy	action of crossing over to the first of the Ushas
3 '*astam nanakshe*' as the house of blind desire which the Ushas should serve	'*punar astam para*' as the ever-renewable home beyond in the space of the Ushas
4 desire based on the imperative act of the piercing penis	desire based on aspect of feminine fusion, luminosity and fluidity

In the subsequent section of the dialogue, the tone of Pururvas' discourse shifts from that of self-reflexivity to supplication, whereas Urvashi's remains explicative. But the major thematic that occurs is the equation of sexuality based on feminine desire with immortality and that of male as mortal. Within this equation one finds the implicit sub-text of the '*amrit asu*' based on the idea of playful sexuality, alongside that of the '*asu mart*' based on the progenic act, which is indirectly implied in Pururvas' statement of:

> *Pururvas*: Flashing like falling lightning (*davidyod*), bringing me the craved waters (*apya kamani*) – from the waters was born a noble lad. May Urvashi grant long life.

Yet the supplication of long life is followed by the desire to return uncovered (*anavrit*) to the womb-lap of Nirrti, the furthest-distant and the first.

> *Pururvas*: The lover throws himself uncovered, going to the furthest distance, to the first, to lie down in the lap of Nirrti.

The pendulumic shift that occurs in Pururvas' discourse on his own desire, from the initial commencement of the assertion of virility to that of the nudity of death in the lap of Nirrti, also invests the idea of death with a masculine projection.

The space of the beyond (*para*), the first (*paramam*) are here associated with Nirrti. In the case of Urvashi they are associated with the plural Ushas. Yet in the act of rape of Usha by Indra, it is Usha who is thrust into Nirrti's space of the extreme beyond. Even spatial categories are embedded in an economy of sexual differences. Consequently if for Pururvas the expression of the beyond is an articulation of coming to terms with 'mortality' and 'nudity', for Urvashi it is the male mortal world that is the other-exile space, and the movement of crossing over to the beyond is the basis for the creation of the ever-renewable home.

Thus 'death', far from referring to a natural, non-gendered event in certain expressions, becomes a cultural, patriarchal act, reflecting the ironic gaze of the feminine other in the arena of sexuality constellated around the gender poles of male progeny and feminine eros. And it is in this context that one can understand the opposition of mortality/immortality: immortality referring to an archetypal continuum, a fusion of the cosmo-social, counter-posed on the other hand to the idea of feminine exile in the male mortal world. Mortality, on the other hand becomes a metaphor for male virility/lordship, which is further implicated in an entire system of dualised oppositions – in particular that of itself; its schizophrenic other half being no other than the nude male corpse: for the motif of nudity in all its entirety can exist only at the moment of death, as a return back to the womb or Nirrti.

Nirrti and the Semiotography of Death and Knowledge

Nirrti = *nirr* (to decay, dissolve, separate, etc.) + the feminine suffix *ti*: it is associated with the topos of Tuonela, the womb-death, the end of male progeny, the begetting only of girl children, female barrenness, and sexual 'deviance'.

> He, who not knowing the wheel (*chakar*), upon perceiving the concealed out of sight (*hiruk*); engulfed in the mother's womb (*matur-yona*) gets possessed by Nirrti and progeny comes to an end. (*RV*, 1.164.32)

Sayan's commentary on this citation states:

> He who has experienced the pains of the womb surrenders himself to Nirrti in the sense of knowing the self form of the knowledge of existence, equivalent to Aditi. To perceive the out-of-sight is to see the concealed – placed between. He of the negative properties of water (*vristi*), the son of the mother and non mother in the interspace of the two *yonas*. To articulate the '*yoni*' is the inter-space. The two forests (*aranyas*: referring to the two *yonas*) are the names and properties of the inter-space; in the one country of the inter-space, in the midst of the (singular) *yoni* occurs progeny when there is an end to the raw-uncooked (blood).(cf.[2])

Death is not seen in the above citation as a teleological event, but as a space placed in between, which must be concealed for the male foetus to be born. This is rendered linguistically by the trans-formation of the word '*antah*' into the compounds of *antar-hita* and *antar-iksh*. The etymological root is the same, but in the compound constructions the 'ah' changes into 'r'. This phonological shift also marks a conceptual shift, from the notion of

   antah: teleological end;

to

   antar: in between, interior, different, interval, hole, etc.

The word '*hit*' designates the action of placing. Death, instead of being the end of life, becomes that which is placed between. In other words, the concealed third point. This is particularly revealing, for possession by Nirrti is equated to the *perception* of the out-of-sight/concealed third point, which marks an end to the ideology of progeny, but not that of fertile birth. For the commentary associates this form of perception with the properties of Aditi and the self form of perception itself. Through the medium of this perception of the third point, a passage space is created between the above dichotomies, thus fusing the patriarchal split between Nirrti and Aditi.

   A triadic mode of cognition emerges, nominated by the motif (*try-ambak*) three eyes/mother or the *yoni*.

   The meaning of 'ambak' as 'eye' may also have a hint to an earlier or primary sense of the word as 'womb' for the eye had been a concept interchangeable with the female yoni.[8]

The motif of *tryambak* as a triadic space creates an entirely different framework of cognition. Instead of oppositions, one has the notions of polarities and the spaces or movements in between. In other words, the triangle as a philosophic image symbolises the constellation of 'opposites' through the mediational point of the apex. The apex becomes both the point of integration (*antar*) and the beyond (*para*). Any form of transference is possible between the three points, as the apex is not fixed, but may be any of the three points.

   As a womb space, the *tryambak* refers to the holistic and integrated womb space, symbolised both by the aspect of giving birth (Aditi), and that of receiving back the foetus-corpse (Nirrti). Aditi and Nirrti are not opposing forces, but are different aspects/faces/eyes of the yonic-womb.

   In the topologies of creation in the gynefocal myths, citations entail not just human creation – which is only one part – but creation as a generative energy. The focus is on an abundance of motifs, for after the initial act of differentiating, a number of different events occur. There is the creation of the intellectual energy of consciousness, the egg, the serpentine energy, the foetus, blood etc. Blood is no longer a raw element, but that which transmits a biological affiliation through women as generatrices in any kinship configuration. The patriarchal affiliation was one that was constructed around the binary oppositions of raw/cultivated or desire/progeny (male).

(The) *parapara* Nirrti, harmful/mischievous kills. Perish along with intense desire (*trishnaya* [f]). (*RV* 1.38.6)

A sacrificial art was hence developed to exile Nirrti and that of her constellation. Of particular significance in this context is the *pashubandh* sacrifice (binding of the animal); the juice or essence of this animal must be appropriated and apportioned only to those gods not connected to the Nirrti constellation.

The animal sacrifice is only for *varun* and Indra. The singing gods, those associated, possessed with/by Nirrti, the seven (to be) restrained.[9]

The raison d'être of the sacrifice was to preserve and protect one's manhood, which meant being freed from the crime of animal sexuality (*pashu-kam*) and Nirrti. This was contrasted to *praja-kam*, or progenic sexuality. Whereas *praja-kam* was associated with (*viry*[a]) virility, light, fixed gender categories, the possession by Nirrti was likened to:

That woman having a male form and that male having a woman's form are possessed by Nirrti. (*MS*, 2.5.5.6)

This text, which is also an invocation to be freed from Nirrti, goes on to elaborate this state of possession by Nirrti as lessening the bull force of Indra, which is equivalent to the sin of *ni-pumsak* (without malehood, neuter). In the *Kathak Samhita*,[10] there is the same formulation, except for the rendering of the word *nipumsak* which becomes *vi-pumsak* (*vi*: contrary), or contrary to malehood. This state is likened to darkness (*tamo*), the dark colour (*krishan*), and above all to death.

Sexuality is to be solely reproductive and transmit the father's *som* (semen).

> He who does not drink the *soma* of the fathers; rather that desire weakens and halves the *virya*. Further this produces the quality of animalness instead of progeny. And this form of inter-course is *ni-pumsak*. (*KS*, 2.5.5.6)

Further, the form of fire and its elements established should be (*ajam*) non-twin, not of the same sex, and not equivalent to the fire of Nirrti-Ahuti or the self-fire. Any form of auto-sexuality is relegated to the sin of Nirrti.

The *Kathak Samhita* has a further elaboration of the above dichotomies and related motifs. Here the zone of Nirrti includes also the associative spectrum of motifs connected with ardent desire which is dwarflike, crooked and thus dangerous. This ardent desire is also expansive (*urva*), and *pashukam* is related to the motif of the pleasure of the waters of the cave (*valam*), waters (*apah*), pleasure (*vrinot*). The compound formation of these motifs contains another set of double meanings, that of the disclosure of the cave. The perception of the space of the beyond is not located in an economy of fear but of pleasure. Instead of the limited and reductive procreative view, there is the liberated visionary opening of the sensual third eye-cave. But instead this energy must be expelled in the patriarchal texts.

> When the mark of the day that is the form of the dark (*krishan*) night possessing both genres, then must be expelled from the senses the vibrating and pulsating sexuality of the 'demoness' (*danavi*) and wandering *asur* (alter-ego of the male god), otherwise the male will become like the qualities of 'woman-hood', like a woman, and will be possessed by Nirrti. His senses will be akin to Nirrti and contrary to malehood (*vipumsak*). (*KS*, 13.5)

The basis of 'cultivated', hence heterosexual, sexuality is also the expulsion of any form of *jamita* (belonging to the same sex). All items belonging to the sacrifice must be (*ajami*) of different sexes, and recreate the gender imbalance of male-active, female-passive.

amaithunam tada aprajanam yada jami

yatha pumsau va sah shayatam striyau va[11]
When (there is) the non-penetrative act (*a-maithunam*), then (there is) no progeny (*a-praja*) and thus it is *jami*; two men or women sleeping (*shayatam*) together (*sah*).

Whereas the word *maithun* had signified various kinds of sexual acts, here the *Jaiminiya Brahman* text is at pains to define what kind of sexuality could be classified as *maithun*. The parameter of this definition is the penetrative *a-jami* act resulting in progeny. The *jami* is the alter-ego/other to this and is now not accorded a sexual status, but is reduced simply to the act of homosexual togetherness or fusion. The word *jami* means twin or being born from the same womb, and is inscribed in the 'same' sexual economy of Nirrti as the auto-erotic. *Jami* also refers to kinship patterns that are based on relations with the collective sisters or mothers.

In *Atharva Ved* 2.10,[12] the male makes a number of invocations to be free from Nirrti's disease (*Kshetriya*) and the sin of *jami-shamsad* (desirous of *jami*). *Kshetriya* also referred to illicit sexual practices, and is described in the commentary to the following *Laws of Manu* as:

A damsel (*kanya*) who pollutes another damsel must be fined 200 panas, pay the double of the bride price to the father and receive 10 lashes with the rod.
But a woman who pollutes another damsel shall instantly have her head shaved or be made to ride through the town on a donkey.[13]

Commentary:

a young woman (*kanya*) who pollutes another *kanya* becomes *yoni-akshatavim*; i.e. the *yoni* becomes invulnerable, unblemished and permanently in the 'virgin' state.
By virtue of this eros, she becomes blemished with the disease of *Kshetriya* and thereby is the wildest woman.[14]

However, the notion of *jami* that emerges outside the heterosexual (*ajami*) gaze is indicative of an entirely different order of kinship relationships, as well as different forms of cognition of sexuality and death. The *jami* state is not interested in mastering the senses, but attaining them in their primal form. For the *jami* state is, above all, the experience of the expansive feminine through the state of fusion. Further, the *jami* state, in its association to a matrifocal kinship framework, does not have to deny the sexual mother, or convert the woman into a fetishised object of exchange between men. Here, on the contrary, it is the experiencing of the feminine as origin that is necessary to establish the primal bond.

The idea of *jami* is a revelatory state of togetherness within the same sex.

> One sister for her generated other sister opens the *yoni* space making it perceptible;
> through the luminous rays, the anointments of the sun, going together like *vrah*. (*RV*, 1.124.8)

Here the act of revelation is for the sister which is akin to the opening of the *yoni* space. Fertility is no longer cleavaged from its psychic generative process, nor is the luminous from the dark.

> this, the arrival of the best of lights, the birth of brilliant luminosity, thus fertility, generativeness as *ratri-usha* (night-dawn) one spoke of the wheel. (*RV*, 1, 113)

The motif of the dual sisters, in its association with the *jami* or *yam* form of eros, is based on the idea of diversity of the same self. This is also expressed in the etymology of the word sister (*sva-sri*), (*sv*) self, (*sri*) to flow, move (*srij*) blood.

> maidens moving together, with adjacent boundaries, sisters (*svasara*), twins (*jami*) in the expansiveness of the manes; they kiss – united, of the (universe's) focal point; (*RV*, 1.85.5)

> similar pathways of the two sisters, treading alternately, not opposing, not tarrying, of one form resplendent (are) *nakta-usasa*, fused yet diverse. (*RV*, 1.113. 1–3)

> twin sisters of various transforming forms, of the two one glowing, the other dark; *syavi* and *arusi*, the two sisters ... (*RV*, 3.55.11)

The *jami* form of sexuality is based on the movement of the diverse variegated ray paths of the self in an eventual fusion. Sexuality is not conceptualised on the basis of the gender opposite but on the diverse within the same self through a flow.

> The still-expansiveness, the foremost variegated tableau of Usha, the self in the ray paths, opening the doors of the stalls of darkness, the gleaming pure fires (*pavaka* [f]) (*RV*, 4.51. 1–2)

In the twin sisters the flow is between the two poles of *syavi* (of the dark Nirrti's domain) and *arushi* (bright red indicative of the blood flower motif). Through the erotic energy of fusion of the twin sisters, tidal flows are generated that bring about the movement of the yonic cycle, and there occurs the transformation of death into life and the inverse. But what really constitutes the imagery and experience of death? The experience of death seems to be above all a libidinal experience of the holistic cyclic womb, its primal waters. In other words, expansive sexuality (*urdhva*) is conceived as an ecstatic climax of material decomposition – into being submerged in/by the cave waters. This is identical to the *jami mulihun* (sexual act) where the libidinal flow is a return to the yonic cave, which re-enacts the primal experience of birth and the state of oneness with the archetypal feminine psyche or self.

> *sv-krit irane jusane nirrti-ev-attu*
> The self made *irane-yoni* (when) satisfied is to be eaten/attained by Nirrti.

> To be eaten/attained (*attu*) is the satisfied (*jusana*) Nirrti in the self made enacted in *irane-yoni* (sacrificial texts)
> in the triangle, of the vibrating state, she, creating reflections, the ever-renewable.[14]

> her (the goddess) libidinal energy, the still *shakti* of the serpent form, the goddess praised for self-desire, of the genre of self desire, the self form (f). (*KK*, 1.109)

Desire when projected as death becomes the all-pervading death. Desire as satiation is the return to the origin, where there is no death, only the multiple plays of transformation, the infinite creations of astral constellations in the many sheaths of form and formlessness, the infinite explorations between the primal feminine *shuny(a)* and the first woman.

(she) enacting the inverted eros (*viprit rati*[*f*]) in the mode of the great 'void' (*maha shuny*[*a*]), the three part serpent-foetus, the six circles, then the cave of the lotus.

GLOSSARY OF TERMS

All translations from ancient texts given here are mine.

'a' as a prefix denotes what is beyond, the other, the triadic point of the rest of the word, e.g. *a-jami, jami*
anamika: beyond nomination
(f): indicates the feminine construction of the original word
nam: nameable
prakriti: feminine principle of materiality
usha: feminine cosmography of light, dawn, etc.
yoni: woman's sexual organ as a totality, origin, cave, water source, etc.

NOTES

1 Wendy O'Flaherty, *Divine Consort*, eds., J S Hawley and D M Wulff, Graduate Theology Union, Berkeley, 1982, p. 132.
2 Sayan was a commentator on the Sanskrit text *Rig Ved*, who lived about 500 BC.
3 Ludwig Wittgenstein, *Tractatus Logico-Philosophicus*, 1922, 7: 'What one cannot speak about must be left silent'.
4 Nelly Sachs, *In den Wohnungen des Todes*, Aufbau-verlag, Berlin, 1947. 'But silence is the dwelling-place of sacrifice'.
The journey of the lesbian reader into time is always through
a passage of the echoes of a silence
a silence beyond nomination
a silence deliberately obscured
a silence inviting excavation – voicing – sculpting – nomination.
5 *Mahabhagvat Puran*: Shaktic text from the period 500 AD to medieval times, 3. 21. The datings of this and other texts cited in this essay are very approximate, and up till now no sure tools of dating exist. Further, since a lot of the women's traditions were passed on orally, their eventual inscription and compilation into a written form came about later, often introducing modifications. However, the following chronology is usually accepted: *Rig Ved;*

Artharva Ved, Sayan's commentary, sacrificial texts; *Laws of Manu*; law commentaries; Shaktic texts.

6 *Rig Ved*, edited by Sitarma Sastri, translated by Sitanatha Pradhana, India Research Institute, Calcutta, 1933. *Rig Ved (RV)*: Sanskrit text dating from earlier than 1500 BC. The (a) at the end of any word indicates a short 'a', which is necessary for the pronunciation of the final consonant; e.g. *chakr(a)*. Where there is no bracket, a long 'a' is indicated. The short vowel at the end of a word in some cases meant a neuter or masculine form of the word, whereas the long vowel meant a feminine form of the word; e.g. shiv = masculine/neuter, and shiva = feminine.

7 *Kalika Khand* (*KK*): Shaktic text from the period 500 AD to mediaeval times. (No modern edition or translation.)

8 P K Aggarwal, *Goddesses in Ancient India*, Prithvi Prakashan, Varanasi, p. 135.

9 *Maitrani Samhita* (*MS*): sacrifical text from about 500 BC, 2.5.6.

10 *Kathak Samhita* (*KS*): sacrifical text from about 500 BC. (No modern edition or translation.)

11 *Jaiminiya Brahman*: sacrifical text from about 500 BC, 1.300. (No modern edition or translation.)

12 *Atharva Ved*: Sanskrit text from about 500 BC, translated by W D Whitney, Harvard Oriental Series, Harvard University, 1905.

13 The *Laws of Manu*, 8.369 and 370, translated by G. Bühler. Clarendon Press, Oxford, 1886.

14 *Yajnavalkya*: a commentary from about 100 AD, II, 288, translated by J R Gharpire, Collection of Indian Law Texts, Bombay, 1936.

15 *Yogini Hradya*: Shaktic text from the period 500 AD to mediaeval times. (No modern edition or translation), p.263.

3

Lesbians   Writing

KATHERINE PHILIPS: SEVENTEENTH-CENTURY LESBIAN POET

Elaine Hobby

Katherine Philips is one of the very few seventeenth-century women writers who have made it even peripherally into the mainstream: a few of her poems are frequently included in anthologies of verse from the period. In part this is because of her relatively high social status, but it is also the case that more biographical information is known about her than most of her female contemporaries. She was born on 1 January 1632, the daughter of Katherine Fowler (née Oxenbridge) and her husband John, a wealthy merchant. She was educated at school in London, where she remained until the age of 15 when, in 1646, her widowed and recently remarried mother called her to her own new home in rural Wales, and married her to a 54-year-old widower, James Philips.[1]

Living in Wales in the 1640s and 1650s she wrote prodigious amounts of poetry, which circulated in manuscript amongst friends; and after 1660, during an extended visit to Ireland, she translated *Pompée*, a play by Corneille, which was performed in Dublin and London with considerable success. Before she died of smallpox in 1664 an unofficial collection of some of her work was published, and in 1667 her friends brought out on her behalf an expanded edition, *Poems by the most deservedly Admired Mrs Katherine Philips, The matchless Orinda.*

I have argued elsewhere[2] that the popularly promoted image of

Philips as a modest and self-effacing poetess is an illusion, one actively created by herself to make more acceptable her unfeminine boldness in writing for publication. In this essay, I want to explore another aspect of her work: its lesbian erotic. In order to do this, I will first provide some historical context for her love for women, and sketch my disagreements with present-day analyses of seventeenth-century (homo)sexuality.

HISTORICAL BACKGROUND

Katherine Philips began to write and publish in the time of the English revolution: those extraordinary years of the 1640s and 1650s when Britain had no king because our ancestors had defied and fought against, and then beheaded, Charles I. This signalled a cultural earthquake that we can barely comprehend today, in our society where the monarch is merely a figurehead of the state, if an astonishingly wealthy one. Charles I asserted to his subjects that he ruled by divine right: that God had personally chosen him to reign, and that to defy the king was to defy God himself. Order in the kingdom was said to be necessary to, and part of, a universal order, one where everyone had their fixed and rightful place in a hierarchy, and where individual households were ruled over by husbands/fathers. Beheading the king, therefore, was an act of huge symbolic significance. If such a thing was possible, what could follow?

Katherine Philips lived, then, in a period of great excitement, change and experimentation, and she was one of very many women who broke into print. The great majority of her fellow female writers (unlike Philips herself) were social radicals, who joined, or even helped form, new churches, which were opposed to the monarchy and its associated hierarchies.[3] These Quakers, Baptists, Seekers, saw it as their God-given task to spread their progressive social messages, and we know that Quakers, in particular, characteristically travelled the country and beyond in single-sex pairs, preaching in partnerships that sometimes lasted for years. Supporting one another through illness, the hardships of travelling, and periods of imprisonment for their activities, they must have loved and trusted each other. Perhaps they were sometimes also lovers. Certainly there is evidence that suggests this. Katherine Evans and Sarah Cheevers, for instance, Quakers who had husbands and children at home in England, were arrested in Malta for their political activities and imprisoned by the Inquisition for three years. Their account of those experiences, published in 1662 whilst they were still in prison, records what happened when their jailers decided to put them into solitary confinement. Katherine Evans writes

> They told us the Inquisitor would have us separated because I was weak and I should go into a cooler room, but Sarah should abide there. I took her by the arm and said, 'The Lord hath joined us together, and woe be to them that should part us'. I said I rather choose to die there with my friend than to part from her.[4]

The echo here of the words of the wedding service – 'Those whom God hath joined together, let no man put asunder' – suggests that the women saw themselves as married, and believed their union to be divinely sanctioned.

There are similar examples of passionate, same-sex bondings in other radical sects. Sarah Davy, for instance, joined her Baptist church after years of isolation and feeling herself to be different from others were ended, when a woman 'of a sweet and free disposition' arrived in her life, and 'it pleased the Lord to carry out our hearts much towards one another'.[5] Hester Biddle, a Quaker arrested for preaching in 1662, told the magistrate at her trial, when he challeneged her with having left her husband for a younger man,

> that was not his business to judge at this time, nor was it fit for him to accuse her, but she went with three women as she was moved of the Lord.[6]

When I first came across such references, I was taken aback, wondering if my modern, lesbian eyes were reading things into the texts that weren't there. Certainly, I'd seen nothing in standard (or even radical) histories of the period that suggested that same-sex love could be part of the picture of social experimentation and change. But on reflection, and as such passages kept appearing, I decided that the existence of such unions is after all unsurprising. A woman wishing to leave the narrow bonds of wifehood and motherhood was offered an adventurous alternative in the radical churches, and the opportunity to justify her commitment to other women as part of a higher divine purpose. I suspect that my current research in this material is going to reveal many other examples.

THE HISTORY OF HOMOSEXUALITY: TODAY'S POLITICAL DEBATE

Reveal many other examples, I say; but examples of what? According to Lillian Faderman, whose *Surpassing the Love of Men* has become a lesbian classic, I certainly won't be finding examples of women who lusted after one another and expressed their desire in sex. Faderman maintains that, whilst women in the past could feel passionately towards one another, they did not believe their emotions to be erotic, and did not act on them sexually. In her reading of Katherine Philips' poetry, Faderman explicitly states the thesis that informs her view of the period:

> Katherine uses the language of erotic love when she is really writing about a spiritual union manifested through verbal declarations and noble actions alone.[7]

Even when Philips uses sexually-charged language, Faderman is saying, all she is expressing is intense friendship. Faderman's grounds for this belief are actually based on a misunderstanding of the history of sexuality. She believes that sex in that period was perceived as necessarily involving a penis (no penis, no sexual encounter), and that 'women in centuries other than ours often internalised the view of females having little sexual passion'.[8] This is certainly wrong. Before about 1700, women were perceived as the more lustful sex, and it was believed that female orgasm was essential for conception to occur. The existence of the clitoris was well known, as was its role in producing female sexual pleasure. I find the suggestion that is implicit in Faderman's thesis simply incredible: that in such a society women would not indulge (heterosexually and homosexually) in sexual activities other than penetrative intercourse, and would not see any resultant pleasure as sexual.

Therefore, whilst it is impossible to know whether any of these seventeenth-century women – Katherine Philips, Katherine Evans,

Sarah Cheevers, Sarah Davy, Hester Biddle – had sexual relations with one another, there are reasons to believe that women's desire for women was thinkable in their society. According to another influential school of thought, however, the existence of such desire does not mean that we can look for 'lesbians' or 'homosexual men' in the past, because although homosexual activity might have existed, the idea that someone could 'be a homosexual' did not. In academic and non-academic gay circles, it is becoming a tenet of faith that there was no such thing as 'homosexual identity' until fairly recently. According to such theories, which find their origins in Michel Foucault's *History of Sexuality*,[9] the possibility of perceiving oneself as a 'homosexual', or as someone whose identity consisted of a 'sexual nature', didn't begin until the second half of the nineteenth century. That was when, so the argument goes, medical science invented the term 'homosexual' and began to categorise people into fixed types according to their sexual preferences and/or sexual characteristics. Before then, it is asserted, people might have indulged in same-sex sexual activity, but they did not see this as defining their identity.

In fact this account of the development of nineteenth-century homosexuality is quite wrong, as has been ably demonstrated by Frederic Silverstolpe and by Chris White.[10] It is easy to see why such an idea, though, would be attractive to some kinds of lesbian and gay rights activism. If, until the quite recent past, people were not seen as 'different' just because of their sexual behaviour, we ought to be able to re-establish a world in which sexual preferences are not used to discriminate legally or socially. It is this application of that field of theory, I think, that in part explains its popular appeal and its tenacity in the face of evidence that ought to dislodge it.

I don't believe that Foucault's model is an accurate picture of the past, because it simply cannot account for some of the references to women's desire for other women that I have come across. Lyndal Roper, an historian of German culture, has brought to my attention this intriguing snippet from the late sixteenth century:

> There was also at that time a poor serving girl at Mösskirch, who served here and there, and she was called Greta by the Market. She did not take any man or young apprentice, nor would she stand at the bench with any such [i.e. work with a man as

husband and wife and sell his goods], but loved the young daughters, went after them and bought them pedlars' goods; and she also used all bearing and manners, as if she had a masculine *affect*. She was often considered to be an herma-phrodite or androgyne, but this did not prove to be the case, for she was investigated by cunning, and was seen to be a true, proper woman. Note: she was said to be born under an inverted, unnatural constellation. But amongst the learned and well-read one finds this sort of thing is often encountered amongst the Greeks and Romans, although this is to be ascribed rather to the evil customs of those corrupted nations, plagued by sins, than to the course of the heavens or stars.[11]

What interests me about this account is the fact that it demonstrates that there was a range of alternative or competing explanations for Greta's behaviour: explanations at least as varied as those employed by heterosexuals today. Why wouldn't she marry, choosing instead to court other girls with pedlars' goods, behaving like a man? The first thought is that she is physically deformed, physiologically not a real woman, so she is 'investigated by cunning' and the belief found groundless. How many people today, I wonder, believe that lesbians are physically peculiar: after all, whatever can we *do* if 'all' we have is women's bits? The very fact that her investigators are looking for a physical difference implies, of course, that it is thought that her attentions to women go further than the giving of gifts. The second explanation suggested for Greta's behaviour has a modern equivalent in 'She's just naturally like that': it's in the stars, 'she was said to be born under an inverted, unnatural constellation'. Third, though, there is the possibility of same-sex courtship being the result of cultural norms: there was a lot of it about in ancient Greece and Rome, the commentator notes. What this brief account suggests, then, is that people who were not themselves involved in same-sex desire knew of its existence, and were puzzled by it. They seem to have believed that this was behaviour peculiar to particular people, whilst at the same time considering the possibility that it might sometimes be made more common by cultural acceptance in 'corrupted nations'. This is a much more complicated and diverse way of thinking about sexual behaviour, and sexual identity, than the model proposed by Foucault would allow.

The belief that there are women who prefer sex with women is also implicit in a passing reference in an English source, Jane Sharp's *The Midwives Book*, which was published in 1671.[12] In the course of her eulogy to the clitoris, Jane Sharp tells us,

> Commonly it is but a small sprout, lying close hid under the wings [labia], and not easily felt; yet sometimes it grows so long that it hangs forth at the slit like a yard [penis (!)], and will swell and stand stiff if it be provoked, and some lewd women have endeavoured to use it as men do theirs. In the Indies and Egypt they are frequent, but I never heard but of one in this country; if there be any they do what they can for shame to keep it close.[13]

What is striking here, apart from Sharp's assumption that if 'they' exist they will keep themselves hidden, is the association of lesbianism with foreignness. It is Black women – women from the Indian subcontinent and North Africa – who are particularly prone to this characteristic, she asserts. This belief might in part find its origin in the practice of clitoridectomy, which was known to be practised in those areas of the world and 'justified' either as a necessary corrective to deformity or as a control of female lust. Seeing lesbianism as a Black characteristic, however, is also a sign of the (white) heterosexual desire to make it something foreign, something unEnglish, something 'uncivilised'. The history of lesbianism in this period, then, must be intimately connected with the history of colonialism, as Britain 'justified' slavery and the rape of other lands by seeing Black people as non-human, non-human in a way that could include being sexually aberrant. Black people and homosexuals were inferior outsiders who must be controlled for civilised society to survive.[14]

KATHERINE PHILIPS' LESBIAN EROTIC

The specific question of whether Katherine Philips' poetry should be read as lesbian has been much disputed, both in our period and her own. When her *Poems* were published in 1667, the book was prefaced by dedicatory verses written by her contemporaries, several of which compared her to Sappho. Anxious that such a comparison should not be seen as inferring lesbianism, however, they also repeatedly assert her 'virtue'. Abraham Cowley's praise of Philips, for instance, involves a particular commendation of her for eschewing Sappho's 'ill manners' (!). The fact that the difference between Philips' poetry and Sappho's is so vehemently asserted, though, implies that there was significant contemporary anxiety about whether the distinction between the two poets was really as great as they would like to think.

Considering the content of Philips' verse, this anxiety is not surprising. She wrote within the traditions of male love poetry, so her verse is full of melancholy lovers longing for kindness from their beloved; railing against her when this is refused or she is believed inconstant; overflowing with delight when the lady responds. What raises the spectre of lesbianism is the fact that both the lover and the beloved in Philips' poetry are consistently and unmistakably female.

It is not the intensity of passion the poems assert that is used as an adjudicating factor in modern discussions of Katherine Philips' verse, however. John Broadbent, for instance, in what is my favourite passage in the whole of mainstream literary criticism, says that her poem 'Orinda to Lucasia parting, October 1661, at London' is 'such sincere blackmailing bitchery that we are bound to think of her work as lesbian'.[15] The editors of *Kissing the Rod*, by contrast, are adamant that 'The flame [of Philips' love] is always pure, the relationship strictly Platonic, a meeting of souls, never the flesh'.[16] They choose to emphasise one element of Philips' use of poetic convention – her use of neo-Platonic tropes where the beloved lady is a source of abstract beauty and perfection – and ignore her diversions from this model. The result is an asexual reading of Philips' verse which is, perhaps, more comfortable to these heterosexual feminists.

These differences between readings of Philips' poetry are not solely attributable to the predispositions of her various readers, however. They are also due in part to the very dynamic of Philips' writings. Her work is riddled with ambiguities, which constantly tease with the promise of revelation and then conceal. This very fact might suggest, of course, that there is more to the poetry than first meets the eye: that the poet is playing a game – rather a dangerous one – where more is available for those who want it. If my contention that Philips' poetry is lesbian is right, such a strategy of concealment would not be surprising: homosexual activity was illegal. A 'closetedness' about sexuality, however, would also be consistent with another crucial characteristic of her writing: its coded royalism.

I have mentioned that Philips was only 15 when her mother married her to the 54-year-old James Philips, removing her from her familiar London environment. Not least of the shocks to her system must have been the fact that, in a period of civil war, she was being bound to her political enemy. Whilst Katherine Philips was a royalist, a position apparently developed whilst she was still at school, her new husband was a parliamentarian, and a prominent one. Her way of dealing with these desperate circumstances – legally, she was practically her husband's property, and those royalists who did not flee the country after the king's execution in 1649 lived in discreet internal exile – was to establish her Society of Friendship. This was a network largely made up of monarchists like herself, all identified by pastoral names (her own was 'Orinda').[17] To these special friends she wrote poems, many of them political. It is to two of the Society's members, Mary Aubrey (whom she addressed as 'Rosania') and Anne Owen (her beloved 'Lucasia') that she also sent her most passionate love poetry.

To understand how lesbian desire is concealed/revealed in Philips' poetry, then, I think it helps to start by examining the encoding of her royalism. The connections between the two are shown most clearly in 'Orinda to Lucasia'.

> Observe the weary birds ere night be done,
> How they would fain call up the tardy sun,
>> With feathers hung with dew,
>> And trembling voices too.
> They court their glorious planet to appear,
> That they may find recruits of spirits there.
>> The drooping flowers hang their heads,
>> And languish down into their beds,
> While brooks more bold and fierce than they
>> Wanting those beams, from whence
>> All things drink influence,
> Openly murmur, and demand the day.
>
> Thou, my Lucasia, art far more to me,
> Than he to all the under-world can be;
>> From thee I've heat and light,
>> Thy absence makes my night.
> But ah! my friend, it now grows very long,
> The sadness weighty, and the darkness strong:
>> My tears (its due) dwell on my cheeks,

And still my heart thy dawning seeks,
And to thee mournfully it cries,
That if too long I wait,
Even thou mayst come too late,
And not restore my life, but close my eyes.

A 1650s royalist reader would know this to be a poem longing for the return of the monarchy. In a manner reminiscent of her fellow royalist and near neighbour Henry Vaughan, Philips has chosen in her first stanza to write about a desire for the return of the sun: an image commonly used to represent the king. The birds, his loyal subjects, are 'weary', and 'court' his reappearance. The fact that the first stanza's real object of desire is the monarchy is also implied elsewhere in the poem. In the second line, the word 'fain' is a pun on 'feign': the birds are only pretending it is the sun they want, their actual yearning is for the king, who is 'glorious'. Whilst they wait, and some subjects hide and 'hang their heads', those who are 'more bold and fierce . . . Openly murmur'. The word 'murmur' is itself significant: the parliamentarian newspapers of the day frequently report the existence in the country of rebellious 'murmur'. What the sun/king will bring is 'recruits of spirits': not just an emotional change in this pastoral scene, but new army recruits (the word was first used to mean 'soldiers' during the 1640s, according to the *Oxford English Dictionary*).

To the royalist reader, then, this is a clear royalist poem. Such a reader might, indeed, see the second stanza's parallel expression of love for a lady as simply part of the disguise of the poem's real politics. The close echoing of the terms of the first stanza – the lady, like the king, is a source of 'heat and light'; the lover's tears are due/dew; dawning is longed for – could be seen by such a reader as reinforcement through repetition of the political message, disguised as a conventional compliment to an absent lady.

My proposition, by contrast, is that the second stanza is as central to the poem's meaning as the first, and that it uses a comparable strategy to disguise its import. Where the political significance of the first stanza is hidden through the use of a conventional pastoral scene – birds in a garden – the erotic significance of the second stanza is disguised through the use of other, related poetic conventions. The assertion that the lover will die if the beloved mistress does not return/respond has become so traditional by the time this poem was written that it could be read as merely conventional. The terms of the description – the poet's tears and the heart's longing – had already come to be the butt of ridicule from some male poets, notably John Donne; and by the 1660s Rochester and his circle were raucously substituting explicit sexual descriptions for such tropes.[18] What Philips' use of these conventions allows, then, is for her reader to believe that they could not be expressive of sexual love, since the expression of such feeling was increasingly being written in a different way by her contemporaries. Her writing, therefore, could be seen as not sexual, but as making a new, desexualised use of a once sexual discourse. By writing in a manner that is so clearly within the terms of a poetry that was becoming obsolete, Philips makes it possible for the reader to assume that sex is not the point at all.

This reasoning might be found tortuous by some. There are other indications, though, both within Philips' verse and in her contemporary reception, that suggest that the dying conventions of male love poetry are being revitalised by Philips to her own, lesbian ends. This is hinted at in the closing lines of the poem John Broadbent loves to hate, 'Orinda to Lucasia parting, October 1661, at London'. The dating of the poem indicates that the parting commemorated is not just a set piece poetic performance but a particular moment. It is, in fact, the occasion when Philips thought she was seeing Anne Owen for the last time, because her beloved was marrying and moving to Ireland.

> Adieu, dear object of my love's excess,
> And with thee all my hopes of happiness,
> With the same fervent and unchanged heart
> Which did its whole self once to thee impart
> (And which, though fortune has so sorely bruised,
> Would suffer more, to be from this excused),
> I to resign thy dear converse submit,
> Since I can neither keep, nor merit it.
> Thou hast to me too long confined been,
> Who ruin am without, passion within.
> My mind is sunk below thy tenderness,
> And my condition does deserve it less:
> I'm so entangled and so lost a thing
> By all the shocks my daily sorrow bring,
> That wouldst thou for thy old Orinda call,
> Thou hardly couldst unravel her at all.

And should I thy clear fortunes interline
With the incessant miseries of mine?
No, no, I never loved at such a rate,
To tie thee to the rigours of my fate.
As from my obligations thou art free,
Sure thou shalt be so from my injury.
Though every other worthiness I miss,
Yet I'll at least be generous in this:
I'd rather perish without sigh or groan,
Than thou shouldst be condemned to give me one;
Nay, in my soul I rather could allow
Friendship should be a sufferer, than thou.
Go then, since my sad heart has set thee free,
Let all the loads and chains remain on me.
Though I be left the prey of sea and wind,
Thou, being happy, wilt in that be kind;
Nor shall I my undoing much deplore,
Since thou art safe, whom I must value more.
Oh! mayst thou ever be so, and as free
From all ills else, as from my company,
And may the torments thou hast had from it
Be all that heaven will to thy life permit.
And that they may thy virtue service do,
Mayst thou be able to forgive them too:
But though I must this sharp submission learn,
I cannot yet unwish thy dear concern.
Not one new comfort I expect to see,
I quit my joy, hope, life, and all but thee:
Nor seek I thence aught that may discompose
That mind where so serene a goodness grows.
I ask no inconvenient kindness now,
To move thy passion, or to cloud thy brow:
And thou wilt satisfy my boldest plea
By some few soft remembrances of me,
Which may present thee with this candid thought:
I meant not all the troubles that I brought.
Own not what passion rules, and fate does crush,
But wish thou couldst have done it without a blush;
And that I had been, ere it was too late,
Either more worthy, or more fortunate.
Ah, who can love the thing they cannot prize?

But thou mayst pity though thou dost despise.
Yet I should think that pity bought too dear,
If it should cost those precious eyes a tear.
Oh, may no minute's trouble thee possess,
But to endear the next hour's happiness;
And mayst thou when thou art from me removed,
Be better pleased, but never worse beloved.
Oh, pardon me for pouring out my woes
In rhyme, now that I dare not do it in prose.
For I must lose whatever is called dear,
And thy assistance all that loss to bear,
And I have more cause than e'er I had before,
To fear that I shall never see thee more.

Several things might strike the lesbian reader, inviting an interpretation of the poem as sexual. The poet refers to her passion, her 'love's excess'; to having given her 'whole self' to her beloved. She is aware that the alternative to marriage she can offer her beloved – lesbian love – is not one that can promise ease or happiness: 'No, no, I never loved at such a rate,/ To tie thee to the rigours of my fate . . ./ I meant not all the troubles that I brought'. In a world where women are so despised, how can she expect her lover to choose her over the safety and status of a good marriage? – 'thou art safe', she reflects, and 'Ah, who can love the thing they cannot prize?'. The poem is indeed manipulative in its use of such observations: it is begging Lucasia to be true to the pleasures of another way of life, and begging perhaps without hope.

What the use of poetic convention allows, initially, is an interpretation that says the poem is not really lesbian at all, though. Neo-Platonic convention[19] could suggest that the 'whole self' once given to Lucasia was the poet's spirit, not her body; it is Lucasia's 'dear converse', not physical contact with her, that will be missed. The references to the lady's 'pity' and the lover's unworthiness are standard tropes in neo-Platonic verse, and can be read as evidence that the beloved is not desired sexually, but as a representative of ideal beauty and virtue. It is in the closing lines of the poem that Philips indicates, though, that it is the very conventionality of these dynamics that allows her to write love poetry at all, and suggests that her use of them is intended to create a smokescreen. She says, 'Oh, pardon me for pouring out my woes/ In rhyme, now that I dare not do it in prose'. 'Dare not do it in prose.' If she wrote about these emotions in prose they could be seen, unmistakably, as expressions of a lover, and now she 'dare not do' that. Instead, she uses the disguise offered by love poetry conventions, producing a poem whose import is comfortably ambiguous.

At least one of Philips' female contemporaries recognised her verse as lesbian, reading through its use of convention, and replied in an equally coded manner. The only poem by a woman to preface Philips' 1667 *Poems* is signed pseudonymously 'Philophilippa' ('lover of Philips'). This opens

> Let the male poets their male Phoebus choose,
> Thee, I invoke, Orinda, for my muse;
> He could but force a branch, Daphne her tree
> Most freely offers to her sex and thee,
> And says to verse so unconstrained as yours,
> Her laurel freely comes, your fame secures:
> And men no longer shall with ravished bays
> Crown their forced poems by as forced a praise.[20]

To understand what Philophilippa is saying here we have to break her code: to know the myth about Phoebus and Diana to which the poem refers. In Ovid's *Metamorphoses*, Daphne is a virgin who is pursued by the god Apollo (another name for Phoebus), who wants to have sex with her. To enable her to escape, the gods turn her into a laurel tree, and Apollo makes himself a crown of its leaves, ordering that the laurel be for ever sacred to him. It is this same laurel crown ('the bays') that came to be a symbol of (male) poetic excellence. What Philophilippa is saying, then, is that Phoebus/Apollo's advances to Daphne are ravishment or rape; this she rejects: Daphne's chosen partner is not a man, but Philips and her sex, to whom she 'freely offers' herself. In Philophilippa's poem, Philips is not only a great poet, crowned with laurel; she is also Daphne's rightful lover.

If it is true that Philips' poetry ambiguously encodes lesbian desire, what kind of erotic is found there? Not surprisingly, it is an erotic formed by the terms of its very existence: in Philips' poetry there is a great deal of concern with, and exploration of, what it means to form relationships within threatening and powerful constraints. In 'A Dialogue of Absence 'Twixt Lucasia and Orinda, set by Mr Henry Lawes', for instance, the poem ends by envisioning a future where women will never again be forced apart by others' desires: 'But we shall come where no rude hand shall sever,/ And there we'll meet and part no more for ever'. This is a love always haunted by the fear of its destruction from outside. At the same time, a fear of loss and rejection becomes crucial to the imagining of this relationship itself, which moves within a tension between real constraints – the existence of husbands and compulsory heterosexuality – and fantasy constraints, which are the emotional power of the lady over her lover. In this context, constraint and the fear of loss become eroticised, and the poetry repeatedly reinvents the attractions and problems of this. In some poems, Philips is gloriously shocking in the way she parades her resultant fixations. The poet plays a sadomasochistic game, headily inside the role and yet never forgetting that it is just a pretence for the sake of the pleasure it brings. In 'Injuria Amicitiae', she angrily fears that her mistress has decided to withdraw her 'strange rigour' and has found someone else to dominate. She laments, 'Must I be subject and spectator too?'. 'Set on fire' by her mistress' cruelty, she anticipates death – a pun on 'orgasm' common in the love poetry of the time. The mistress cannot go too far in her teasing, however: the lover reminds her that the continuation of the dynamic between them is dependent on the active participation of them both. 'You must undo yourself to ruin me', she warns, an ambiguous observation which courts the undoing/undressing of the mistress, which will 'ruin' the poet with desire; even whilst it reminds the mistress that to 'ruin' the passive partner by being too unkind will also end the relationship and so 'undo' her dominant role too. It is also a dynamic formed crucially by the poet herself: it is her worship, her singing 'to the swains' about the lady that has given her her power, and this worship can always be withdrawn. If she falls silent, the lady's dominant role would cease to exist. This might suggest that it is really the poet-lover who is the more powerful partner in this play. The pleasure she finds in her mistress' sternness is such, though, that despite her assertion that having 'died' she has stopped caring, the poem ends with a re-enactment of desire, obeisance, and orgasm: 'I'll adore the author of my death/ And kiss the hand that robs me of my breath'.

Injuria Amicitiae

Lovely apostate! what was my offence?
Or am I punished for obedience?
Must thy strange rigour find as strange a time:
The act and season are an equal crime.
Of what thy most ingenious scorns could do,
Must I be subject and spectator too?
Or were the sufferings and sins too few
To be sustained by me, performed by you?
Unless (with Nero) your uncurbed desire
Be to survey the Rome you set on fire,
While wounded for and by your power, I
At once your martyr and your prospect die.
This is my doom, and such a riddling fate
As all impossibles doth complicate.
For obligation here is injury,
Constancy crime, friendship a heresy.
And you appear so much on ruin bent,
Your own destruction gives you now content:
For our twin-spirits did so long agree,
You must undo yourself to ruin me.
And, like some frantic goddess, you're inclined
To raze the temple where you are enshrined.
And, what's the miracle of cruelty,
Kill that which gave you immortality.
While glorious friendship, whence your honour springs,
Lies gasping in the crowd of common things;
And I'm so odious, that for being kind
Doubled and studied murthers are designed.
Thy sin's all paradox, for shouldst thou be
Thyself again, th'wouldst be severe to me.
For thy repentance coming now so late
Would only change, and not relieve my fate.
So dangerous is the consequence of ill,
Thy least of crimes is to be cruel still.
For of thy smiles I should yet more complain,
If I should live to be betrayed again.
Live then (fair tyrant) in security,
From both my kindness and revenge be free;
While I, who to the swains had sung thy fame,

And taught each echo to repeat thy name,
Will now my private sorrow entertain,
To rocks and rivers, not to thee, complain.
And though before our union cherished me,
'Tis now my pleasure that we disagree.
For from my passion your last rigour grew,
And you killed me because I worshipped you.
But my worst vows shall be your happiness,
And not to be disturbed by my distress,
And though it would my sacred flames pollute,
To make my heart a scorned prostitute;
Yet I'll adore the author of my death,
And kiss the hand that robs me of my breath.

Philips' lesbian erotic might include an exploration of the pleasures of differential role-playing, but it is not limited to this. Although the fantasy power of the mistress can sometimes be a source of pleasurable pain, pleasurable too are the real equality of the lovers and their sense of sameness. In 'Friendship's Mystery', the poet celebrates the fact that both lover and beloved are equally committed to the relationship, wearing 'fetters whose intent/ Not bondage is, but ornament'. The implicit contrast, here, is with the chains of matrimony, which for a woman are as true bondage. Their lesbian fetters, by contrast, are part of an equal erotic dynamic, where 'both diffuse [pour out], and both engross [absorb]'. The dynamic of their relationship could serve as an example to 'the dull angry world'.

Friendship's Mystery

Come, my Lucasia, since we see
    That miracles men's faith do move,
By wonder and by prodigy
    To the dull angry world let's prove
    There's a religion in our love.

For though we were designed to agree
    That fate no liberty destroys,
But our election is as free
    As angels', who with greedy choice
    Are yet determined to their joys.

Our hearts are doubled by the loss,
    Here mixture is addition grown.
We both diffuse, and both ingross:
    And we, whose minds are so much one,
    Never, yet ever are alone.

We court our own captivity,
    Than thrones more great and innocent:
'Twere banishment to be set free,
    Since we wear fetters whose intent
    Not bondage is, but ornament.

Divided joys are tedious found,
    And griefs united easier grow:
We are ourselves but by rebound,
    And all our titles shuffled so,
    Both princes, and both subjects too.

Our hearts are mutual victims laid,
    While they (such power in friendship lies)
Are altars, priests and offerings made:
    And each heart which thus kindly dies
    Grows deathless by the sacrifice.

Specifically, here, Philips is comparing the freedom of playing roles in a relationship where both partners know they are playing and the power between them is in fact equal, with the constraints of marriage. This is signalled in part by her echoing of a poem by her influential predecessor John Donne, who crows in 'The Sun Rising', 'She is all states, all princes I'. In the relationship celebrated by Philips the 'fetters' are taken with 'greedy choice', and the lovers are, in terms of their social power, 'Both princes, and both subjects too'. As woman loves woman, a new identity comes into existence in their mirroring of one another: 'We are ourselves but by rebound', she affirms.

This mirroring and sense of sameness that runs alongside the erotic pleasure of role-playing is also central to Philips' most anthologised poem, 'To my Excellent Lucasia, on our Friendship'.

I did not live until this time
    Crowned my felicity,
When I could say without a crime,
    I am not thine, but thee.

> This carcase breathed, and walked, and slept,
>   So that the world believed
> There was a soul the motions kept;
>   But they were all deceived.
>
> For as a watch by art is wound
>   To motion, such was mine:
> But never had Orinda found
>   A soul, till she found thine;
>
> Which now inspires, cures and supplies,
>   And guides my darkened breast:
> For thou art all that I can prize,
>   My joy, my life, my rest.
>
> No bridegroom's nor crown-conqueror's mirth
>   To mine compared can be:
> They have but pieces of this earth,
>   I've all the world in thee.
>
> Then let our flames still light and shine,
>   And no false fear control,
> As innocent as our design,
>   Immortal as our soul.

The general terms of the poem are conventional: it is the lady's soul that brings the lover to life; in the perfect union of lovers, both become immortal. Within this framework, though, a very particular love, one quite different from the heterosexual desire of poetic tradition, is celebrated. The beloved woman is a source specifically of joy and rest; she is inspirational and curative. The 'I' who opens the poem becomes part of an immortal 'our soul'; she is no longer a mechanical watch 'wound/ To motion' – an image, by implication, of the tedious and inhuman dynamics of heterosexuality. This merged identity is set in contrast to the 'bridegroom's . . . mirth': the controlling, self-satisfied male figure who fills so much of John Donne's verse.

CONCLUSION

Katherine Philips' poetry, then, is 'closet' lesbian verse. It has qualities that not all lesbians today would celebrate: I am repelled by her royalism (which even infects the last poem quoted, in its use of 'Crowned' and its despising of 'crown-conquerors'). Had she been on the other side of the political divide, she would have had access to women like Katherine Evans, Sarah Cheevers, Sarah Davy and Hester Biddle. But the lesbian community then, as now, had its divisions, it would seem. Other present-day lesbians might be disturbed by Philips' delight in the dynamics of domination and submission.

It seems to me crucial, if we are really to recover our lesbian past that we begin, at least, by allowing the evidence to challenge our pre-existing commitments to what we want to find. The past is a complicated place, a place with as many conflicting cultures as our own. It has much to teach us.

This essay has had a number of previous incarnations as talks and conference papers, and I owe much to those who came to my talks and discussed Philips' poetry with me, especially the Lesbian History Group, Sappho, the Higher Education Teachers of English Conference 1986, the London University Early-Modern History Seminars. Jonathan Dollimore, Kathryn Harriss, Lyndal Roper, Jan Sellers, Alan Sinfield, Simon Shepherd, Mick Wallis and Chris White, most particularly, have taught me a great deal.

NOTES

1 More information on Katherine Philips' life – most of it accurate – can be found in Philip Souers, *The Matchless Orinda*, Harvard University Press, Cambridge, Massachusetts, 1931.

2 Elaine Hobby, *Virtue of Necessity: English Women's Writing 1649–1688*, Virago, London, 1988.

3 The demands of these radical groups are outlined in Christopher Hill, *The World Turned Upside Down: Radical Ideas During the English Revolution*, Penguin, Harmondsworth, 1975; and J F McGregor and B Reay, eds., *Radical Religion in the English Revolution*, Oxford University Press, Oxford, 1984. For more information on women's roles in the sects, see Mabel Brailsford, *Quaker Women 1650–1690*, Duckworth and Company, London, 1915; Phyllis Mack, 'Women as Prophets During the English Civil War', *Feminist Studies 8*, 1982; and Elaine Hobby, *Virtue of Necessity*.

4 Elspeth Graham, Hilary Hinds, Elaine Hobby and Helen Wilcox, eds., *Her Own Life: Autobiographical Writings by Seventeenth-Century Englishwomen*, Routledge, London, 1989, p. 125.

5 *Ibid.*, p. 174.

6 *A Brief Relation of the Persecutions and Cruelties that have been Acted upon the People called Quakers*, London, 1662.

7 Lillian Faderman, *Surpassing the Love of Men: Romantic Friendship and Love Between Women from the Renaissance to the Present*, The Women's Press, London, 1985, p. 71.

8 *Ibid.*, p. 16.

9 Michel Foucault, *The History of Sexuality Volume I: An Introduction*, Penguin, Harmondsworth, 1981.

10 Frederic Silverstolpe, 'Benkert Was Not a Doctor: On the Non-Medical Origin of the Homosexual Category in the Nineteenth Century', in *Papers of the Conference 'Homosexuality, Which Homosexuality?'* (a conference in lesbian and gay studies), Free University/Schorer Foundation, Amsterdam, 1987; Chris White, 'The Organisation of Pleasure: British Homosexual Discourse, 1869–1914', Nottingham University PhD unpublished thesis, 1992.

11 Hans-Martin Decker-Hauff, ed., *Die Chronik der Grafen von Zimmern* in three volumes, Stuttgart, 1967, vol. 2, p. 212, translated by Lyndal Roper.

12 Jane Sharp's *The Midwives Book* is very rare. I am editing it for the Oxford University Press series of Brown University Women Writers Project, expected publication date 1994/5.

13 *Ibid.*, p. 45.

14 For more information on racist constructions of Black sexuality, see Peter Fryer, *Staying Power: The History of Black People in Britain*, Pluto Press, London, 1984.

15 John Broadbent, ed., *Poets of the Seventeenth Century*, two volumes, Signet Classics, New York, 1974, vol. 2, p. 317.

16 Germaine Greer, Jeslyn Medoff, Melinda Sansone, Susan Hastings, eds., *Kissing the Rod: An Anthology of 17th Century Women's Verse*, Virago, London, 1988, p. 191.

17 So-called 'pastoral' works were popular in the late sixteenth and early seventeenth century in England. They generally have idealised countryside (or garden) settings, sprinkled with loving shepherdesses and shepherds, and are characterised by a nostalgia

for the simple life of an imaginary past, and a rejection of the strife and ambition of the court.

18 For the rejection by Philips' male contemporaries of these poetic conventions, see Peter Malekin, *Liberty and Love: English Literature and Society, 1640–88*, Hutchinson, London, 1981.

19 Neo-Platonism is a literary convention that has as its central image the beautiful and perfect lady, who is loved by the poet not for carnal ends, but in order to 'ascend' to pure and abstract beauty, or to God. It was a literary style encouraged at the English court in the 1630s by Queen Henrietta Maria, in resistance to the increasing sexual explicitness of male writing.

20 The full text of Philophilippa's poem can be found in *Kissing the Rod*, pp. 204–13.

READING GENESIS
Patricia Duncker

The grammar of heterosexuality is articulated in the myths of western culture. And the Bible is the text at the root, a vast encyclopaedia of stories, the book of patriarchy. It is a text that has been perpetually re-translated, re-imagined, re-written. But it is not, as many women may be tempted to think, a monolithic slab of sexist dogma. It is a checkerboard of contradictions, a text whose meaning has been fought over for centuries. What I have to say here, about Paradise, Eve, John Milton and the structures of heterosexuality, is part of that struggle for meaning. The Eden story in Genesis is crucial for any analysis of heterosexuality, because it is there that women's subordination to men within marriage as a sexual union and the very fact of heterosexual pairing, are mystified and justified, with all the spurious authority of Biblical myth. Myths are the incarnation of the unseen, 'the expression of unobservable realities in terms of observable phenomena'.[1] Usually the myths to which the greatest significance is attached are the least probable. But myths have a more sinister function. They are used to legitimate power relationships, to justify cruelty, injustice and an existing social order. Throughout history, Genesis has been used to do precisely these things.

Mythologies have a tendency to divide essences into opposites, and this is true of the creation myths in Genesis. The binary oppositions emerge: Heaven and Earth, Adam and Eve, male and female, good and evil, natural and supernatural, immortal and mortal, life and death. Heterosexuality too, necessarily thrives upon the insistence that we exist within dualities, as opposites. The middle ground which exists between the two poles is always abnormal, non-natural, holy. It is a land full of monsters, virgin mothers and incarnate gods. Eden reflects this: here is a garden with speaking serpents and magical trees. The middle ground is also the land where our culture has chosen to locate homosexuality, the magic garden, the forbidden space.

There are of course two creation stories in the first chapter of Genesis. There is what Christian scholars describe as the Priestly Narrative, which shows God as the Author of All Things, the maker who creates not with his hands, but through his will. The passage is precise, repetitive, abstract. The narrative perspective is cosmic and remote. This is a myth about pure power, the power to call forth into being. 'And God said, Let there be light: and there was light' (Genesis 1:3). The second story is what is known as the Jahwist document, the narrative of Eden. This is the older story; the written form dates from the ninth or tenth century BC, but behind it there is likely to have been a more ancient oral tradition, or even several stories, woven together.[2] And here God becomes YHWH,[3] God incarnate, the speaking, breathing creator, walking in his garden. This God makes mistakes. He is arbitrary, cruel and despotic. He denies his creatures knowledge, he is envious, fearful, the jealous God. The association of the serpent with Satan is a later interpretation of the narrative. All that we have in the text is that the serpent was 'more subtil than any beast of the field' (Genesis 3:1). There are malevolent reptiles in Semitic demonology, and the serpent in Genesis does tell lies. He promises Eve knowledge without the penalty of death, a promise that is not fulfilled. But Adam and Eve do not die from the fruit of the tree. They die because YHWH carries out his threat and condemns them to death. The final verses of Genesis 3 endorse the serpent. YHWH fears that they will eat of the tree of life, live for ever and become gods. The serpent's assessment of the fruit and the reasons why it was forbidden prove to be utterly accurate. His only miscalculation was of the unpleasantness of the Lord's temper.

The two creation stories in Genesis present a patchwork of problems. In the first story women and men are both created in the image of God, 'male and female created he them' (Genesis 1:27), but in the Eden narrative Eve is an afterthought: 'an help meet' for

Adam. The Eden narrative is a text full of gaps, like a ballad; a mesh of unspoken motives and circumstances, perplexing and peculiar. Each story is perfectly consistent within its own narrative perspective, but, taken together, we have two radically different versions of human being, and different versions of God. While we have two alternative accounts of creation, we have only one of the Fall. And it is that version, the Garden of Eden and the Fall of Man which children illustrate at school, it is that version which has been painted again and again throughout Christian history, and it is that version which John Milton chose for the action of *Paradise Lost*.

Paradise Lost is a poem written by a revolutionary in defeat. It was first published in 1667 and Milton was paid five pounds for it by the bookseller. It is a rationalist epic, a search for a first cause, by a man trained in both logic and philosophy. Milton wrote his own treatise on logic, *Ars Logica* (1672)[4]; for him logic was the handmaiden of theology. *Paradise Lost* is also the fruit of an enormous poetic ambition, to write a greater and more original epic than anyone else had ever done. It was to be original in both senses of the word, that is, unlike any other poem and dealing with the origins of all things. It was to embody a critique of classical epics and yet surpass them. Theodicy (Theos/Dikê) is not just the justice of God, but his justification. Milton knew that in order to do this he must gather up all human history. He was writing within a tradition of Christian myth where we cannot understand Eden without Golgotha, nor can we justify God's creation without Apocalypse and the image of Paradise Regained. No one part of God's plan can be seen to be just without the vision of Eternity, that perspective which can only be God's. *Paradise Lost* had, of necessity, to commence with the first creation, the fall of the rebel angels, the narrative of Eden, through the Crucifixion to the end of all things, from Eden to Apocalypse.

> Of man's first disobedience, and the fruit
> Of that forbidden tree, whose mortal taste
> Brought death into the world, and all our woe,
> With loss of Eden, till one greater man
> Restore us, and regain the blissful seat,
> Sing heavenly Muse . . .[5]

Notice that it is 'a greater man' who is to save us, not a god. But

Milton is on God's side, one of the saints, God's soldiers. He says he is.

> . . . what in me is dark
> Illumine, what is low raise and support;
> That to the height of this great argument
> I may assert eternal providence,
> And justify the ways of God to men.

(PL, i, 22–26)

But did Milton ever justify the ways of God to women? And who can presume to fathom the justice of God? I want to cast a fundamental doubt on the nature of the enterprise of *Paradise Lost*.

The key words in the poem are reason, justice, free will. Milton desperately needed to believe in a God who is benevolent and intelligible, a God who can be grasped by human intellect and understanding. His concept of Providence and Divine Justice is legalistic. The law of God binds both parties, God and human beings, to a sequence of mutual obligations. For Milton YHWH is desperately problematic. The God to whom the Hebrew Bible bears witness is passionate, unguessable, apparently irrational and capricious. The God of the Psalms has to be wooed, implored, cajoled and begged like a lover. And it is in the nature of love that we are vulnerable and at risk, without security and at the mercy of one another's pleasure. Milton could not be in love with the God he incarnated in *Paradise Lost*. The attempt is doomed precisely because it is anthropomorphic. If we limit our conception of God to the political metaphors by which we name him, then we are left with a monster of theological sadism whose laughter, which echoes throughout *Paradise Lost*,[6] is savage, malicious and unjust. But even God's laughter is Biblically based. 'He that sitteth in the heavens shall laugh: the Lord shall have them in derision' (Psalm 2:4). The myth of Eden is too frail a thing to carry the experience of human history and the bitterness of human suffering. No amount of gratuitous theological exposition can ever match the eating of the apple to the misery of the world.

As women, we are burdened with this myth. It touches us whether we do accept and believe in Christian myth or whether we don't. We are interpreted and harassed by the structures of heterosexuality articulated and mythologised in Genesis even if we define ourselves as Lesbian. It is therefore important to look the monster in the face and to question the ways in which myths are used. Lesbians usually read both the margins and the gaps in the heterosexual text. We listen for silences, echoes, inconsistencies, contradictions. We listen for lies. Most Lesbians have to live, speak and write lies. Most Lesbians have to lie about who it is they love. I listened for Milton's lies. If he didn't love God, who was it that he loved?

Poetry is an incarnational art. Milton's imagination reveals that with which he was truly in love, the sensuality of creation. Book vii of *Paradise Lost* is the story of God's creating word. It is the Son – Milton never refers to him as Christ or Jesus – who creates, the Father who condemns. In book vii we watch the 'six days' work, a world' (*PL*, vii, 568), the circle drawn with the golden compasses, God's cosmic geometry; creation rises out of chaos, and poetry from raw imagination – the animals struggle into being from the earth.

> . . . now half appeared
> The tawny lion, pawing to get free
> His hinder parts, then springs as broke from bonds
> And rampant shakes his brinded mane . . .
>
> (*PL*, vii, 463–466)

Man – Adam – is the crown of creation. And it is here that Milton's creation theology becomes dangerous. The Priestly Narrative in Genesis is explicit.

> So God created man in his own image, in the image of God created he him; male and female created he them. (Genesis 1:27)

I would have thought that this simple statement of equality in the hands of God was unambiguous. But so is that of Milton. Man is in the image of God, woman is *created* inferior, as a sexual necessity. She does not reflect her male creator. We first saw Eve and Adam in book iv, through Satan's voyeuristic eyes.

> . . . for in their looks divine
> The image of their glorious maker shone,
> Truth, wisdom, sanctitude severe and pure,
> Severe but in true filial freedom placed;

> Whence true authority in men; though both
> Not equal, as their sex not equal seemed;
> For contemplation he and valour formed,
> For softness she and sweet attractive grace,
> He for God only, she for God in him.
>
>   (*PL*, iv, 292–299)

The marriage of Adam and Eve and their relationship of power and subordination exactly mirrors the hierarchy of power between God the Father and his hapless creation. And for this too there is ample scriptural support. 'The head of every man is Christ, and the head of the woman is the man; and the head of Christ is God.' (1 Corinthians xi: 3).[7] But Milton did not take the doctrine of natural inequality for granted. He insists upon it with neurotic intensity, as if this assumption was unproven, challenged and in doubt. As indeed it was during his times. The creation of Eve, described in book viii, is an extraordinary piece of male pornographic fantasy. And it is here that the contradictions begin to splinter the text. Adam begs God, explicitly, for an equal companion.

> Hast thou not made me here thy substitute,
> And these inferior far beneath me set?
> Among *unequals* what society
> Can sort, what harmony and true delight?
> Which must be mutual, in proportion due
> Given and received . . .
>
>   (*PL*, viii, 381–386. My emphasis)

But God promises 'Thy wish exactly to thy heart's desire' (PL, viii, 451), and produces the inferior sex, Eve.

God's injustice is not in question here, because Adam's dream is of woman as 'the spirit of love and amorous delight' (PL, viii, 477), and how can women and men ever be equals if woman is the dream made flesh as erotic object? The Fall takes place in book ix; so here, at Eve's creation, before she stands in front of us with the apple in her hand, Milton takes care to point out Adam's vulnerable heel, sex.

> . . . here passion first I felt,
> Commotion strange, in all enjoyments else
> Superior and unmoved, here only weak

Against the charm of beauty's powerful glance.

(PL, viii, 530–533)

Sexual desire so unhinges Adam that he is in danger of forgetting her subservient status. And in case we too become so bewitched that we forget, Milton says it all again.

> For well I understand in the prime end
> Of nature her the inferior, in the mind
> And inward faculties, which most excel,
> In outward also her resembling less
> His image who made both, and less expressing
> The character of that dominion given
> O'er other creatures . . .

(PL, viii, 540–546)

Here, neatly articulated, is one of the foundations of heterosexuality. To pursue that obscure object of desire, woman and her sex, is to desire something less than perfect, less than man and less than God. The other side of male heterosexual desire is contempt.[8]

Milton was a revolutionary. He supported a republican government, the execution of the king, the freedom of the press, the separation of Church and State. Yet he could not unthink the most fundamental political oppression of all, the subjection and exploitation of women by men. He was married to Mary Powell in June 1642. Within a month she abandoned him and went back to her mother. She could not be persuaded to return. During the next three years Milton published a series of books urging that the law be reformed so as to permit divorce not only for gross breaches of matrimony on the woman's part – such as adultery or frigidity – but also for personal incompatibility. Divorce was, however, to be for men only. Milton even argued for legally and socially sanctioned polygamy. Here again, he found ample scriptural justification in the 'Old Testament'. It has been suggested that Milton's first marriage was never consummated during the brief weeks that Mary Powell was with him in London. This speculation is based on a passage in the *Doctrine and Discipline of Divorce* (1643).

> Whereas the sober man honouring the appearance of modesty, and hoping well of every social virtue under that veil, may easily

chance to meet, if not with a body impenetrable, yet often with a
mind to all other due conversation inaccessible.[9]

It is disturbing, but not surprising that Milton's idea of marriage in
this passage, is coercive. Women's bodies are there to be
penetrated, preferably with their consent, their minds to be
influenced and controlled. 'Conversation' could also mean 'intercourse'. So minds were presumably there to be penetrated too. In
his commonplace book, Milton wrote: 'Marriage: see Of Divorce'.
Another entry reads: 'Official Robbery or Extortion: see Pope'. He
could question an existing ecclesiastical hierarchy; but not a sexual
one. Milton was quite clear about what men could expect from
marriage and what women deserved. What women wanted or
needed was not his concern and at any rate, he never asked them.

Mary Powell eventually returned to Milton three years later, in
the summer of 1645. Her reasons were very clearly economic and
political. Her family had royalist allegiances. They needed a
Puritan ally in the Civil War. Eventually they all moved into
Milton's London house. Mary bore Milton four children and died
giving birth to the last in May 1652. Milton's second wife,
Katherine Woodcock, the 'late espoused saint' of his sonnet,
'Methought I saw my late espoused saint/Brought to me', also
died in childbirth after 15 months of marriage. The child, another
daughter, Katherine, died six weeks later. Milton's third wife,
Elizabeth Minshull, cleverly avoided bearing any of his children
and survived him. She lived to be 90. We do well to remember that
for our foresisters, marriage and heterosexual sex was, very often,
a sentence of ill health and early death.

It is not true to say that mainstream Protestantism was
necessarily liberating for women. Certainly the reformers, women
among them, did attack the old Catholic ideology of regarding
women – if they didn't happen to be virgin mothers – as carnal
temptresses and vessels of sin incarnate. Instead, however, they
created the image of woman as the good wife, the symbol of
domestic purity, spirituality, helpfulness and loyalty – Eve's image
cleaned up. Neither Catholic nor Protestant priests or theologians
denied that woman was created inferior. She was naturally suited
to a life of submission and obedience. Prelapsarian Eden was not a
paradise of equality. Eve's transgression made the burden of her
sex more painful, but the yoke was already there. The Protestant
notion of the priesthood of all believers did, however, mean that

religion was not safely confined in a spiritual space. The Christian life – all aspects thereof – had to be lived in godly, righteous and sober ways. This made family life a critical area in the struggle for godliness. The family becomes 'a little church . . . a little state'. William Gouge, a prominent Puritan preacher, celebrated marriage in the following terms.

> Marriage is the Preservative of Chastity, the seminary of the Commonwealth, seed plot of the Church, pillar (under God) of the world, right-hand of providence, a supporter of lawes, states, orders, offices, gifts and services.[10]

Gouge also argued that the husband's adultery was as bad as that of the wife, so chastity was to be preserved by men as well as by women.[11] But Puritan marriage was built upon an intractable contradiction. As Milton's Adam supposedly desired, husband and wife should enjoy the close and loving mutual companionship of working partners, yet the marriage relation should nevertheless be based on the inexorable subordination of the woman to the man. This is the contradiction at the heart of heterosexuality and of marriage. 'Among unequals what society/ Can sort, what harmony or true delight?' (*PL*, viii, 383–384). Yet the Protestants turned to St Paul for his most unequivocal statements on the subordination of women, and so did Milton. Man is the image and glory of God, God's substitute on earth, woman is the glory of the man. 'He for God only, she for God in him . . .' (*PL*, iv, 299). Here is William Whateley, another Puritan.

> Every good woman must suffer herselfe to be convinced in judgement that she is not her husband's equall. 'Out of place, out of peace'; and woe to those miserable aspiring shoulders, which will not content themselves to take their room below the head.[12]

So the law of patriarchy was not challenged; the Puritans merely shifted the terms of the argument. The Catholics relied on priests to shepherd their flocks; the Puritans saw this duty of discipline and authority passing to fathers and husbands. One person's authority necessarily means another's submission – and the dethroning of female images of divine power, the Virgin and her sisters, all the martyred heroines of the Catholic Church, left only the ruling male Gods, God the Father, God the Son. The disbanding of women's religious houses, which had at least given women some small measure of power and control over their lives as the brides of Christ – the absent husband – left women with the paradigm of natural rather than spiritual marriage – and present husbands. We were to define ourselves in relation to men – as maids, wives, widows, mothers. And marriage was to be a sweet friendship within a coercive structure of power. The subversive contradiction within all this was of course, the Holy Spirit. If women are at least spiritually equal, and equally likely to receive God's messengers, might a wife not, in all righteousness, be forced to disobey her husband in matters of conscience? Some women did.

The most insidious threat to family life was adultery. Even the more moderate Puritans prescribed a single standard of sexual behaviour. More radical libertarian groups even advocated free love. But the problem with libertarian sexuality as well as simple straightforward adultery is that women always have the worst of it. Gerrard Winstanley warned women against the groups he regarded as extremists.

> Therefore you women beware, for this ranting practice is not the restoring but the destroying power of the creation . . . by seeking their own freedom they embondage others . . .[13]

The seventeenth century radicals were warm advocates of heterosexual sex, marital love patterned on devotion to God, and stable, life-long, non-adulterous marriages. They were deeply suspicious of lust, which was possible even between husband and wife. This is an important point in *Paradise Lost*, and the first consequence of the Fall, the first fruit of sin.

> Carnal desire inflaming, he on Eve
> Began to cast lascivious eyes, she him
> As wantonly repaid; in lust they burn . . .
>
> > (*PL*, ix, 1013–1015)

Postlapsarian sex, no longer honourable and innocent, becomes carnal lust. The problem here is that the language which Milton and the radicals used to describe lust is the same language used by Anglicanism to describe sex. In Milton's fallen Paradise postcoital tristesse ensues.

Milton's misogyny is most clearly stated in book iv, where, long before the Fall, heterosexuality is hymned as the source of all joy.

> Hail wedded love, mysterious law, true source
> Of human offspring, sole propriety
> In Paradise of all things common else.
> By thee adulterous lust was driven from men
> Among the bestial herds to range, by thee
> Founded in reason, loyal, just, and pure,
> Relations dear, and all the charities
> Of father, son and brother first were known.
>
> (*PL*, iv, 750–757)

There are some remarkable assertions here. Married love is the only aspect of Eden that includes property rights. Eve is Adam's property. Lust is brute desire and confined to the animals, in whom, presumably, it is made perfect as befits their unfallen state. If mutual desire is impossible between unequals – and Milton himself begged that question – then surely, given that Eve is property within marriage, heterosexuality in Paradise is, at best, coercive sex. Eve cannot bargain. She can only submit. The language of heterosexual eroticism is pitched in terms of conquest and surrender – in Paradise, just as it is everywhere else. '. . . he in delight/ Both of her beauty and submissive charms/ Smiled with superior love' (*PL*, iv, 497–499). And the only charities (affections) that can exist within the family institution, according to Milton, are those appertaining to relationships between men: fathers, sons, brothers. The exclusion of mothers, daughters, sisters, is pointed, and I suspect, deliberate.

The most usual and insidious device male writers and some of their female collaborators use to belittle, humiliate and stifle women is to place the expression of delight at our own oppression in women's mouths. Thus Eve:

> . . . O thou for whom
> And from whom I was formed flesh of thy flesh,
> And without whom am to no end, my guide
> And head . . .
>
> (*PL*, iv, 440–443)

Throughout all literary history women sing hymns to the phallus, praise obedience to men, advocate utter submission, worship male gods. Eve sounds like the abject sexual robot of pornography, infinitely pliable, infinitely desiring whatever the gentlemen desire.

> My author and disposer, what thou bid'st
> Unargued I obey; so God ordains,
> God is thy law, thou mine: to know no more
> Is woman's happiest knowledge and her praise.
>
> (PL, iv, 635–638)

For us then, there would obviously be no point whatever in reading Milton if he were simply one more massive block on that pyramid of misogyny otherwise known as Theology and Literature. But Eve doesn't simply wander through Genesis and *Paradise Lost*, swathed in tendrils of erotic hair, muttering, 'Unargued I obey . . .'. Milton's reading of Genesis is most interesting at those moments where he interprets the gaps in the Biblical narrative, the moments where he invents. It is here that the poem begins to explode, it is here that he becomes subversive and contradictory. The margins invade the page. The Lesbian enters the text.

The first person Eve sees is not Adam but herself, reflected in the 'liquid plain'. And the face she sees returns 'answering looks/ Of sympathy and love' (*PL*, iv, 465). Eve's first desire is for a female image, for another woman. Milton is being imaginatively honest here. The first body we know is a woman's, that of our mother. Eve is of no woman born, yet her first love is for a woman. God's voice pursues her, pointing out that her great role as mother of the race awaits and that her destiny is Adam, 'whose image thou art'. But Eve, upon seeing Adam, knows at once that she is not made in his image. Amazingly, Milton says so. Eve is speaking.

> Till I espied thee, fair indeed and tall,
> Under a platan, yet methought less fair,
> Less winning soft, less amiably mild,
> Than that smooth watery image; back I turned . . .
>
> (PL, iv, 477–480)

There is a structural echo here with Adam's assertion in book viii that he perceives Eve ' . . . resembling less/ His image who made both . . .' (*PL*, viii, 543–544). But we hear Eve first – refusing to acknowledge that they are one bone, one flesh. Eve's response to

Adam is unequivocal. She runs. And she takes considerable persuading before she will have anything to do with him.

Milton's first love was a man, Charles Diodati, whom he knew from his schooldays at St Paul's. Diodati's family were originally Italian Protestants from Lucca who abandoned Italy during the Counter-Reformation.[14] The main branch of the family settled in Geneva where Giovanni Diodati became a professor of Hebrew, an internationally famous theologian, who translated the Bible into Italian. Milton adored Charles. His early death in 1638, while Milton was in Italy, was a terrible blow. The Latin elegy for Charles, the *Epitaphium Damonis* (1640)[15] was the first poem Milton published separately. In the poem he not only suggests that he saw himself married to Charles (line 65 – 'innube'), he imagines his dead friend admitted to erotic Bacchic orgies in Paradise. The heterosexism of Genesis may indeed have troubled Milton; the politics of heterosexuality certainly did. Marriage as a sacrament, a symbol, a mystery, interestingly and thoroughly confused with compulsory heterosexuality and a coercive institution for the policing of women, is deeply bound into the mythology of the Christian religion. The metaphor of marriage stretches from Genesis to Apocalypse.

> For this cause shall a man leave his father and mother and shall be joined unto his wife, and they two shall be one flesh. This is a great mystery: but I speak concerning Christ and the Church.
>
> (Ephesians v: 31–32)

This great mystery remains satisfyingly invisible; the dispute of power and authority between women and men, disturbingly close to the bone of daily existence. Milton married three times. He had three daughters. He abused his first wife in his divorce pamphlets. Although he did teach his daughters to read, his pamphlet *Of Education* (1644) has nothing whatever to say on the education of women. And this is a stark omission because most other education reformers of the period did discuss the issue. We do have some independent comments from Milton's daughters. Deborah, who eventually became a school-mistress, tells us that her father was a tyrant and that he forced them to read to him in languages they did not understand. His first mother-in-law described him as a harsh and choleric man. His daughter Mary, aged 15, said that 'her father's death would be better news than his third marriage'.[16]

Milton neither liked nor respected women. But his unrelenting contempt did not bring him complacency or peace. If we really were all one in Christ Jesus then he was faced with an irresolvable problem. And he had the intelligence and sense to acknowledge this.

He saw in Genesis what every woman sees, a myth which legitimates male power and ensures male access to women, to our bodies, our labour, our energy and our strength. Even Satan becomes sexually involved with Eve in Milton's version, as he approaches her to tempt her and bring about her 'ruin' (*PL*, ix, 493). She is 'pleasure not for him ordained' (*PL*, ix, 470), but by implication a 'pleasure' created for someone else.[17] The slave is unconditionally accessible to the master, in whatever way he pleases. Total power is unconditional access, sexual and otherwise. Milton knew this. And I think that this insight is at the root of one of the finest, most extraordinary passages in the poem. I don't read Milton for his intellectual consistency, but for his capacity to articulate his imaginative fears. We are preoccupied with the same questions, the same issues of sexual politics; we are simply on different sides. Eve confronts the serpent alone. This is a crucial incident in the theology of the Fall. Why was she alone? Where was Adam? Again, Milton, without guidance from the Scriptures, invents.

Eve decides to do some gardening alone. She proposes a sensible division of labour on the grounds of efficiency. In book ix it emerges that Eve had heard the Angel Raphael's warning. She was listening in the bushes. She knows that God's enemy may try to assault or seduce them. But she insists that this does not justify Adam's initial prohibition on her departure. If, as he argues, it is best that

> The wife, where danger or dishonour lurks,
> Safest and seemliest by her husband stays,
> Who guards her, or with her the worst endures . . .
>
> (*PL*, ix, 267–269)

is she then less able to withstand temptation? Ironically, Eve's temptation has already begun, for Satan, upon his first incursion into Eden, 'Squat like a toad' (*PL*, iv, 800) – a traditional image of male sexuality – had hovered close at her sleeping ear, filling her mind with 'phantasms and dreams', vain hopes, vain aims, 'high conceits engendering pride', dreams of power. Now Eve insists,

> And what is faith, love, virtue, unassayed
> Alone, without exterior help sustained?
>
> (*PL*, ix, 335–336)

Milton envisaged human virtue as developing and dynamic. In *Areopagitica* (1644) he rejected 'cloistered virtue'.[18] Reason, his other God, is on Eve's side. Adam is caught in his own logic. If God has made them free, able to judge and choose for themselves, then it would be blasphemy to doubt the creator's capacities and purposes.

> . . . his creating hand
> Nothing imperfect or deficient left
> Of all that he created, much less man,
> Or aught that might his happy state secure,
> Secure from outward force; within himself
> The danger lies, yet lies within his power . . .
>
> (*PL*, ix, 344–349)

And thus, Adam's relation to Eve, one of supposed authority and love, exactly mirrors his own relationship to God. And his dismissal follows the pattern of God's insistence on their free will in book iii: '. . . of freedom both despoiled,/ Made passive both, had served necessity/ Not me' (*PL*, iii, 109–111). Quite so. Adam, reluctantly, and against his better judgment, not underestimating the risk, lets her go. 'Go; for thy stay, not free, absents thee more' (*PL*, ix, 372). We all know what happened. But is *this* moment in fact the Fall? The Separation Scene shows Adam's refusal to exert the power he undoubtedly has over Eve, and within the inevitable outcome of the story, and the story stands irrefutably, unchangeably, according to the Scriptures, this failure of his will is disastrous. Or we could argue the other side. Milton is using that story, the story of Genesis, to lay the sin even more firmly at the woman's door. The original sin is Eve's; and that sin is separatism.

Genesis is about power, authority, obedience, domination, submission, rebellion. So is *Paradise Lost*. Woman's powerlessness ends when separation begins; for the moment of 'conscious and deliberate exclusion of men, from anything' – even as in this case, from a bower of myrtle and roses in Paradise, is blatant insubordination.[19] It is also the moment of self-definition. It is the moment when Eve refuses to acquiesce submissively, refuses to mouth her given formula 'Unargued I obey'. There are two rebellions in *Paradise Lost*: Satan's and Eve's. Both are regarded by Christian theology, and by Milton, as falls from perfection and grace. Both are defiant assertions of self against an authority that has not been chosen, but arbitrarily imposed. Both Satan and Eve are on the receiving end of the realities of power. Their rebellions are moments of separation, separation from God and separation from man. Satan and Eve are natural allies. Milton's accusation – against an individualism that was as uncompromising as his own – was this savage re-telling of Genesis. You, woman, my wife, turned away from me and betrayed the whole world for all time and in all eternity. For a woman's duty is submission to men. It says so in the Bible. See also John Dod and Robert Cleaver, *A Godley Form of Household Government* (1630),

> So then the principal duty of the wife is, first to be subject to her husband (Ephesians 5:22, Colossians 3:18, 1 Peter 3: 1–2). To be chaste and shamefast, modest and silent, godley and discreet. To keep herself at home for the good government of her family and not to stay abroad without good cause.[20]

My reply to Milton's accusation is simple: we are the women who make it our just cause 'to stay abroad', to leave home. Separation from men and from the institutions which give men access to our bodies and our minds is the barrier reef surrounding Lesbian identity. Heterosexuality, marriage, motherhood: these are the institutions which most obviously maintain the power structure which makes women accessible to men. They form the core triad of all anti-feminist and anti-Lesbian ideology – in the seventeenth century, and in our own.

Men have always used the Bible against women. And we, the women, have always answered back. Across hundreds of years we have answered Genesis and Milton. Mary Wollstonecraft picks out Milton's contradictions in *A Vindication of the Rights of Woman* (1792). As she says – Adam asked for an equal partner. Why then was his Eve created subject? Why should sexual difference necessarily entail injustice and subordination? My own generation of feminists has also struggled with Genesis. Michelene

Wandor's *Gardens of Eden: Poems for Eve and Lilith* (1984)[21] is a
game for women's voices, arguing, challenging, questioning, God,
men, other women, each other. The poems score off the aggression
of the individual voice, which answers God back. These poems
take Genesis and the Hebrew Bible seriously. They work within
the terms of the old stories. But the shadows of Milton's
anthropomorphism still encircle the text and circumscribe the
limits of Wandor's thinking. Here, in 'Lilith takes tea with the
Lord', the conventional metaphors used in the Bible to invoke the
power of God, become Hollywood special effects.

> you fly upon the wings of the wind
> you hail stones and coals of fire
> you shoot arrows of lightning
> and the breath from your nostrils
> burns
>
> you have all the good bits
> and I scare easy.[22]

The theological sadist lurks on the edge of the page. These poems
make good polemical points for women. But they offer no new
thinking of God. At the end of her sequence Wandor unites the
two women, Lilith and Eve, appropriating the marriage metaphor
of the Song of Songs. 'Eve to Lilith',

> your mouth is a pomegranate
> ripening in smile
>
> I can see into the garden
> my sister, my love.[22]

The Lesbian implications of the last poems are not spelt out.
Elsewhere in the sequence Wandor capitulates to the coerciveness
of the old stories. These are the wives talking to each other,
Adam's wives.

Monique Wittig and Sande Zeig have neither Wandor's scruples
nor her inhibitions. They bind Lilith and Eve to one another in
their exuberant dictionary text, *Lesbian Peoples* (1976).

Eve and Lilith

Two famous companion lovers who lived in Palestine during the Bronze Age. Their love was so strong it is said, that it survived a long, forced sojourn in the desert. There they developed their legendary endurance.[23]

But, humorously, Wittig and Zeig dispense with God, creation and all the rest of the myth. Genesis rises, only to be finally dismissed. Here is their entry for FALL.

Fall

If it is a question of falling, better to do it into the arms of one's companion lover, forward or backward, with eyes open or closed. If this is not possible, one would be best to fall upon piles of leaves, sand, hay, snow.[24]

Wittig and Zeig, like myself, are the inheritors of Genesis. For us this myth recounts the beginning of the spiritual history of patriarchy; which is the beginning of division. It is of no use in the enterprise we have undertaken, the imagining and the creation of a world where we are free.

John Milton did not believe that it was necessary to belong to any Christian community or congregation. He was in himself a temple of the Holy Spirit, a solitary pillar of righteousness. Early on in his career he had planned to become an Anglican priest, but his disillusionment with the state church became complete. He supported the sectarian Protestants, the visionary Utopians, the religious radicals. From the 1640s onwards he was working on his *De Doctrina Christiana*. This heterodox theological tract was never published in his life time. He called it his 'dearest and best possession'. It is the theological basis for *Paradise Lost*. In the Preface to *De Doctrina Christiana* he denounces 'those two repulsive afflictions, tyranny and superstition'.[24] It is not only the right, but the duty of the oppressed to fight for their freedom. On this point Milton never recanted. And I believe that we should take this insight from him if we take nothing else.

Milton created a monstrous God, who in his turn could only fashion a man in his own monstrous image, the image of injustice and tyranny. Adam's sin is neither rebellion nor disobedience, but sexual weakness. His eventual capitulation is pitched in terms of heroic matrimony.

> I feel
> The bond of nature draw me to my own,
> My own is in thee, for what thou art is mine;
> Our state cannot be severed, we are one,
> One flesh; to lose thee were to lose my self.
>
> (*PL*, ix, 955–59)

I want you to read this passage cynically. Adam's love is based on property and possession, 'my own' – 'what thou art is mine'. And Milton is articulating one of his deepest terrors: that women do not in fact need men and if not properly disciplined might choose each other, or worse still, serpents, first.

The original sin is Eve's, mine, ours, whether as feminists, Lesbians or lovers of serpents: separation. Our insistence on our own integrity as separate beings, on the possession of our own bodies, on our own freedom, places us outside male rule. It is our necessary heresy. It is not negotiable. And there, my Lord God, John Milton and Gentleladies of the Jury, my case rests.

NOTES

1 Edmund Leach, *Genesis as Myth and Other Essays*, Cape, London, 1969, p.7.

2 See J M Evans, *Paradise Lost and the Genesis Tradition*, Clarendon Press, Oxford, 1968, chapter 1.

3 Christian commentators and Christian translators of the Bible often translate the tetragrammaton as 'Yahweh' or 'Jehovah'. This is tactless and often offensive to Jewish people because YHWH is the unpronounceable name of God, which cannot be spoken, nor translated.

4 See Christopher Hill, *Milton and the English Revolution*, Faber and Faber, London, 1977, p. 239 ff.

5 *Paradise Lost*, in *The Poems of John Milton*, eds. John Carey and Alastair Fowler, Longman, London, 1968. Book l, ll, 1–6 pp. 458–599.

6 See *Paradise Lost* xii, 59–60. ' . . . great laughter was in heaven . . .'

7 Women have always contested the meanings men have given to the Scriptures. Priscilla Cotton's and Mary Cole's pamphlet *To the Priests and People of England* (1655) uses the Bible to argue against the limitations placed upon women's power and women's rights to speak within the religious community. The arguments – equating 'woman' with 'weakness', and therefore including men, who might well give way to 'weakness' – are far-fetched, but ingenious. See Elaine Hobby, *Virtue of Necessity: English Women's Writing 1649-88*, Virago, London, 1988, p.43.

8 For further feminist thoughts on Adam, Eve, versions of Genesis and the mystifications of 'equal' creation see Mary Nyquist, 'The Genesis of Gendered Subjectivity in the Divorce Tracts and in *Paradise Lost*', *Remembering Milton: Essays on the Texts and Traditions*, eds. Mary Nyquist and Margaret W Ferguson, Methuen, New York & London, 1987, pp. 99-127.

9 Cited in Edward Le Comte, *Milton and Sex*, Macmillan, London, 1978, pp. 26-27.

10 See Roberta Hamilton, *The Liberation of Women: A Study of Patriarchy and Capitalism*, Allen and Unwin, London, 1978, p.56.

11 William Gouge not only argued that the husband's adultery was as bad as that of the wife, he also argued against wife-beating. See Christopher Hill, *The World Turned Upside Down: Radical Ideas During the English Revolution* (1972), Peregrine Books, Harmondsworth, 1985, pp.308.

12 Hamilton, p.58.

13 *Ibid.*, p.67. See also Hill, *The World Turned Upside Down*, especially chapter 7; and J F McGregor and B Reay, eds., *Radical Religion in the English Revolution*, Oxford University Press, Oxford, 1984, especially chapter 5 'Seekers and Ranters'.

14 See Christopher Hill, *Milton and the English Revolution*, pp.30-31.

15 *Paradise Lost* op. cit. pp. 267-283

16 *Ibid.*, p.144.

17 In the following discussion of the Separation Scene in book ix I am endebted to Marilyn Frye, *The Politics of Reality: Essays in Feminist Theory*, The Crossing Press, Trumansburg, 1983, and especially her essay in that volume 'Some Reflections on Separatism and Power'.

18 John Milton, *Areopagitica: A Speech for the Liberty of Unlicenc'd Printing*, in *Complete Poetry and Selected Prose of John Milton*, Random House, New York, p. 691.

19 See Frye, p. 103.

20 Cited in David Aers and Bob Hodge, 'Rational Burning: Milton on Sex and Marriage', *Milton Studies* vol 12, 1979, pp. 3–33.

21 Michelene Wandor, *Gardens of Eden: Poems for Eve and Lilith*, Journeyman/Playbooks, London, 1984, p. 37.

22 *Ibid.*, p.60.

23 *Lesbian Peoples: Materials for A Dictionary*, Virago, London, 1980, p. 52.

24 *Ibid.*, p. 53.

25 John Milton, *De Doctrina Christiana* 'Epistle', in *The Complete Prose Works of John Milton*, Vol. 6 edited by Maurice Kelley, Yale University Press, London, 1973.

FROM MY EYES . . . ZAMIS
PUBLISHING POETRY 1984–1988

Dorothea Smartt

Pulled from dusty history
dusty draws chewed envelopes tablenapkins . . .
Laying down words to record
   that we do not forget –
forget how much is different in our paths

Each of us having innumerable battles
with monsters inside –
not to mention those outside . . .

These are the words
quartered, divided and whole
whose contradictions
line our souls.
Words of resistance
which in sharing
we move forward
claiming what is ours.
   Gabriela Pearse, 'Black Women Talk Poetry'

My primary motive for this modest documentation is to continue
to resist the death by silence that is imposed on this aspect of Black
British writing; to continue the chorus of voices challenging the

homogeneity of the Black experience in contemporary Britain. Also, to upset the projection of the 'lesbian' experience as dictated by this euro-centric definition of the possibilities and parameters of female bonding.

From my eyes, many of the most vocal and challenging voices within Blackfeminism have been zami, and writing poetry has been one aspect of their multifaceted creativity. I've focused on poetry as this is a popular form of expression among Blackwomen writing, whether for publication, in writing support groups, or for peace of mind. In the 1980s I experienced the growing confidence of zami-inspired writing and publishing. The following selection of writers reflects my own personal choice of writers; zamis and poetry that inspired me. It also represents the contacts I had available to me from New York, where I was when I began this project in 1988.

In compiling their biographies, I have consulted with mes'zamis myself and each is listed with her consent. It is no coincidence that some of these writers are known to each other, we have fostered and encouraged each others' voices, as zamis, as Blackwomen, allowing us to use our imaginations to recreate from the totality of our realities. Many of us have appeared in the same anthologies. A few have had their words published exclusively. I have tried to stress similarities in levels of education, overlapping artistic, cultural, and political involvements.

There have been countless small and/or exclusive readings and performances of zami poetry that have offered validation and affirmation. Most have gone unrecorded, surviving only in the memories of those who were there. A tide of inspiration waves in the face of silence and distortion; their words a distillation of a raw hard experience.

These short biographies and select bibliographies represent a signpost to works by zamis. Do not assume about our sexuality; it may not always remain a pivotal focus in our writing; but become integrated into all the same difference of being a Blackwoman in a white society. Labels may become straitjackets; mono-dimensional. Selfhood is primary, a healthy wholeness; the sum of the whole being greater than the parts – even the 'lesbian' bit. Zami; loving ourselves/Blackwomen. Blackpeople are experts at piecing jigsaws together, and know that parts alone can be deceptive, however intriguing.

What follows is part of a larger, yet to be completed project; a selection for the context of this publication. Ultimately I hope this paper (which is by no stretch of the imagination definitive) can offer a starting point for critical discussion; a source for further research, re-membering, reading and inspiration primarily for zamis and other Blackwomen who care to know.

SELECTED SELF-IDENTIFIED ZAMI WRITERS

Adjoa Andoh (b. 1963)

Biography

Ghanaian/English Blackwoman. Born in Bristol and raised in the Cotswolds. 'Lover of Woman and Womanspirit', *Black Women Talk Poetry*.[1] Studied law for a year and a half, before emerging as an actress, singer and writer. She was also an active member of Bristol Black Women's Group, before moving to London in 1984. Was one of the original members of Sistahs In Song (a Black-women's a cappella group). She has toured nationally and internationally with various theatre groups, including The Women's Theatre Group, Akimbo, Theatre Centre, Birmingham Repertory and Gay Sweatshop. As a musician she has recorded for Temba Theatre and Teatro del'Angolo. Adjoa is currently writing her first play, *Just My Luck* (unpublished), for Theatre Centre, about a young mixed-race girl moving from the countryside to the city accompanied by her two guardian spirits. Recently she also began writing critical reviews of Black/lesbian fiction.

Published Poetry

In *Black Women Talk Poetry*:[2]
   'Abortion is not the easy option don't assume' (p. 76)
   'C'mon Jesse' (p. 58)
   'For Papy' (p. 52)
   'I'd also like to say' (p.30)
In *Charting the Journey*:[3]
   'My True Name' (pp. 222–223)

Barbara Burford (b. 1945)

Biography

Blackwoman, active feminist and medical researcher. Has written not only poetry, but short stories, a novella and a play. She has the distinction of being the only British zami to have had her own collection of short stories published (*The Threshing Floor*).[4] She has also edited a collection of poetry for The Women's Press (*Dancing the Tightrope*),[5] as well as writing critically on Blackwomen's writing. In the past she has worked with The Women's Theatre Group, and has led discussions on Blackwomen's writing/writing workshops for Theatre of Black Women.

Published Poetry

In *A Dangerous Knowing*[6]:
 'Christine' (p. 13)
 'Daughters of Eve' (p. 14)
 'Fallow Time' (p. 16)
 'In my gift' (p. 5)
 'In Solitary' (pp. 11–12)
 'Introspection blues' (pp. 8–9)
 'State of the Art' (p. 6)
 'Sisterwrite' (p. 10)
 'The Nth day of Christmas' (p. 7)
 'The Other' (p. 15)
 'Untitled' (p. 4)
 'Women Talking' (p. 3)
In *Dancing the Tightrope*:
 'Manumissions' (p. 5)
 'Reflections' (p. 14)
 'Sheherazade' (p. 9)
 'September Blue' (p. 7)
 'You' (p. 6)

Bernardine Evaristo (b. 1959)

Biography

Nigerian (Yoruba)/English Blackwoman. Trained in drama at Rose Bruford College, where she met Patricia St Hilaire, the co-founder of Theatre of Black Women (TBW), which was formed in 1982. TBW has toured nationally, and Bernardine's work has also been featured at the Royal Court Black Writers' Festival. She has written several plays, including two co-authored with Patricia St Hilaire. She was one of the four co-editors of *Black Women Talk Poetry*, and has more recently moved into theatre administration.

Published Poetry

In *Black Women Talk Poetry*:
  'Ameland' (p. 123)
  'Dream Sequence' (p. 129)
  'Mombasa Old Town' (p. 83)
  'Movements' (p. 122)
  'Tribal Girl' (p. 19)
In *Charting the Journey*:
  'Grandmother' (p. 111)
  'Mother is . . .' (p. 144)
In *Beautiful Barbarians*:[7]
  'Flame Dance' (p. 108)
  'Olu-A-Day' (pp. 103–104)
  'Sun Clouds Dry' (pp. 106–107)
  'The Blonde in Buki' (pp. 101–102)
  'Tiger Teeth Clenched Not To Bite' (p. 105)

Shabnam Grewal (b. 1963)

Biography

Born in India, first came to England aged two, returning aged seven before finally settling in West London aged 12. Her A-level education was interrupted by the Southall uprisings of 1981. She became an active member of Southall Black Sisters. Has consistently written poetry, and has been writing zami poems since she was 19. Shabnam was an early member of Black Woman Talk Collective, and via this took a job with Sheba Feminist Publishers, where she worked for a year and a half, including working with Jackie Kay on the First International Feminist Bookfair. She remained involved with Sheba for over three years through her co-editing of *Charting the Journey*. She has read her poetry in and outside London, and was an early member of the Asian Women's

Writing Group. More recently she has been working in film/video.

Published Poetry

In *Black Women Talk Poetry*:
  'Because' (p. 126)
  'For Sandra' (p. 125)
  'Mutilation' (p. 82)
  'Old wisdom' (p. 118)
  'Sister' (p. 86)
  'The Women loving Women' (p. 111)
In *Charting the Journey*:
  'Because' (p. 114)
  'My Hair and I' (pp. 252–253)
  'Rejection' (pp. 239–240)
In *Turning the Tables*: [8]
  'Shabnam's Parathas' (p. 53)

Savitri Honoman (b. 1962)

Biography

Born in Colombo, Sri Lanka, and came to England in 1964. A Chemical Engineering graduate, she has worked as a laboratory technician, a science and mathematics tutor, a proof-reader and a copy-editor, and for the past four years has worked for the London Blacklesbian and Gay Centre Project. She has been involved in many groups and campaigns, including the Migrant Media Collective. She read one of her poems on a Channel Four documentary on East London writers. She still writes poetry, though not prolifically. She has contributed articles on lesbian and gay issues to publications such as *Spare Rib* and the *Lesbian and Gay Christian Movement Journal*. She has written a number of short stories, including an unpublished collection set in Sri Lanka and Britain.

Published Poetry

Flood at the Door[9]
In *You'll Love This Stuff*: [10]
  'Monsoon' (p. 78)
In *Hear Me Out*: [11]
  'The Cage' (p. 191)

Patricia St Hilaire (b. 1960)

Biography

Of Caribbean parentage, born in London. Studied drama at Rose Bruford College where she met the co-founder of Theatre of Black Women, Bernardine Evaristo. She has written several plays, including those co-written with Bernardine Evaristo, which were produced by TBW. During 1987–88 she worked with the English National Opera's education programme, creating, writing and directing opera for young people.

Published Poetry

In *Black Women Talk Poetry*:
  'A Poem for Black women' (p. 133)
  'An open letter' (p. 62)
  'Just thinking' (p. 119)
  'No regrets' (p. 68)

Jackie Kay (b. 1961)

Biography

Born in Edinburgh, and raised in Glasgow. An English graduate, she has worked as a tutor in creative writing, has toured nationally reading her poetry, and has been interviewed on national radio. She was a member of the Black Lesbian Group in the early 1980s, and worked for Sheba Feminist Publishers during the First International Feminist Bookfair, with Shabnam Grewal. Her first play, *Chiaroscuro,* in *Lesbian Plays*,[12] was commissioned by Theatre of Black Women (TBW). The original draft was elaborated by input from workshops organised by TBW; personnel included Gabriela Pearse and Bernardine Evaristo. Jackie's second play, *Twice Over*,[13] was produced by Gay Sweatshop and featured Adjoa Andoh. Both plays toured nationally and had Black/lesbian main characters. She has also published short stories, interviews, and is one of the editors of *Charting the Journey*. Currently Jackie is enjoying a writer-in-residence position in London. Her latest collection of poems, *The Adoption Papers*, is due for publication in 1991 by Bloodaxe Press.

Published Poetry

In *Angels of Fire*[14]
In *Black Women Talk Poetry*:
  'Blue notes for Billie' (p. 38)
  'Memory Track' (p. 46)
  'Some Nights in Brooklyn and the Blood' (p. 42)
  'Waiting for the 171' (p. 16)
In *Dancing the Tightrope*:
  'Diary days for Adjoa' (p. 43)
  'Peony' (p. 45)
In *A Dangerous Knowing*:
  'And I still cannot believe it' (pp. 64–65)
  'Dustbins and dreams' (pp. 60–61)
  'Happy ending' (pp. 56–57)
  'Intensity' (p. 63)
  'Remi' (pp. 66–67)
  'So you think I'm a mule?' (pp. 53–54)
  'The sky changes every second now' (p. 62)
  'Tulips' (p. 55)
  'We are not all sisters under the same moon' (pp. 58–59)
In *Feminist Review 17*: [15]
  'happy endings' (p. 52)
  'So you think I'm a mule?' (p. 80)
In *Beautiful Barbarians*:
  'Aisha's Poem (pp. 42–44)
  'InterCity Through Spring' (pp. 38–39)
  'Opal's Poem' (pp. 46–47)
  'Some Nights in Brooklyn and the Blood' (pp. 39–41)
  'Witness' (pp. 36–37)
  'Yomi's Poem' (pp. 45–46)

Gabriela Pearse (b. 1963)

Biography

A Trinidadian/English Blackwoman. Born in Columbia, and raised in South America, the Caribbean and England. Studied Comparative American Studies at Warwick University, and was a member of the Women's Group, before moving to London. She has worked around women's employment and training. She was

one of the original members of Sistahs in Song, with Adjoa
Andoh, Dorothea Smartt and Carmen Tunde Williams. Also,
together with Theatre of Black Woman (TBW), Gabriela was one
of the workshop participants involved in developing Jackie Kay's
Chiaroscuro. She has read her poems publicly in and outside
London. With her mother Jean Pearse she wrote a play for
children, *Miss Quashie and the Tiger's Tail*, which was performed
and toured nationally by TBW in early 1987 (unpublished). She is a
co-editor with Black Woman Talk, and is working on their next
anthology of short stories. Currently she is leading workshops in
creative writing, and, as an extension of her spiritual practice,
workshops in self-empowerment for Blacklesbians.

Published Poetry

In *Black Women Talk Poetry*:
  'Black Women Talk Poetry' (p. 11)
  'El Salvador march' (p. 36)
  'Patricia' (p. 127)
  'Sistahs' (p. 131)
  'This cat' (p. 130)
  'Today' (p. 98)
In *A Dangerous Knowing*:
  'Alice' (p. 30)
  'Autobiography' (pp. 23–24)
  'Credo' (p. 28)
  'Grenada . . . Heathrow . . . London' (pp. 32–33)
  'Hot Summer' (p. 32)
  'Mother' (p. 21)
  'Queiro — (I want/love)' (pp. 19–20)
  'Soft evening blues' (p. 27)
  'St Helen's, and St Catherine's school for girls' (p. 22)
  'Turning back is no longer possible' (p. 29)
  'Wedding Guest' (pp. 25–26)

Dorothea Smartt (b. 1963)

Biography

Barbadian parentage. Born and raised in South London. A
graduate in Social Science from South Bank Polytechnic. She was

a member of Brixton Black Women's Group, and was a founding member of the Black Lesbian Support Network. She has written critical reviews of zami and Blackwomen's literature and theatre. Two of her reviews are featured in *Let It Be Told*. [16] As part of a collective she organised the 1984 'We Are Here' Blackfeminist Conference. She was also an original member of Sistahs In Song for three years. Dorothea has worked with 'I-Spirit', a zami drum/dance/poetry performance group, which included Carmen Tunde Williams. She sat on the Theatre of Black Women's advisory board. She has read and performed in London, Leicester, and in New York (where she worked for the Audre Lorde Women's Poetry Center). Currently one of her jobs is as a Black Arts Worker, and she is completing her MA in Anthropology for Hunter College (City University of New York).

Published Poetry

In *Black Women Talk Poetry*:
   'My mother's hands' (p. 47)
   'Part of me is a stranger' (p. 34)
   'Summer breeze' (p. 128)

Maud Sulter (b. 1960)

Biography

Born and raised in Glasgow, Scotland, Maud first came to London to study at a fashion college. Her first collection of poetry, *As a BlackWoman*, was published by Akira Press in 1985 as a result of the title poem winning the 1984 Vera Bell Prize (Black Penmanship Awards). [17] She was the first Blackwoman on the Sheba collective, before moving on to create the Blackwomen's Creativity Project (at the Women and Education Group Centre). Through this in 1984 she organised 'Check It!', a two-week celebration of Blackwomen's performance/arts in London. That featured Barbara Burford and created the original Sistahs In Song. Maud has also used her poetry with her photography and short experimental video. She is featured in *Let It Be Told*, and has published critical reviews, essays and interviews. Currently she is Artist-in-Residence at the Liverpool Tate Gallery, is developing Urban Fox Press and exhibiting internationally.

Published Poetry

As A Blackwoman [18]
In *Dancing the Tightrope*:
   'The Dance' (p. 90)
   'Full Circle' (p. 91)

In *Let It Be Told*:
   'As a Black Woman' (p. 66)
   'Headstone' (p. 55)
   'Under attack' (p. 65)
In *Watchers and Seekers*:[19]
   'Babe' (p. 129)
   'Once' (p. 73)

Carmen Tunde Williams (b. 1957)

Biography

St Kitts/English Blackwoman born and raised in London. Studied Sociology and Social Anthropology at the University of Hull. She has been active in women's, socialist, Black and Blackwomen's organisations, including Southall Black Sisters and OWAAD. In 1983, along with several other Blackwomen including Shabnam Grewal, she was instrumental in setting up Black Woman Talk. She performed and co-wrote music for Theatre of Black Women's *Pyeyucca* (unpublished), and toured nationally with the production in 1984–85. Carmen has drummed and performed her poetry as a member of 'I-Spirit' (a drum/dance/poetry trio of zamis that performed periodically in London during 1986–87). From 1985 to 1990 she was an original member of Voices for Oya (née Sistahs In Song). Carmen has worked in a number of women's organisations offering support to women in crises, and/or emotional distress.

Published Poetry

In *We Are Here: Blackfeminist Newsletter*: [20]
   'Another dirty silence'
In *Black Women Talk Poetry*:
   'An open letter' (p. 87)
   'Bus stop (p. 18)

'Contradictions' (p. 94)
'I long to be pregnant' (p. 59)
In *Charting the Journey*:
'Dreadlocks Lesbian' (pp. 205–206)
'Shutdown' (pp. 43–44)
'The Violation in Secret' (pp. 48–51)
In *Feminist Review 17*:
'White woman, hey' (p. 79)
In *MotherTongue 4/5*: [21]
'I hope you'll both be very happy'
'Moon eyes'
In *Sweeping Statements*:[22]
'Black Rebel Sistren' (pp. 280–281)

CONTACT ADDRESSES

Black Woman Talk: Box 32, 190 Upper Street, London N1 1RG
Sheba Feminist Publishers. 10a Bradbury Street, London N16 8JW
Theatre of Black Women: Box 6, 136–8 Kingsland High Street,
London, E8 2NS
Urban Fox Press: PO Box 2, Hebden Bridge, West Yorkshire,
HL7 6LW

NOTES

1 Da Choong, Olivette Cole-Wilson, Bernardine Evaristo and
Gabriela Pearse, eds., *Black Women Talk Poetry*, Black Womantalk, London, 1987, p. 135.

2 *Ibid.*

3 Shabnam Grewal, Jackie Kay, Liliane Landor, Gail Lewis and
Pratibha Parmar, eds., *Charting the Journey: Writings by Black and
Third World Women*, Sheba Feminist Publishers, London, 1988.

4 Barbara Burford, *The Threshing Floor*, Sheba Feminist
Publishers, London 1987.

5 Barbara Burford, Lindsay MacRae, Sylvia Paskin, eds.,
Dancing the Tightrope; New Love Poems by Women, The Women's
Press, London, 1987.

6 Barbara Burford, Gabriela Pearse, Grace Nichols and Jackie
Kay, *A Dangerous Knowing: Four Black Women Poets*, Sheba
Feminist Publishers, London, 1985.

7 Lilian Mohin, ed., *Beautiful Barbarians: Lesbian Feminist Poetry*, Onlywomen Press, London, 1986.

8 Sue O'Sullivan, ed., *Turning the Tables: Recipes and Reflections from Women*, Sheba Feminist Publishers, London, 1988.

9 Savitri Hensman, *Flood at the Door*, Centreprise Trust Ltd, London, 1979.

10 Morag Styles, ed., *You'll Love This Stuff*, Cambridge University Press, Cambridge, 1986.

11 Roy Blatchford, ed., *Hear Me Out*, Longman, Harlow, 1987.

12 Jackie Kay, *Chiaroscuro*, in *Lesbian Plays*, ed. Jill Davis, Methuen, London, 1987.

13 Jackie Kay, *Twice Over*, in *Gay Sweatshop: Four Plays and a Company*, ed. Philip Osmet, Methuen, London, 1989.

14 Sylvia Paskin, J Ramsay, J Silva, eds., *Angels of Fire: Anthology of Radical Poetry in the 1980s*, Chatto and Windus, London, 1986.

15 *Feminist Review* 17, 1984.

16 Laura Ngcobo, ed., *Let It Be Told: Black Women Writers In Britain*, Virago, London, 1988.

17 Maud Sulter, *As A Black Woman*, Akira Press, London, 1986; Urban Fox, Hebden Bridge, West Yorkshire, 1989.

18 *Ibid.*

19 Rhonda Cobham and Merle Collins, eds., *Watchers and Seekers: Creative Writing by Black Women in Britain*, The Women's Press, London, 1987.

20 *We Are Here: Blackfeminist Newsletter*, 1985.

21 Kris Black, Sarah Magen, Rebecca Stein, Lily Brighton, *MotherTongue* 4/5, 1986.

22 Hannah Kanter, Sarah Lefanu, Shaila Shah and Carole Spedding, eds., *Sweeping Statements: Writings from the Women's Liberation Movement 1981–83*, The Women's Press, London, 1984.

THE PROCESS OF WRITING
THREE PLY YARN
Caeia March

When I am asked to examine how and why I wrote a novel, I have to move back into the complex relationship between the individual and the social: between my inner world as a creative artist and the social world into which, and from which, I was writing.

The social/individual connections are flexible, changing and shifting. There are many unknowns, and the areas that I think I do know about I may wish to consider differently 10 or 20 years from now.

The social world is not beyond us, static, waiting to be defined. When I analyse an earlier part of my process it is not separated from myself now analysing it, nor from any part of my present social world.

Writing a novel, any novel, has an extraordinary appeal for me in its infinite potential for learning. Creativity involves discovery: moving nearer and nearer to the intuitive and risk-taking centres from which my most powerful writing may emerge.

However, creativity in the sense of being delighted by an initial 'splurge' is only 10 per cent of the final product. The rest is 90 per cent discipline through editing, re-writing and research. The excitement and the risk make the 90 per cent possible, worthwhile and alluring. The sense of adventure and discovery are what fuel the hard graft.

One August morning in 1983, I woke up with an image – three

strands of knitting wool twisted around each other, held in a woman's hand. A phrase – Three Ply Yarn – repeated itself, with the names Deanne, Lotte and Esther. The hand holding the wool was Nell.

Such realisations followed from 15 months of unstructured, unfinished writings, including letters, diaries, a half-hatched play (*Loom Stories*) and two linked but undeveloped manuscripts called Betrayals.

But now, names that had arisen only briefly, became real characters, with voices, faces and separate identities, starting to interact in a framework.

The challenge for me at the beginning of any novel lies in the long-term commitment to a process that is both social and individual. Here is the paradox: at the very heart of the solitary writing is the desire to communicate, which is social. Discussions with friends whilst writing are social; and although the *act* of putting pen to paper, fingers to keys, is individual, disciplined, solitary, even isolated, yet in the very moment of creation, the reference point (audience/reader) is social. The writing room, corner, desk, alcove, becomes crowded with voices, full to bursting, peopled: one writer in a room full of characters.

Three Ply Yarn, is entirely fictional.[1] As the characters settled themselves and began to unfold their lives, I wrote both in longhand and directly on to the typewriter. I finished the fifth and sixth drafts (re-writes) in the early summer of 1984 ready for the manuscript to be re-typed and then submitted for consideration to The Women's Press.

It was months before a reply came. When it did, I couldn't tell if it was yes or no. I psyched myself up and rang the Press. They did want it, but with more rewriting. No contract as yet.

The insecurity and the periods of waiting were difficult. I re-submitted the seventh draft in summer 1985, received a contract and was asked to rewrite the last 50 pages. The final script went to the Press nine months before publication,[2] which was set for August 1986.

Meanwhile the book jacket for *Three Ply Yarn* was being designed. I had in mind some suggestions and I was definite about what I didn't want. Bryony Jenkins[3] did three roughs in chalk on black sugar paper. When I saw them I felt as if she'd been sitting inside my head looking out. I loved the picture that was chosen for the cover from the first moment that I saw it. The colours, the long desolate sweep of the beach, the blurred outlines of the hotels, the countryside beyond Coombebury, all were exactly how I knew the place to be.

To feel that the book and cover were harmonious meant that for both author and artist the process was sound: that the match of the artist's style with what the author wanted from the book had been made carefully by those responsible at the Press. There are horror stories, for many authors. Mine was a happy one.

Three Ply Yarn was a selected title for Feminist Book Fortnight 1987; and was part of Feminist Book Fortnight and Gay Pride Week in the summer of 1988, coinciding with Clause 28 passing into law.

I would now like to explore some of the social contexts which I feel were crucial to me at the time when I began to write *Three Ply Yarn*.

In the early 1980s in London and throughout this country, there was excitement and debate around women's lost heritage, including (amongst many themes) links between art/fabric/myth/legend/storytelling; and specific research about lesbian 'her' story.

It was acknowledged by lesbians that one of the most powerful weapons held by homophobic men and women is the denial both that lesbians have a history and that a fascinating cultural diversity is part of that history. Without knowledge of our history lesbians can have no sense of continuity so a sense of community and culture becomes far more difficult to develop.

In that context of excitement/reclaiming/research/talking of the early 1980s, I wanted to contribute to the lesbian heritage by writing through fiction some parts of our history that have been left unrecorded or stolen or hidden.

One central theme of *Three Ply Yarn* was women and work – in the widest sense – paid work/unpaid work/unemployment. However, whereas my unfinished *Loom Stories* had a woman weaver in it, I chose knitting, a more ordinary, everyday version of work with yarn, for *Three Ply Yarn*. During childhood, I was used to seeing women knitting; and in my family background on both sides were tailors and seamstresses. We sewed for work or because it was cheaper to clothe ourselves.

The novel now led me again to the Manx museum,[4] where I read the history of thread on the island; made links between the raw materials of knitting and the landscapes from which they came; and learned about the wild flowers and other plants used for dyes. As I re-explored the Celtic and Viking history of the island, I recognised that my image of twisting strands of yarn was an adult development from my childhood memories of stone dragons with coils and cables, like Aran jumpers, carved on Manx runic crosses. Research now told me that the dragons came with the Vikings from Scandinavia, and had been imposed (by violent means) on the Celtic thread of life.

My love of music including jazz,[5] and the idea of call and response, now suggests to me that *Three Ply Yarn* was part of a very wide call and response echoing through the women's liberation movement during the early 1980s, when many very different women responded to a complex theme of 'broken and (re)connected threads of women's history', through film, video, dance, poetry, all forms of writing, theatre and music.

For example, Barbara Burford wrote the historical/mythical play *Patterns* set in a closed-down textile factory; and created the fictional Black woman, Pearl, in her short story 'Coming of Age' (in *The Threshing Floor)*[6]. Pearl was drawn to the museums – the bronze head of the Queen Mother; the necklace; the bird mask; and the pictures and symbols woven into carpets and rugs. Pearl thought that the people must have no shame, they who stole from other cultures all over the world then built store houses for their plunders.

During my own research for *Three Ply Yarn* I saw many such stolen weavings. I went to exhibitions of spinning, weaving, tapestry, political patchwork and the history of knitting. I visited the Dinner Party exhibition when it was in London, became immersed in the books which accompanied it,[7] and let the new knowledge flow into my fiction writing.

Many other books are important to the history of the writing of *Three Ply Yarn*, including some that I read long before I consciously started work on the novel.

In October 1980 just after I came out as a lesbian, Adrienne Rich read her poetry and prose in London. I bought *The Dream of a Common Language*; was given *On Lies, Secrets and Silence*;[8] and slept with both those books by my bed. The words of the poem 'Hunger', written for Audre Lorde, are still with me now a decade later. From the start of my first fiction writing, that autumn, I wanted my work to reflect the international issues raised in that poem. I still do.

Discovering lesbian poetry, including much loved works by Pat Parker and Judy Grahn,[9] affected *Three Ply Yarn* immediately, through a desire for an economic form of language. It was amazing that such a thing as lesbian poetry was there for me, when I needed it. Now, a decade later, it is important to name just how crucial the words of those writers were to me then. The honesty, openness, outness, the challenge and the hope fed me, when I'd been hungry for a long time. As discoveries happened I felt an overwhelming love for the lesbian writers who wrote words with which I could identify, as a lesbian who longed to write. *Three Ply Yarn* was formed in that context.

In Germany, November 1980, Karin Schönewolf, for whom I wrote 'Ms World' (in *Dancing the Tightrope*[10]) introduced me to Jane Rule's work – a copy of *Lesbian Images*; and my first lesbian novel: *Desert of the Heart*.[11] I can still feel the heat of the desert; the love of the two women for one another; the weight of the money machine the younger one wore in the casino. I can't recall whether that particular book made me want to write a lesbian novel, but I remember thinking it was written especially for me. I felt wonderful reading it.

In December 1980, two months after I came out, I read *The Well of Loneliness*.[12] I'd never before heard of Radclyffe Hall. Now, as I write this article, I can recognise the many, varied and sometimes intense, effects of Radclyffe Hall's life and work on my life and work.

In the early 1980s, I felt both compassion and admiration for Radclyffe Hall. They have increased: across both class and time, I imagine her courage. She would have fought Clause 28. She keeps me strong.

When I read *The Well of Loneliness*, I became determined to learn to write fiction. Not only were the non-fiction books I was coming across causing me to meet fictional characters in my mind whenever I put pen to paper, but also I was certain it was not only the upper-class Unas and Radclyffes who lived and loved together; nor even only the middle-class women writers, sharing flats and working hard.

I felt that wherever women were together as close friends/ companions, and certainly where women shared beds in servants' quarters and slums, that some of them loved each other's bodies.

I decided to assume that before the second world war many working class women who had not heard of the sexologists, continued to create passionate equal sex, oblivious to the horrible things being written about lesbians/inverts.

My aim: to use fiction to represent the 'unrecorded examples', the ones that 'everybody knows': the two women who ran the corner shop and were companions and shared a bed; the two who said they were sisters, new to the area, lived in a one-room flat above a mice-infested greengrocers; the two mothers, one a widow, one single, who moved in together and raised their children together; the prostitutes (like Corrine and Maggie), who loved one another, not their clients; the market traders (Red Heather); the bus conductresses (Rene); the chamber maids (Deanne and Dora): the list is endless if it's true that any woman can be a lesbian.

They were heady times, the early 1980s, full of women's poetry, theatre, dancing, art and craft, music and political work . . . But before sentimental nostalgia creeps into an account of *Three Ply Yarn*, it should be said they weren't easy times. Women as wives/mothers/lesbians/tenants/workers/ claimants, were experiencing violence; evictions; awful lesbian custody cases; harassment at work, on the social and on the dole.

I wanted *Three Ply Yarn* to challenge patriarchy, both patriarchy as a system, and patriarchy as represented by individuals: men as landlords, bosses, line managers, judges, ex-husbands, brothers, fathers, sons . . . any man can be a representative of patriarchy.

I also wanted to explore the fact that not all women are equally betrayed under patriarchy, and not all women collude equally in their own betrayal without personal and collective resistance.

Nell's group was one form of resistance. It was composed of individual women with different emphases, needs and reactions to each other and to male power. Her daughter Tracey's resistance to Nell's heterosexism (Why can't you find a nice boyfriend and settle down?) as well as Tracey's raw energy for confronting things, was a problem for the older women, who had juggled for years with compromises and negotiations.

While I was writing *Three Ply Yarn*, resistance was a central theme for theatre groups such as The Cunning Stunts (resistance to nuclear power); The Scarlet Harlots (resistance to psychiatry and male medicine); and Theatre of Black Women (resistance to racism, colonialism and imperialism) whose work I followed closely and whose influence on my writing was inspirational.[13]

It can also be stated clearly here that the networking among women around overtly political issues (e.g. Greenham) overlapped with the networking around creativity, so that the linking of politics and creativity was integral to what I've termed the call and response of the women's liberation movement. These links are, under patriarchy, claimed to be inappropriate, contradictory, naive and/or silly, in an attempt to invalidate or minimise the effect of challenges that feminists make to the status quo.

Meanwhile, I had had full-time then part-time work as a clerical assistant/receptionist for the London Borough of Lewisham.

Clerical work itself was a dead dogfish but on reception I was surrounded by voices. People from all kinds of backgrounds told me of their lives, to get things off their chests; to be chatty; and to complain. At night, working as a tutor,[14] I was encircled by women's voices, wanting and needing to be heard.

Slowly I was naming *my own* voice, my own background, speeded on by a workshop on voice at the Feminist Writers' Conference 1983; by working in various political groups with women from working-class backgrounds; and by visits (sometimes with my two sons) to my parents in the Isle of Man, where land/sea/sky images filled my mind.

In my creative writing classes, it was quite common for women to begin by saying that they didn't write much: 'only diaries, or letters', which were actually amazing volumes. Historically, when unvoiced women wrote diaries and letters, being of low status in patriarchy, they weren't archived. Sometimes they were stored, treasured by friends, kept, handed down – only very rarely were they made public. But, amazingly, in the early 1980s, letters between Ruth Slade and Eva Slawson, were rediscovered. The Women's Theatre Group performed *Dear Girl*,[15] researched by Tierl Thompson, (and co-devised for stage with Libby Mason) from the correspondence begun in 1897, in north-east London. I laughed and cried during the play – it had a profound effect – I was already writing *Three Ply Yarn*, in which Dee and Lotte spoke their lives on to tape; Esther wrote her diary and letters to her women friends; and Rene had kept copies of her own letters and replies from Red Heather, with a newscutting of Red Heather's death in the blitz on Sheffield.

In 1982, on holiday in the USA, I had found the just published hardback of Alice Walker's *The Color Purple*[16] and Anne Cameron's *Daughters of Copper Woman*.[17] In 1983, when the title of *Three Ply Yarn* came to me, these two books contributed to my decision to include letters and some form of oral history in my novel. I felt that in everyday life women used spoken stories and letters as strong but invisible stitches holding together the patchwork pieces of their worlds.

Thus, before and during my own writing, a framework was being developed, in which oral history and women's letters, real and fictionalised, were regarded as very important in the women's liberation movement.

I began to read Audre Lorde's writings: starting with *Zami*, followed by the essay 'Uses of the Erotic – The Erotic as Power',[18] *The Cancer Journals*, and much of her poetry.

When I read *Zami*, I felt empowered, creatively. I searched and studied everything I could about women as leaders and goddesses, women in myth, legend and history, cutting through patriarchal lies. *Zami* inspired me to continue.

I found that in many legends, myths and languages, the words for blood/flow/thread/river/stream and water overlap. Women of the past as goddesses and leaders wove destinies *and* threads, spun words *and* images. I was fascinated. I turned my various findings into creative writing materials for women, and wove the goddesses into the developing tapestry of *Three Ply Yarn*.

I am indebted to Audre Lorde for the concept, throughout her work, of the spiritual as inseparable from the political; and (especially in the above mentioned essay) to the distinction she makes between women's creative life-force and the abuse of this through male violence, including pornography.[19]

When the issue of pornography became included in *Three Ply Yarn*, through Lotte's experiences of her husband using porn, huge questions arose for me as a fiction writer.

My experience of living as a lesbian means that I have political perspectives and hopes. But I was writing a novel not an essay. So, how could I be true to myself, whilst avoiding making women characters say or do 'proper' political things that a 'right-on' feminist 'should' say or do – whatever those might be?

I wanted to maintain a clear distance between fiction writing and political essay writing, but the problem for fiction is that it isn't (and can't be) free of judgments, assumptions or values. I don't believe that any research, non-fiction or fiction writing is value free.

My decision was to respect the integrity of the characters, which means that they had to be real and whole, sometimes internally unsure or contradictory, different from each other, and not simply reflections of me, or parts of me, obedient to me.

This also meant that sometimes I would have to stop and ask myself who was in control, me or the characters? I experienced it as a process of negotiation between myself (as writer) and the women (as characters). The political dimension of this is but one facet of the total negotiations required.

I read and re-read Audre Lorde's essay, mentioned above, giving me a grounding in my own politics, whilst Lotte, who was not a feminist, was getting on with her own journey. The essay strengthened me in negotiating with Lotte – a powerful character, whom I liked and felt close to; and when *she* was being hurt *I* sometimes found that the writing process was very painful.

Meanwhile, I carried through the decision to trust Lotte to be herself, which meant her claiming her own space, her own timing, her particular place on stage.[20] Very slowly, Lotte began to think beyond herself as individual, coming to terms with her increasing identification as women-centred.

Lotte had no background in recognising pornography as violence against women. Some women might argue that she was betrayed by her own mother, Rene, who could have 'brought her up to understand this'. I was committed not only to respecting the integrity of Lotte's journey, (i.e. through her character) but also to not allowing Rene to be blamed when Lotte was going through violence and deep distress over James' use of pornography. Bad mothers/inadequate mothers/mothers to blame are often the scapegoats in books by men and non-feminists, and I rejected that short-cut.

Lotte didn't want feminism and wasn't looking for it. She met feminist ideas through Hazel and Marie at secretarial school, which she went to behind James' back, on the first independent steps along her escape route. When she met Dee and fell in love, it was a physical response. Dee's nearness made Lotte's breasts sing. Many lesbians have their introduction to their lesbian bodies in this way. Sex between women is created against all odds, contrary to all conditioning.

I began this section by acknowledging Audre Lorde's influence on my fiction, and I shall now refer to another 'political' dimension influenced by my reading of *Zami* whilst writing *Three Ply Yarn*. I refer to the implicit and explicit assumptions in my novel about role-playing by lesbians in the 1950s and 1960s.

My reading of *Zami* became crucial in my writing life because of what it does over this issue. *Zami* validated for me the strong hunch that not all 'previous dykes' accepted the role-play model.

Zami suggested to me that there were women searching for equal partners, for creativity and fulfilment in their lives and beds, despite the restrictions imposed on them in a woman-hating world.

Three Ply Yarn has a number of underlying assumptions. These include the belief that some of the women of the 1950s and 1960s were non-role-playing like Dee and Dora; that others such as Micky and Pol down The Feathers Pub, were role-playing but not setting out to get 'into pain' nor to link pain with desire, nor submission and dominance with desire. They were not into S&M. For example, Pol did *not* see herself as submitting to Micky. Related to this is the belief that there were yet others such as Charlie who would have been into role-play with lovers, but they were loners.

I loved those women of The Feathers Pub. They came to my mind as a varied group, all working-class women, some of whom were role-playing as a structure of survival in what Dee called The Good Old Bad Old Days. Their lives were not romantic and they had no privileges. Some found alternative methods of survival. Corrine, for instance, was a lesbian prostitute who, bereaved of her lover who died of syphilis, became the mistress of Ralph Edmund Dove. She says, 'With men you do it for money – with women for love.' Writing fiction, I listened to the characters, watched them struggling to go forward without pain; struggling to pay the rent, go to work, clothe the kids; struggling for definitions of sex, love and friendship that were alive, changing, passionate, real, and not destructive; struggling for lesbian/gay identity: the power of fiction is to go beyond stereotypes.

Non-stereotypical characters are free to behave in non-stereotypical ways. As I go back into history through fiction, I can feel a strong connection, linking, love for the real women behind the fictional women.

Worldwide and stretching through time I am certain that wherever women are friends they are potentially lovers.

In some societies such as those documented by Anne Cameron (*Daughters of Copper Woman*); Audre Lorde (*Zami*); Judy Grahn (*Another Mother Tongue*);[21] and Janice Raymond (*A Passion for Friends*);[22] this love (and sex) between women was socially validated.

Three of the lesbian characters in *Three Ply Yarn* are Black women: Isobel, Marion and Zella. The other Black women characters are Laura, Hortense and Beth.

This raises immediately the question of my integrity as a white woman writer in a novel with Black characters.

It is central to my life that I do not live in an all-white world. The love and support of Black women both lesbian and heterosexual was an integral part of the process of writing *Three Ply Yarn*, giving me encouragement and confidence to write the scenes as the book was transformed from draft to draft.

My questions were (and are) how could I write a book without Black characters and why would I want to? And then, given that I don't know what it feels like to be Black, how could I know what was happening to the Black women in the novel, and would I attempt to write any Black characters from the inside?

I had to make political decisions about these issues, faced with my questions to myself about my power as a white woman writer and my potential abuse of that power.

As I commented in note 2, a first novel is sometimes called a birthing process – of oneself as a writer. With respect to writing about race and racism, it's important to state how significant to me was the birth of Isobel Beale, Dora's baby. As the daughter of a central character (her non-biological mother, Deanne) Isobel is also central to me. Her personality, her physicality, her childhood as a Black child in a white town, her adult work, her sexuality, her return to this country from scientific/political work abroad, all of these things foreground her in my consciousness, from near the start to the very end of *Three Ply Yarn*.

Isobel Beale began something in my writing life: *Three Ply Yarn* was a first step, setting out some of the parameters, some of the dimensions. There will be creative and political decisions to make for the rest of my life because Isobel will never not challenge me.

It would be meaningless, I decided, to write the novel without Laura or Isobel, Marion or Zella, Hortense and Beth.

Laura's husband and children were central to Laura's life, and as she was Esther's close friend since her teens, they were important to Esther too.

Hortense and Beth's children were part of Esther's and Nell's social environment as well as central to their mothers' lives.

From the initial phases of draft one, the novel had an international focus, through the lives of several of the characters, and it seemed within that framework essential not to collude in the lies about the legacy of colonialism and imperialism. The UN figures for the 1970s and 1980s show that of the millions of war refugees world wide, 90 per cent are women and children. The phrase 'refugees' hides their real identity – that the women and children are Black and live in the 'Third World'.

Isobel, Marion and Zella all work to challenge that legacy.

Further, international relationships exist in many families in this country. Many women such as Laura have connections with other countries that give them a world view often denied or made to seem unimportant during their schooling here. Such women in *Three Ply Yarn* link with themes begun in my unpublished novel, *Tarn Wood*,[23] and I felt a sense of continuity for myself as writer, carrying the themes through.

However, with respect to, and for, the internal knowledge the Black characters had of themselves, I decided that unless the Black women were revealing their thoughts to the white women they knew, I could not possibly have access to such internal knowledge. That decision having been made, it remained steady, a base line from which to write different drafts.

It affected the structure. For example, I couldn't be with Laura in Bristol; Isobel, Marion and Zella in Mozambique; Hortense in her kitchen, in London. So if Hortense said to Mo and Esther: 'Come for a cuppa'; or if Isobel wrote to her non-biological mother, Deanne; or Laura wrote to Esther; or Esther went to visit Laura, only then could I as a writer know what was going on.

This was very dynamic, not always easy, always challenging. As a base line it has remained firm throughout the rest of my work. It was about bridges across difference, ways through anger and hurt, and a recognition of all the work that goes into friendships between Black women and white women.

As I wrote the interactions between Black women and white

women for *Three Ply Yarn*, I experienced being part of the book that I was writing. I felt that I was engaging with the struggles of the characters for dignity and respect, each of the other, without liberal sentiment. To write about race and racism as a white woman writer is essential to me, from both a political and a personal/creative perspective. This is part of my life, part of who I am. Engaging in this dynamic, in this struggle, in this learning, will take me all of my life.

The whole process of writing, editing, re-writing is one of continual change and growth. New friendships developed through my writing *Three Ply Yarn*; and responses to me as an image-writer led to more self-knowledge of my involvement with image.

The writing of this article made me think consciously, slowly, deliberately about aspects of writing *Three Ply Yarn* and how they link to me as author, now, after a second published novel, *The Hide and Seek Files*; at the point of finishing a third, *Fire! Fire!*; and having already begun my next novel.

Some aspects of writing *Three Ply Yarn* were about being new to fiction writing, and will of necessity change now, as I do research for future fiction.

As the women in *Three Ply Yarn* unfolded on to paper, they fascinated me, but in early drafts, I tried sometimes, out of 'newness', to intervene, to impose places, timings, meetings, partings. I was amazed at how the women argued with me, refusing to co-operate if I interfered too much.

Often they took me completely by surprise. I had no idea that Lotte and Dee were going to meet and certainly not to fall in love. Completely taken aback, I got out of their way, and trusted myself to go along with them. Readers wrote that they loved the surprise element of the meeting. They also believed in Dee and Dora cuddling behind the hay barn while Nellie collected eggs; the relationship between Isobel and Deanne in their everyday life; and the difficulties faced by Isobel, Marion and Zella trying to construct friendship in a non-monogamous context. This was as real to readers as the I-never-want-to-see-her-again experience of Esther and Christine. It is not simply that couples can and do split up. Rather, the feedback verifies my own feeling that there is a need for lesbian literature that goes beyond a narrow 'couples' romanticism. Couples would be part of a wider reality, rather than the definition of what is real.

Meanwhile in my own real life, my process of writing fiction was not free, easy, undirected: it was interrupted by family commitments, work, dole, struggles with the DSS, and eventually myalgic encephalo-myelitis (ME).

ME started in April 1988, and was diagnosed as soon as I sought diagnosis, September 1988, five months before publication of *The Hide and Seek Files*, and halfway through the writing of *Fire! Fire!*

Immobilised during nine months, unable to sit up or pick up a pen, I re-trained myself, transposing the earlier discipline (of words on to paper) into a new form: inner image/film. I began to recognise that I'd been 'filming' spontaneously and intuitively, as an integral but unnamed part of my writing process. Now, on a screen in my mind, I watched the characters, until, knowing them so well, I could live with them in *their* film, which I could then re-run and re-member. The re-training was itself tiring because memory loss is one of the symptoms of ME. Once I accepted the fact that parts of the new film might fade and have to be re-made, it was such an improvement on being unable to write that, with a real sense of excitement, this became increasingly a discovery of a writing self in a non-writing expression.

After months and months flat on my back filming internally, I was able to write again – *Fire! Fire!* was ready to go straight on to a word processor, albeit at a rate of less than an hour a day.

The process of letting the characters take me with them, has been developed out of my earlier process of writing *Three Ply Yarn*: a method of writing fiction which suits me. The excitement of that: mentally always having a place to go; the place always being new; the fact that there might always be something round the corner, and I could go and explore it . . . that's what I found that the writing of *Three Ply Yarn* gave me. Further, although assessment is important, so is flexibility – the process goes on changing, *because I want it to*.

Other changes have happened to me too, since I first came out as a lesbian: my children have grown up.

I am a lesbian feminist mother of two young men. I shall go on dealing with the contradictions of that. I still find it a blessed relief not to have given much space in *Three Ply Yarn* to men, nor am I interested in devoting many lines here to them. The issue of men in lesbian books is one which I periodically review, as new characters emerge in new work. Also, I recognise that although some readers, usually straight, want more men in my books, other readers, usually lesbian, don't want *any*!

Experiencing the fun/humour of *that* contradiction is to move a long way from the anguished mother of the short stories, though this is perhaps a see-saw of contradictions with, let's say, anguish/anger at one end, amusement at the other. There will be times when men's world news (e.g. the Gulf War) tips the balance to such an extent that anguish/anger for mothers/lesbians/women peace campaigners is heavily increased.

I was 40 the summer that *Three Ply Yarn* was published.

Now, at 44, I have come through with no less contradictions in my life, but a deep, personal happiness. This is wonderful after a decade of coming out, being out and proud, being immersed in busycitymotherhood, whilst determined to make a contribution as a lesbian novelist.

February 1991

NOTES

1 The only aspect taken directly from 'real' life, is the voice of Nell Winters – whose voice was that of my friend Penny Holland, from oral history tapes made in the late 1970s. Penny wanted her voice to be in one of my novels. She loved *Three Ply Yarn*, and came to the launch. Nell Winters herself is fiction.

2 As a lesbian mother I noted 'nine months' with some amusement – birthing a novel! Within *Three Ply Yarn*, babies are born to Dora and to Nell, but not to Lotte, who at first longs for a child.

3 This refers to the cover of the first edition of *Three Ply Yarn*. The autumn 1991 reprint was rejacketed.

4 Research is ongoing, and leads along varied and unexpected paths. For example, Manx natural history and crofters' ways of life shown in the rural museums there, fed an interest in pre-industrial times. I took many notes used later for *Fire! Fire!*

5 When I'm writing I work without background music. I experience novel writing as a moving film with a soundtrack. My task is to put that on to the page – external voices or music would usually interfere with what I 'hear' as I write.

6 Barbara Burford, *The Threshing Floor*, Sheba Feminist Publishers, London, 1986.

7 Judy Chicago, *The Dinner Party: a Symbol of Our Heritage*, Anchor/Doubleday, New York, 1979; Judy Chicago with Susan Hill, *Embroidering Our Heritage: The Dinner Party Needlework*, Anchor/Doubleday, New York, 1980.

8 Adrienne Rich, *The Dream of a Common Language: Poems 1974–77*, W W Norton, New York, 1978. *On Lies, Secrets and Silence: Selected Prose 1966–78*, Virago, London, 1980.

9 Pat Parker and Judy Grahn, *Where Would I Be Without You: the Poetry of Pat Parker and Judy Grahn*, Olivia Records, 1976. See Bibliography for further works by these poets.

10 Barbara Burford, Lindsay MacRae and Sylvia Paskin, eds., *Dancing the Tightrope: New Love Poems by Women*, The Women's Press, London, 1987.

11 Jane Rule, *Lesbian Images*, The Crossing Press, Trumansburg, 1982. Jane Rule, *Desert of the Heart* (1964), Pandora, London, 1986.

12 Radclyffe Hall, *The Well of Loneliness*, Virago, London, 1982.

13 Theatre of all kinds was a primary influence on my work. The Cunning Stunts' influence, including Ova Music Group's live music, came through into my creative writing tutoring, through use of movement, music and the freeing up of our bodies for the physical work of writing. Maggie Nichols' voice workshops helped free my own voice. The Scarlet Harlots' play – *We Who Were The Beautiful* – mirrored the experience of Dora in *Three Ply Yarn*, already in manuscript; and Theatre of Black Women incorporated so many strands of lyrical poetry, image, history, political comment, and dramatic tension, particularly in the plays *Silhouette* and *Pyeyucca*.

Theatre workshops led by Nancy Diuguid for Women in Entertainment; and by Sistren Theatre company from Jamaica, helped me explore concepts of body space/body energy. Crucially when writing fiction, I became fascinated by the varied forms of body language through which characters might communicate.

14 Tutoring women's groups began in 1982, as community education via everyday English, at the Albany Community Centre, Deptford. The syllabuses were designed each term, by the women in the Discussion and Support Group based on women's studies. This led to additional work tutoring women's writing groups.

15 Unpublished. An edition of the letters has been published as *Dear Girl: The Diaries and Letters of Two Working Women, 1897–1917*, Tierl Thompson, The Women's Press, London, 1987.

16 Alice Walker, *The Color Purple*, The Women's Press, London, 1983; Harcourt, Brace Jovanovich, New York, 1982.

17 Anne Cameron, *Daughters of Copper Woman*, The Women's Press, London, 1984; Press Gang Publishers, Vancouver, 1981.

18 Now published in the book *Sister Outsider*. I read it as *Out & Out* pamphlet no. 3, published by The Crossing Press, Trumansburg, 1978. For Audre Lorde's work, see Bibliography.

19 Sarah Daniels' play, *Masterpieces*, (Methuen Modern Plays Series, London, 1982), Alice Walker's short story, 'Porn', and Mary Dorcey's poem 'Photographs', helped me find my own words/write my own experience of pornography, in the story: 'Photographs' (in *Girls Next Door*, eds. Jan Bradshaw and Mary Hemming, The Women's Press, London, 1985). I am unlikely to be won over by *any* contemporary pro-porn arguments: e.g. *Feminist Review* no. 34, 1990. But it's also essential to make the point that in every society where human rights are being seriously infringed, known to Amnesty International, censorship is a weapon of patriarchal state oppression. As a lesbian mother/woman writer/lesbian writer I have nothing to gain from the current censorship lobby of the Campaign Against Pornography. Further, any potential alliance between the left and the far right, e.g. embracing Dame Jill Knight (of Clause 28), is highly unlikely to be supportive of lesbian culture, continuity or community.

20 This was very much the case with Moss and Biff of *The Hide and Seek Files* (The Women's Press, London, 1989). They arrived unexpectedly in the middle of the Miners' Strike in summer 1984, while I was writing *Three Ply Yarn*. Instead of remaining the first two women of a seven-woman saga, they refused to leave centre stage and demanded a whole book, taking me with them. Before that novel was finished, I met the women from *Fire! Fire!* (The Women's Press, London, 1991), some of whom were in the seventeenth century.

21 Judy Grahn, *Another Mother Tongue: Gay Words, Gay Worlds*, Beacon Press, Boston, 1984.

22 Janice Raymond, *A Passion for Friends*, The Women's Press, London, 1986.

23 Tarn Wood was an attempt to turn into fiction diaries I'd made while teaching social studies to Black and white young women, during 1978, in a south-east London comprehensive, where institutionalised racism and homophobia were rife. The young women read the diaries and wanted them published as fiction, but I was too inexperienced as a writer for that particular task. The manuscript has remained unpublished.

NOTES ON CONTRIBUTORS

LYNDIE BRIMSTONE was born into a white working-class Coventry family in 1951. Already rubber-stamped 'beyond parental control' and institutionalised by the time she was 13, she can't honestly say that she's changed a great deal. Certainly she remains as sensitive to oppressive power structures (or 'nets' if we must, it all *feels* the same) as she was then but with a little less bewilderment. Without any formal qualifications she began a degree in English in 1981, has published a number of critical pieces, and is currently working on a Ph.D. thesis. She lives a very real and rewarding life with her 'pretended family' in London and, with the support of lover and children alike, she is back on the soul-destroying job trail with renewed hope and vigour.

PATRICIA DUNCKER was born in Jamaica in 1951. Her father is Jamaican, her mother English. She writes fiction and radical lesbian feminist criticism. Her published work includes 'James Miranda Barry 1795–1865', in the *The Pied Piper: Lesbian Feminist Fiction*, Onlywomen Press, London, 1989. She edited *In and Out of Time: Lesbian Feminist Fiction*, Onlywomen Press, London, 1990, and is the author of *Sisters and Strangers: Contemporary Feminist Fiction*, Basil Blackwell, Oxford, 1991. She now lives and writes in south-west France where she teaches for the University of Poitiers.

GABRIELE GRIFFIN was born in Cologne, Germany, in 1957; she is white. At present she is a senior lecturer in English at Nene College, Northampton, where she teaches women's writing of the twentieth century but also of earlier periods (in-print-ness allowing). Her research centres on various areas of women's writing, currently focusing on lesbian writing and the work of contemporary women's theatre groups.

GILLIAN HANSCOMBE was born in 1945 in Melbourne, Australia, though since 1969 she has lived and worked in Britain. She is white. She has published in a variety of modes, principally poetry, literary studies, polemic and journalism. Her books include *The Art of Life: Dorothy Richardson and the Development of Feminist Consciousness*, Peter Owen, London, 1982; *Writing for Their Lives: The Modernist Women 1910–1940* (with Virginia L Smyers), The Women's Press, London, 1987; and *Flesh and Paper*, a sequence of lesbian love lyrics written with Suniti Namjoshi, Jezebel, Seaton, Devon, 1986.

ELAINE HOBBY is a socialist and a feminist who finally admitted she was also a lesbian some time in the early 1980s. (Almost everyone she knew said they had known *that* for years!) She is white, and was born in England in 1956 but raised by Welsh parents who gave her a strong and proud sense of herself as Welsh. She is lecturer in Women's Studies in the Department of English and Drama, Loughborough University, where, as an out lesbian, she teaches a variety of explicitly feminist courses and is ridiculously happy. Her research is principally in seventeenth-century women's writing, and her publications include *Virtue of Necessity: English Women's Writing, 1649–1688*, Virago, London, 1988; *Her Own Life: Autobiographical Writings by Seventeenth-Century Englishwomen* (co-edited with Elspeth Graham, Hilary Hinds and Helen Wilcox), Routledge, London, 1989. She lives in Beeston, Nottingham, with her lover Chris White.

CAEIA MARCH was born of white working-class parents in the Isle of Man, 1946. She grew up in industrial south Yorkshire, graduated from London University in Social Sciences, 1968, and became a social science teacher. She has tutored women's discussion and support groups, pensioners' writing groups, women's and lesbian creative writing workshops; and women's international history.

She came out as lesbian in October, 1980 and currently divides her time between London and Cornwall.

Her stories have been published in *Everyday Matters, I*, Sheba Feminist Publishers, London, 1983; *The Reach*, Onlywomen Press, London, 1984; *Girls Next Door*, The Women's Press, London, 1985; and her articles in *Spare Rib* and *In Other Words*, Hutchinson, London, 1987. Her poetry is included in *Dancing the Tightrope*, The Women's Press, London, 1987, and *Naming the Waves*, ed. McEwan, Virago, London, 1988. She is the author of *Three Ply Yarn* (1986); *The Hide and Seek Files* (1989); and *Fire! Fire!* (1991), all published by The Women's Press, London. She is working on another novel, a collection of short stories and a collection of poetry.

PAULINA PALMER teaches an undergraduate course in 'Feminist Approaches to Literature' at the University of Warwick and contributes to the teaching of the Women's Studies MA. Her publications include *Contemporary Women's Fiction: Narrative Practice and Feminist Theory*, Harvester Wheatsheaf, Brighton, 1989; an essay on 'Lesbian Fiction' in Linda Anderson, ed., *Plotting Change: Contemporary Women's Fiction*, Edward Arnold, 1990; and a lesbian feminist reading of Antonia White's *Frost in May*, in Susan Sellers, ed., *Feminist Criticism: Theory and Practice*, Harvester Wheatsheaf, Brighton, 1991. She has a story in Jan Bradshaw and Mary Hemming, eds., *Girls Next Door*, The Women's Press, London, 1985. She is a member of Cambridge Lesbian Line.

JAN SELLERS juggles a range of jobs – teaching creative writing at Goldsmiths College, at Newham Community College and for the Workers Educational Association; deputy head of Barclay Hall Centre (Newham Community College); and performance poet. She is white, a socialist and feminist, and lives in London, but hopes eventually to return to northern England where she has, if not roots, definitely tendrils. Her poems have been published in several anthologies, journals and magazines. She began performing with 'Alice's Cabaret' in 1990 and, after an unsuccessful stage debut (age nine) as a yellow butterfly, is delighted to be back on stage again at 39, even without the frilly dress and the wings.

DOROTHEA SMARTT is a Capricorn Zami, completing her MA in Anthropology. She has contributed articles and reviews to several publications, including *Spare Rib, New Statesman,* and *Let It Be Told: Black Women Writers in Britain.* Recently, her poetry was anthologised in *An Intimate Wilderness*, Eighth Mountain Press, Oregon, 1991.

GILLIAN SPRAGGS was studying Greek at school when a friend lent her Sappho's poems in translation and she was fired with enthusiasm to read the originals. This began an obsession which has lasted 20 years. She is a former teacher and has published essays and articles on a number of educational and literary topics, including 'Section 28 and Education', with Sue Sanders, in *Learning Our Lines: Sexuality and Social Control in Education,* eds. Carol Jones and Pat Mahoney, The Women's Press, London, 1989; and 'Exiled to Home: the Poetry of Sylvia Townsend Warner and Valentine Ackland' in *Lesbian and Gay Writing: An Anthology of Critical Essays*, ed. Mark Lilly, Macmillan, London, 1990. She is a regular contributor to *Rouge* magazine.

GITI THADANI: born in 1961, a product of tropical fire, a school and institutional dropout negotiating the spaces between that of a nomadic intellectual and international bum. Thriving on ecstatic madness and lesbian eros in all its plural manifestations.

CHRIS WHITE has been queer for as long as she can remember, and a lesbian since 1986. She is from a white working-class Hampshire family, and now lives with her lover Elaine Hobby in great happiness. She is a part-time lecturer at Loughborough University, and has published an essay on Michael Field, to be reprinted in *Sexual Sameness: Textual Differences in Lesbian and Gay Writing*, ed. Joseph Bristow, Routledge, London, 1992. She is currently finishing a Ph.D. thesis on nineteenth-century homosexual and lesbian writing.

LIZ YORKE was born in 1941, of white working-class parents – mother a psychiatric nurse and a socialist, father a bricklayer and a musician. She worked for six years as a general nurse before doing the expected thing. After having three children, she returned as a mature student to Manchester Polytechnic, where she has worked as a part-timer teaching women's writing (among other things) since 1982. Coming out as a lesbian has been a long-drawn-out process, but at last she is out in the teaching context. She is also interested in using creative writing (of poetry) as therapy and works part-time as a counsellor. Her forthcoming book is called *Impertinent Voices: Strategies of Subversion in Contemporary Women's Poetry,* Routledge, London, 1991. Her recently completed PhD thesis is entitled 'Re-Visionary Mythmaking in the Work of Adrienne Rich and Other Women Poets'.

BIBLIOGRAPHY

Unless otherwise specified, the place of publication is London.

Abbott, Sidney and Barbara Love, *Sappho was a Right-On Woman: A Liberated View of Lesbianism*, Stein and Day, New York, 1985; first published 1972

Aers, David and Bob Hodge, 'Rational Burning: Milton on Sex and Marriage', *Milton Studies* 12, 1979

Aggarwal, P K, *Goddesses in Ancient India*, Prithvi Prakashan, Varnasi, India

Alcyonius, Petrus, *Medices Legatus De Exsilio*, Aldus, Venice, 1522

Arnold, June, *Sister Gin*, The Women's Press, 1979; first published 1975

Atharva Ved, Sanskrit text dating from about 500 BC tr. W.D Whitney, Harvard Oriental series, Harvard University, 1905

Baker, Ida, *Katherine Mansfield: The Memories of L M*, Michael Joseph, London, 1971

Balmer, Josephine, trans., *Sappho. Poems and Fragments*, Brilliance Books, London, 1984

Blatchford, Roy, *Hear Me Out*, Longman, Harlow, 1987

Bowlby, Rachel, *Virginia Woolf: Feminist Destinations*, Basil Blackwell, Oxford, 1988

Bowra, C M, *Greek Lyric Poetry from Alcman to Simonides*, second edition, Clarendon Press, Oxford, 1961

Brailsford, Mabel, *Quaker Women 1650–1690*, Duckworth, 1915
   *A Brief Relation of the Persecutions and Cruelties that have been
   Acted upon the People called Quakers*, 1662
Brittain, Vera, *Radclyffe Hall: A Case of Obscenity?* Femina
   Books, 1968
Broadbent, John, ed., *Poets of the Seventeenth Century*, two
   volumes, Signet Classics, New York, 1974
Brome, Vincent, *Havelock Ellis, Philosopher of Sex: A Biography*,
   Routledge and Kegan Paul, 1979
Browne, F W Stella, 'The Sexual Variety and Variability among
   Women and their Bearing upon Social Reconstruction', *The
   British Society for the Study of Sex Psychology: No. 3*, 1917
Broumas, Olga, *Beginning with O*, Yale University Press, New
   Haven, 1977
Bühler, G., *The Laws of Manu, Translated with Extracts from Seven
   Commentaries*, Clarendon Press, Oxford, 1886
Bulkin, Elly, 'An Interview: Audre Lorde and Adrienne Rich', in
   Sister Outsider, vol. 1, no. 1, p.98
— 'An Interview with Adrienne Rich: Part 2', *Conditions*, vol. 1,
   no. 2, 1977
Burford, Barbara, *The Threshing Floor*, Sheba Feminist Pub-
   lishers, 1986
Burford, Barbara, Jackie Kay, Grace Nichols and Gabriela
   Pearse, *A Dangerous Knowing: Four Black Women Poets*, Sheba
   Feminist Publishers, 1985
Burford, Barbara, Lindsay MacRae and Sylvia Paskin, eds.,
   Dancing the Tightrope: New Love Poems by Women, The
   Women's Press, 1987
Burnett, Anne Pippin, *Three Archaic Poets: Archilochus, Alcaeus,
   Sappho*, Duckworth, 1983
Calder-Marshall, Arthur, *Havelock Ellis: A Biography*, Rupert
   Hart-Davis, 1959
Cameron, Anne, *Daughters Of Copper Woman*, The Women's
   Press, 1984, Press Gang Publishers, Vancouver, 1981
Campbell, David A, ed., *Greek Lyric*, volume 1, Loeb Classical
   Library, Harvard University Press, Cambridge, Massachusetts,
   1982
Chicago, Judy, *The Dinner Party: A Symbol of Our Heritage*,
   Anchor/Doubleday, New York, 1979
Chicago, Judy, with Susan Hill, *Embroidering Our Heritage: The
   Dinner Party Network*, Anchor/Doubleday, New York

Choong, Da, Olivette Cole-Wilson, Bernardine Evaristo and Gabriela Pearse, eds., *Black Women Talk Poetry* Black Womantalk, 1987

Cixous, Hélène, 'The Laugh of the Medusa', *Signs: Journal of Women in Culture and Society*, vol. 1, no. 4, 1976; reprinted in Elaine Marks and Isabelle de Courtivron, eds., *New French Feminisms: An Anthology*, Harvester Press, Brighton, 1981

Cobham, Rhonda and Merle Collins, eds., *Watchers and Seekers: Creative Writing by Black Women in Britain*, The Women's Press, 1987

Colvin, Madeleine, *Section 28: A Practical Guide to the Law and its Implications*, National Council for Civil Liberties, 1989

Cook, Blanche Wiesen, ' "Women Alone Stir My Imagination": Lesbianism and the Cultural Tradition', *Signs: Journal of Women in Culture and Society*, vol. 4, no. 4, 1979

Cotton, Priscilla, and Mary Cole, *To the Priests and People of England*, 1655

Coward, Rosalind, and Linda Semple, 'Tracking down the Past. Women and Detective Fiction', in Helen Carr, ed., *From My Guy to Sci Fi: Genre and Women's Writing in the Postmodern World*, Pandora Press, 1989

Day, Gary, 'Investigating the Investigator: Hammett's Continental Op', in Brian Docherty, ed., *American Crime Fiction*, Macmillan, Basingstoke, 1988

Decker-Hauff, Hans-Martin, ed., *Die Chronik der Grafen von Zimmern*, three volumes, Stuttgart, 1967

DeJean, Joan, *Fictions of Sappho, 1546–1937*, University of Chicago Press, Chicago, 1989

Devereux, George, 'The Nature of Sappho's Seizure in Fr. 31 LP as Evidence of Her Inversion', *Classical Quarterly*, new series, 20, 1970

Dollimore, Jonathan, 'The Dominant and the Deviant: A Violent Dialectic', *Critical Quarterly*, vol. 28, nos. 1/2, 1986

D[oolittle], H[ilda], *Collected Poems 1912–44*, Carcanet, Manchester, 1984; first published 1925

Dorcey, Mary, 'Photographs', in *Kindling*, Onlywomen Press, 1982

Dover, K J, *Greek Homosexuality*, Vintage Books, New York, 1980; first published 1978

Dreher, Sarah, *Stoner McTavish*, Pandora, 1987

DuPlessis, Rachel Blau, 'For the Etruscans', in Elaine Showalter, ed., *The New Feminist Criticism: Essays on Women, Literature and Theory*, Virago, 1986

Edmonds, J M, ed., *Lyra Graeca*, volume 1, Loeb Classical Library, Heinemann, 1922

Edwards, M J, 'Greek into Latin: A Note on Catullus and Sappho', *Latomus*, vol. 48, no. 3, 1989

Ellis, Edith, 'Eugenics and the Mystical Outlook', in Edith Ellis, *The New Horizon in Love and Life*, 1921

— *The Mine of Dreams: Selected Short Stories* A & C Black, 1925

— *The New Horizon in Love and Life*, A & C Black, 1921

— *Stories and Essays* I, Free Spirit Press, New York, 1924

— *Stories and Essays* II, Free Spirit Press, New York, 1924

— *Three Modern Seers: James Hinton, Frederic Nietzsche, Edward Carpenter*, Stanley Paul and Co., 1910

Ellis, Havelock, *My Life*, Heinemann, 1940

Ellis, Havelock, and John Addington Symonds, *Sexual Inversion*, Wilson and MacMillan, 1897

Evans, J M, *Paradise Lost and the Genesis Tradition*, Clarendon Press, Oxford, 1968

Evans, Mari, ed., *Black Women Writers: Arguments and Interviews*, Pluto Press, Sydney, 1985

Faderman, Lillian, *Surpassing the Love of Men: Romantic Friendship and Love Between Women from the Renaissance to the Present,* Junction Books, 1981; The Women's Press, 1985

Feminist Review 17, 1984

Forrest, Katherine V, *Amateur City*, Naiad Press, Tallahassee, 1984; Pandora, 1987

— *Murder at the Nightwood Bar*, Pandora, 1987

Foucault, Michel, *History of Sexuality Volume One: An Introduction*, Penguin, Harmondsworth, 1979

Fox, Robin Lane, *Pagans and Christians in the Mediterranean World from the Second Century AD to the Conversion of Constantine*, Penguin, Harmondsworth, 1988

Franks, Claudia Stillman, *Beyond the Well of Loneliness: The Fiction of Radclyffe Hall*, Avebury, 1982

Freeman, Jo, *The Politics of Women's Liberation: A Case Study of an Emerging Social Movement and Its Relation to the Policy Process*, Longman, Harlow, 1975

Frye, Marilyn, *The Politics of Reality: Essays in Feminist Theory*, The Crossing Press, Trumansburg, 1983

Fryer, Peter, *Staying Power: The History of Black People in Britain*, Pluto Press, 1984

Gardiner, Judith Kegan, 'Mind Mother: Psychoanalysis and Feminism', in Gayle Greene and Coppélia Kahn, eds., *Making a Difference: Feminist Literary Criticism*, Methuen, 1985

Gearheart, Sally, and Susan Rennie, *A Feminist Tarot*, Persephone Press, Massachusetts, 1981

Giacomelli, Anne, 'The Justice of Aphrodite in Sappho Fr. 1', *Transactions of the American Philological Association* 110, 1980

Graham, Elspeth, Hilary Hinds, Elaine Hobby and Helen Wilcox, eds., *Her Own Life: Autobiographical Writings by Seventeenth-Century Englishwomen*, Routledge, 1989

Grahn, Judy, *The Work of a Common Woman*, Onlywomen Press, 1985

— *Another Mother Tongue: Gay Words, Gay Worlds*, Beacon Press, Boston, 1984

Grahn, Judy, and Pat Parker, *Where Would I Be Without You: The Poetry of Pat Parker and Judy Grahn*, Olivia Records, Los Angeles, 1976

Greene, Gayle and Coppélia Kahn, eds., *Making a Difference: Feminist Literary Criticism*, Methuen, 1985

Greer, Germaine, Susan Hastings, Jeslyn Medoff and Melinda Sansone, eds., *Kissing the Rod: An Anthology of 17th Century Women's Verse*, Virago, 1988

Grewal, Shabnam, Jackie Kay, Liliane Landor, Gail Lewis and Pratibha Parmar, eds., *Charting the Journey: Writings by Black and Third World Women*, Sheba Feminist Publishers, 1988

Griffin, Susan, *Made From This Earth: Selections from her Writings 1967–1982*, The Women's Press, 1982

Grosz, Elizabeth, *Sexual Subversions: Three French Feminists*, Allen and Unwin, Sydney, 1989

Hall, Radclyffe, *The Unlit Lamp*, Virago, 1981; first published 1924 *The Well of Loneliness*, Virago, 1982; first published 1928

Hallett, Judith P, 'Sappho and Her Social Context: Sense and Sensuality', *Signs: Journal of Women in Culture and Society*, vol. 4, no. 4, 1979

Hamilton, Roberta, *The Liberation of Women: A Study of Patriarchy and Capitalism*, Allen and Unwin, 1978

Hemming, Mary and Jan Bradshaw, eds., *Girls Next Door: Lesbian Feminist Stories*, The Women's Press, 1985

Hensman, Savitri, *Flood at the Door*, Centreprise, 1979

Hill, Christopher, *Milton and the English Revolution*, Faber and Faber, London, 1977

— *The World Turned Upside Down: Radical Ideas During the English Revolution*, Penguin, Harmonsdworth, 1975

Hobby, Elaine, *Virtue of Necessity: English Women's Writing 1649–1688*, Virago, 1988

Hurcombe, Linda, *Sex and God: Varieties of Women's Religious Experience*, Routledge and Kegan Paul, 1987

Irigaray, Luce, 'Women's Exile', translated by Couze Venn, *Ideology and Consciousness* 1, 1977

— 'When Our Lips Speak Together', translated by Carolyn Burke, *Signs: Journal of Women in Culture and Society*, vol. 6, no. 1, 1980

Jacobus, Mary, 'The Difference of View', in Mary Jacobus, ed., *Women Writing and Writing about Women*, Croom Helm, 1979

Jaiminiya Brahman, sacrificial text dating from about 500BC

Jeffreys, Sheila, *Anticlimax: A Feminist Perspective on the Sexual Revolution*, The Women's Press, 1990

— *The Spinster and Her Enemies: Feminism and Sexuality 1880–1930*, Pandora, London, 1985

Jenkyns, Richard, *Three Classical Poets: Sappho, Catullus and Juvenal*, Duckworth, 1982

Joreen, 'The Tyranny of Structurelessness', in Anne Koedt, Ellen Levine and Anita Rapone, eds., *Radical Feminism*, Quadrangle, New York, 1973

Kalika Khand, Shaktic text written between 500 AD and mediaeval times

Kanter, Hannah, Sarah Lefanu, Sheila Shah and Carole Spedding, eds., *Sweeping Statements: Writings from the Women's Liberation Movement 1981–83*, The Women's Press, 1984

Kaplan, Cora, 'An Unsuitable Genre for a Feminist?', *Women's Review* 8, 1986

Kathak Samhita, sacrificial text dating from about 500 BC

Kay, Jackie, *The Adoption Poetry*, Bloodaxe Books, Newcastle-upon-Tyne, 1991

— *Chiaroscuro*, in *Lesbian Plays*, ed. Jill Davis, Methuen, 1987

— *Twice Over*, in *Gay Sweatshop: Four Plays and a Company*, ed. Philip Osmet, Methuen, 1989

Kennard, Jean E, 'Ourself behind Ourself: A Theory of Lesbian

Readers', in Estelle B Freedman, et al, eds., *The Lesbian Issue: Essays from Signs*, University of Chicago Press, Chicago, 1982

Kirkwood, G M, *Early Greek Monody: The History of a Poetic Type*, Cornell Studies in Classical Philology 37, Cornell University Press, Ithaca, 1974

Knight, Stephen, ' "A Hard Cheerfulness": An Introduction to Raymond Chandler', in Brian Docherty, ed., *American Crime Fiction*, Macmillan, Basingstoke, 1988

Lacan, Jacques, *The Four Fundamental Concepts of Psychoanalysis*, ed. by Jacques-Alain Miller, trans. by Alan Sheridan, Penguin, Harmondsworth, 1979

Leach, Edmund, *Genesis as Myth and Other Essays*, Cape, 1969

Le Carré, John, *Smiley's People*, Hodder and Stoughton, 1980

Le Comte, Edward, *Milton and Sex*, Macmillan, 1978

Lee, Hermione, *The Novels of Virginia Woolf*, Methuen, 1977

Light, Alison, 'Writing Fictions: Femininity and the 1950s', in Jean Radford, ed., *The Progress of Romance: The Politics of Popular Fiction*, Routledge, 1986

Lobel, Edgar, and Denys Page, eds., *Poetarum Lesbiorum Fragmenta*, Clarendon Press, Oxford, 1955

Lorde, Audre, *The Black Unicorn: Poems*, W W Norton and Company, New York, 1978

— *The Cancer Journals*, Spinsters Ink, San Francisco, 1980

— *Chosen Poems: Old and New*, W W Norton and Company, New York, 1982

— 'My Words Will Be There', in Mari Evans, ed., *Black Women Writers: Arguments and Interviews*, Pluto Press, 1983

— *Sister Outsider: Essays and Speeches*, The Crossing Press, Trumansburg, 1984

— *Zami: A New Spelling Of My Name*, Sheba Feminist Publishers, 1982

McDermid, Val, *Report for Murder*, The Women's Press, 1987

McGregor, J F, and B Reay, eds., *Radical Religion in the English Revolution*, Oxford University Press, Oxford, 1984

Mack, Phyllis, 'Women as Prophets During the English Civil War', *Feminist Studies 8*, 1982

MacLachlan, Bonnie, 'What's crawling in Sappho Fr. 130', *Phoenix*, vol. 43, no. 2, 1989

Mahabhagvat Puran, Shaktic text written between 500 AD and mediaeval times

Maitrani Samhita, sacrificial text dating from about 500 BC

Malekin, Peter, *Liberty and Love: English Literature and Society, 1640–88*, Hutchinson, 1981

Manning, Rosemary, *The Chinese Garden*, Brilliance Books, 1984; first published 1962

— *A Corridor of Mirrors*, The Women's Press, 1987

— *A Time and a Time: An Autobiography*, Marion Boyars, 1986; first published 1971

Mansfield, Katherine, *Journal of Katherine Mansfield*, ed. by J Middleton Murry, Constable, 1962

March, Caeia, *Three Ply Yarn*, The Women's Press, 1986

— *The Hide and Seek Files*, The Women's Press, 1989

— *Fire! Fire!* The Women's Press, 1991

Marcovich, M, 'Sappho Fr. 31: Anxiety Attack or Love Declaration?', *Classical Quarterly*, new series, 22, 1972

Marks, Elaine, and Isabelle de Courtivron, *New French Feminisms: An Anthology*, Harvester Press, Brighton, 1981

Milton, John, *Paradise Lost*, ed. Alastair Fowler, Longman, Harlow, 1968

Mohin, Lilian, ed., *Beautiful Barbarians: Lesbian Feminist Poetry*, Onlywomen Press, 1986

Mort, Frank, *Dangerous Sexualities: Medico-Moral Politics in England since 1830*, Routledge and Kegan Paul, 1987

MotherTongue 4/5, Brighton Polytechnic Women's Group, eds. Kris Black et al, Brighton, 1986

Munt, Sally, 'The Investigators: Lesbian Crime Fiction', in Susannah Radstone, ed., *Sweet Dreams: Sexuality, Gender and Popular Fiction*, Lawrence and Wishart, 1988

Murry, John Middleton, ed., *Letters of Katherine Mansfield to John Middleton Murry*, Constable, 1951

Nestle, Joan, 'Butch-Femme Relationships: Sexual Courage in the 1950s', in *A Restricted Country*, Firebrand Books, New York, 1987; Sheba Feminist Publishers, 1987

— 'My History with Censorship', in *A Restricted Country*, Firebrand Books, New York, 1987; Sheba Feminist Publishers, 1987.

Newton, Esther, 'The Mythic Mannish Lesbian: Radclyffe Hall and the New Woman', *Signs: Journal of Women in Culture and Society*, vol. 9, no. 4, 1984

Ngcobo, Laura, ed., *Let It Be Told: Black Women Writers in Britain*, Virago, 1988

Nicolson, Nigel, and Joanne Trautmann, eds., *The Letters of*

Virginia Woolf, Volume 3, Harcourt Brace Jovanovich, New York, 1977

Noble, Vicki, *Motherpeace: A Way to the Goddess through Myth, Art and Tarot*, Harper and Row, San Francisco, 1983

Nyquist, Mary, 'The Genesis of Gendered Subjectivity in the Divorce Tracts and in *Paradise Lost*', in Mary Nyquist and Margaret W Ferguson, eds., *Re-Membering Milton: Essays on the Texts and Traditions*, Methuen, New York & London, 1987

O'Flaherty, Wendy, *Divine Consort*, ed. J S Hawley and D M Wulff, Graduate Theology Union, Berkeley, 1982

Oram, Alison, ' "Embittered, Sexless or Homosexual": Attacks on Spinster Teachers 1918–1939', in The Lesbian History Group, eds., *Not a Passing Phase: Reclaiming Lesbians in History 1840–1985*, The Women's Press, 1989

O'Rourke, Rebecca, *Jumping the Cracks*, Virago, 1987

— *Reflecting On The Well of Loneliness*, Routledge, 1989

Ostriker, Alicia, *Writing Like a Woman*, University of Michigan Press, Ann Arbor, 1983

— *Stealing the Language: The Emergence of Women's Poetry in America*, The Women's Press, 1987

O'Sullivan, Sue, *Turning the Tables: Recipes and Reflections from Women*, Sheba Feminist Publishers, 1988

Page, Denys, *Sappho and Alcaeus: An Introduction to the Study of Ancient Lesbian Poetry*, Clarendon Press, Oxford, 1955

Palmer, Jerry, *Thrillers: Genesis and Structure of a Popular Genre*, Edward Arnold, 1978

Parker, Pat, *Movement in Black*, The Crossing Press, Trumansburg, 1983

Parker, Pat and Judy Grahn, *Where Would I Be Without You: The Poetry of Pat Parker and Judy Grahn*, Olivia Records, Los Angeles, 1976

Paskin, Sylvia, J Ramsay and J Silva, eds., *Angels of Fire: An Anthology of Radical Poetry in the 1980s*, Chatto and Windus, 1986

Pearson, K, *Darwinism, Medical Progress and Eugenics: The Cavendish Lecture: An Address to the Medical Profession*, University College, 1912

Philips, Katherine, *Poems*, 1667

Raymond, Janice, *A Passion for Friends*, The Women's Press, 1986

Rich, Adrienne, 'Compulsory Heterosexuality and Lesbian

Existence', in Ann Snitow, Christine Stansell and Sharon Thompson, eds, *Desire: The Politics of Sexuality*, Virago, 1984

— *The Dream of a Common Language: Poems 1974–1977*, W W Norton and Company, New York, 1978

— *Of Woman Born: Motherhood as Experience and Institution*, Virago, 1977

— *On Lies, Secrets and Silence: Selected Prose 1966–1978*, Virago, 1980

Rig Ved, Sanskrit text dating from earlier than 1500 BC ed. Sitarma Sastri, trans. Sitanatha Pradhana, India Research Institute, Calcutta, 1933

Robbins, Emmet, ' "Every time I look at you . . .": Sappho Thirty-One', *Transactions of the American Philological Association*, 110, 1980

Rollason, Christopher, 'The Detective Myth in Edgar Allen Poe's Dupin Trilogy', in Brian Docherty, ed., *American Crime Fiction*, Macmillan, 1988

Rolley, Katrina, 'Cutting a Dash: The Dress of Radclyffe Hall and Una Troubridge', *Feminist Review* 35, 1990

Rose, Phyllis, *Life of Virginia Woolf*, Routledge and Regan Paul, 1978

Ruehl, Sonja, 'Inverts and Experts: Radclyffe Hall and the Lesbian Identity', in Rosalind Brunt and Caroline Rowan, eds., *Feminism, Culture and Politics*, Lawrence and Wishart, 1982; reprinted in Judith Newton and Deborah Rosenfelt, eds., *Feminist Criticism and Social Change*, Methuen, 1985

Rule, Jane, *Desert of the Heart*, Pandora, 1986

— *Lesbian Images*, The Crossing Press, Trumansburg, 1982; Pluto Press, 1989; first published 1975

— *Memory Board*, Pandora, 1987

Ryan, Joanna, 'Psychoanalysis and Women Loving Women', in Sue Cartledge and Joanna Ryan, eds., *Sex and Love: New Thoughts on Old Contradictions*, The Women's Press, 1983

Sachs, Nelly, *In den Wohnungen des Todes*, Aufbau-verlag, Berlin, 1947

Saïd, Edward W, *Orientalism*, Penguin, Harmondsworth, 1985; first published 1978

Sastri, Sitarma, ed., *Rig Ved*, trans. by Sitanatha Pradhana, Indian Research Institute, Calcutta, 1933

Scaliger, Joseph, *Scaligeriana: Editio Altera*, The Hague, 1666

Shepherd, Simon, and Mick Wallis, eds., *Coming on Strong: Gay Politics and Culture*, Unwin Hyman, 1989

Showalter, Elaine, *The New Feminist Criticism: Essays on Women, Literature and Theory*, Pantheon Books, New York, 1985; Virago, 1986

Silverstolpe, Frederic, 'Benkert Was Not a Doctor: On the Non-Medical Origin of the Homosexual Category in the Nineteenth Century', in *Papers of the Conference 'Homosexuality, Which Homosexuality?'* (a conference in lesbian and gay studies), History Volume 1, Free University/Schorer Foundation, Amsterdam 1987

Souers, Philip, *The Matchless Orinda*, Harvard University Press, Cambridge, Massachusetts, 1931

Spearhead Nov/Dec 1968

Spretnak, Charlene, ed., *The Politics of Women's Spirituality: Essays on the Rise of Spiritual Power Within the Feminist Movement*, Anchor Books, New York, 1982

Stetson, Erlene, ed., *Black Sister: Poetry by Black American Women, 1746–1980*, Indiana Press, Bloomington, 1981

Stigers, Eva Stehle, 'Romantic Sensuality, Poetic Sense: A Response to Hallett on Sappho', *Signs: Journal of Women in Culture and Society*, vol. 4, no. 4, 1979

Stimpson, Catherine R, 'Zero Degree Deviancy: The Lesbian Novel in English', in Elizabeth Abel, ed., *Writing and Sexual Difference*, Harvester Press, Brighton, 1982

Styles, Morag, ed., *You'll Love This Stuff*, Cambridge University Press, Cambridge, 1986

Sulter, Maud, *As A Black Woman*, Akira Press, 1986; Urban Fox, Hebden Bridge, West Yorkshire, 1989

Symons, Julian, *Bloody Murder: From the Detective Story to the Crime Novel: A History*, Penguin, Harmondsworth, 1972

Tey, Josephine, *Miss Pym Disposes*, Peter Davies, 1946

Thompson, Tierl, *Dear Girl: The Diaries and Letters of Two Working Women 1897–1917*, The Women's Press, 1986

Vicinus, Martha, 'Distance and Desire: English Boarding-School Friendships', in Estelle B Freedman, et al, eds., *The Lesbian Issue: Essays from Signs*, University of Chicago Press, Chicago, 1982

Walker, Alice, *The Color Purple*, The Women's Press, 1983
You Can't Keep a Good Woman Down, The Women's Press, 1982

Wandor, Michelene, *Gardens of Eden: Poems for Eve and Lilith*, Journeyman/Playbooks, 1984

We Are Here: Blackfeminist Newsletter, 1985

Weeks, Jeffrey, *Coming Out: Homosexual Politics in Britain*, Quartet Books, 1977

Weigall, Arthur, *Sappho of Lesbos: Her Life and Times*, Thornton Butterworth, 1932

West, M L, 'Burning Sappho', *Maia* 22, 1970

White, Chris, 'The Organisation of Pleasure: British Homosexual Discourse, 1869–1914', Nottingham University Ph.D. thesis, 1992

Whitlock, Gillian, ' "Everything Is Out of Place": Radclyffe Hall and the Lesbian Literary Tradition', *Feminist Studies*, Vol. 13, no. 3, 1987

Wilde, Oscar, *De Profundis and Other Writings*, with an introduction by Hesketh Pearson, Penguin, Harmondsworth, 1973

Williams, Raymond, *Marxism and Literature*, Oxford University Press, Oxford, 1977

Wills, Garry, 'Sappho 31 and Catullus 51', *Greek, Roman and Byzantine Studies*, 8, 1967

Wilson, Barbara, *Ambitious Women*, Spinsters Ink, New York, 1982; The Women's Press, 1983

— *Murder in the Collective*, Seal Press, Washington, 1984; The Women's Press, 1984

— *Sisters of the Road*, The Women's Press, 1986

Wings, Mary, *She Came Too Late*, The Women's Press, 1986

Winkler, John J, 'Double Consciousness in Sappho's Lyrics', in *The Constraints of Desire: The Anthropology of Sex and Gender in Ancient Greece*, Routledge, 1990

Wittgenstein, Ludwig, *Tractatus Logico-Philosophicus*, 1922

Wittig, Monique, and Sande Zeig, *Lesbian Peoples: Materials for a Dictionary*, Virago, 1980

Wollstonecraft, Mary, *Mary and The Wrongs of Woman*, Oxford University Press, Oxford, 1983; first published 1788

— *Vindication of the Rights of Woman*, ed. Miriam Kramnick, Penguin, Harmondsworth, 1975; first published 1792

Woolf, Virginia, *Collected Essays I*, Chatto and Windus, 1967

— *The Common Reader*, Penguin, Harmondsworth, 1938; first published 1925

— *A Haunted House*, Granada Publishing, 1982; first published 1944

— *Mrs Dalloway*, Granada Publishing, 1976; first published 1925
— *Orlando*, Penguin, Harmondsworth, 1963; first published 1928
— *A Room of One's Own*, Granada Publishing, 1981; first published 1929
— *Women and Writing*, The Women's Press, 1979
— *A Writer's Diary*, Triad Panther, St Albans, 1978
Yogini Hradya, Shaktic text written between 500 AD and mediaeval times
Zimmerman, Bonnie, 'Exiting from Patriarchy: The Lesbian Novel of Development', in Elizabeth Abel, Marianne Hirsch and Elizabeth Langland, eds., *The Voyage In*, University of New England Press, Hanover, 1983

INDEX

Abbott, Sidney 141
academic curriculum *see* mainstream academic curriculum
Adam 205–7, 209, 209–10, 211, 213, 214–17, 218–19, 220, 223
Aditi 171, 172
Africa 39, 45; *see also* Egypt; Ghana; Nigeria; Rhodesia
Aggarwal, P K 179
Akimbo 228
Alcaeus 51, 53
Alcyonius, Petrus 66
Anactoria 53
Anchises 57
Andoh, Adjoa 228, 232, 233
androgyny 69, 72, 73, 188
Aphrodite 57–64, 65
Apollo 196
Archilochus 56
Arnold, June 26
Asian Women's Writing Group 230
Atharva Ved 175, 179
Artemis 53
Atthis 53

Aubrey, Mary (Rosania) 191
autobiography 53, 61, 146, 150; *see also* biography

Baker, Ida (L[esley] M[oore]) 115–16, 118, 119–23, 125, 126, 130–1, 133
Balmer, Josephine 64
Baptists 184, 185
Barbados 234
Barney, Natalie 91
Bax, Daphne 71, 72–3
Beauchamp, Leslie 115, 116–18, 121, 123
de Beauvoir, Simone 33
Benkert, K M 70
Bible 142, 148, 205–7, 208, 216, 217, 219, 220–1, 224
Biddle, Hester 185, 186–7, 202
biography 3, 112, 113–14; *see also* autobiography
Birmingham Repertory 228
bisexuality 45, 47, 112, 130
Blacklesbian and Gay Centre Project, London 231
Black Lesbian Group 232

Blacklesbianism 3, 4, 38–9, 88, 189, 249; *see also* zamis
Black Lesbian Support Network 234
Black Woman Talk Collective 230, 234, 236, 237
Black Women's Creativity Project 235
Blackwomen's movement 226–7
Blake, William 61, 135
Blatchford, Roy 238
Boa, Elizabeth 5
body, theories of 28–46
Bowden, George 119
Bowlby, Rachel 106
Bowra, C M 61, 66
Brailsford, Mabel 202
Brimstone, Lyndie 2, 3, 256
Brittain, Vera 94
Brixton Black Women's Group 234
Broadbent, John 190, 193
Brome, Vincent 84
Bromley, De 5
Brontë, Charlotte *Jane Eyre* 147
Broumas, Olga 36–8, 42, 43, 47
Browne, F W Stella 78, 95, 96
Burford, Barbara 228–9, 235, 242
Burnett, Anne Pippin 65, 67
butch 19–20, 139, 140, 144, 248
Byron, Lord George Gordon Noel 135

Calder-Marshall, Arthur *Havelock Ellis: A Biography* 84
Cameron, Anne, *Daughters of Copper Woman* 246, 249
Campaign Against Pornography 255
Campbell, David A 64, 65, 66
capitalism 11, 16, 18, 80
Caribbean 231, 233, 234, 236, 254
Carpenter, Edward 73, 77, 95
Chandler, Raymond 10, 11, 14, 16
Charles I 184, 211
Charles II 192
Cheevers, Sarah 184–5, 186–7, 202

Choong, Da 237
Christianity 37, 51, 52, 117, 139, 150, 158, 184, 206, 207, 212–13, 222, 231; *see also* Bible; God; Jesus Christ
Christie, Agatha 10, 11, 25
Cixous, Hélène 46, 47–8
class 10, 33, 77, 78, 98; *see also* middle class; working class
Clause 28 of the Local Government Act 1988 146–7, 241, 243, 255; *see also* Section 28 of the Local Government Act 1988
Cleaver, Robert *A Godley Form of Household Government* 220
Cleopatra 138, 139
Cobham, Rhonda 238
Cole, Mary 224
Cole-Wilson, Olivette 237
Coleridge, Samuel Taylor 135
Collecott, Diana 153
Collins, Merle 238
colonialism 149, 160, 189, 245, 250; *see also* eurocentrism; racism
Colombia 233
Colvin, Madeleine 107–8
Corneille, Pierre, *Pompeé* 183
Cotton, Priscilla 224
Coward, Rosalind 26
Cowley, Abraham 189–90
cummings, e e 135
Cunning Stunts, The 244–5

Daly, Mary 29, 34, 46
Dane, Clemence 135, 138–9, 153
Daniels, Sarah *Masterpieces* 255
Daphne 196
Davy, Sarah 185, 186–7, 202
Day, Gary 26
Deem, Rosemary 154
Deighton, Len 15
DeJean, Joan 65
desire: cultural specificity of 2; hidden 92, 112–13, 114, 125–9,

desire (cont.)
131, 141–2, 147, 148, 191, 195–
6; historical variants in 2, 57;
for husband 116, 131; and
identity 30, 158, 177; and
language 1, 2, 34, 142–3; male
heterosexual 211; and pain 56–
7; power of taboo desire 129; in
Sappho's poetry 54–8; *see also*
eroticism; gaze; sensuality
Devereux, George 66
Dickens, Charles 14
Diodati, Charles 217
divinities 155–9; see also
goddesses; gods; Kali
Dod, John *A Godley Form of
Household Government* 220
Dollimore, Jonathan 202
domination and submission 3, 22;
see also sadomasochism
Donne, John 193, 200, 201
Doolittle, Hilda (H D) 112, 138,
148
Dorcey, Mary 255
Douglas, Lord Alfred (Bosie) 85
Dover, Kenneth 62, 66
Doyle, Sir Arthur Conan 11, 14,
24
Dreher, Sarah 12; *Stoner
McTavish* 25
Duiguid, Nancy 254
Duncker, Patricia 2, 3, 256
Du Plessis, Rachel Blau 28
Duras, Marguerite 46

Eden, Garden of 1, 116–17, 118–
19, 142, 205–7, 212, 215
Edmonds, J M 65
Edwards, M J 67
Egypt 189
Eliot, T S 135
Ellis, Edith 2, 68–85
Ellis, Havelock 68–9, 73–5, 77,
79, 82, 95, 98, 140
English National Opera 232
Eros 58, 64
eroticism: butch–femme 20;

eroticism (cont.)
heterosexual 210–11; history of
20, 57; and language 43–4;
lesbian 20, 29, 30, 41–2, 43–4,
53, 103, 125, 162–4, 184, 186,
189–202; mystical 123, 156; and
reading 161; sub-eroticism 72–
3; suitable subject for poetry
53–4; *see also* desire;
sadomasochism; sensuality; sex
essentialism 21, 69–70
eugenics 68, 69, 76–83
eurocentrism 149, 226; *see also*
colonialism; racism
Evans, Katherine 184–5, 186–7,
202
Evans, J M 223
Evans, Mari, *Black Women
Writers* 48
Evaristo, Bernardine 229–30,
231–2, 232
Eve 205–7, 209–10, 211, 212, 214–
17, 218–20, 220–2, 223, 229

Fabian Society 77
Faderman, Lillian 66, 107, 186
Fellowship of the New Life 77
femininity 12, 15, 69, 75, 80–1, 98,
134, 144, 165–78
femme 20, 139, 140, 144, 248
Fleming, Ian 10, 15, 21, 24
Forrest, Katherine V 12–13, 22;
Amateur City 22, 24; *Murder at
the Nightwood Bar* 13, 19–21,
23, 24, 25
Foster, Jeannette H 153
Foucault, Michel 69–70, 187, 188
see also Foucauldian theory
Foucauldian theory 3, 70
see also Foucault Michel
Fowler, John 183
Fowler, Katherine (Oxenbridge)
183, 191
Fox, Robin Lane 67
France 119, 120
Franks, Claudia Stillman 90
Freeman, Jo 26

friendship between women 20, 54, 71, 120–3, 125, 146, 147, 184–6, 191, 243, 249
Freud, Sigmund 30, 39, 95, 96; *see also* Freudian theory
Freudian theory 29, 30, 101; *see also* Freud, Sigmund
Frye, Marilyn 224
Fryer, Peter 203

Galton, Francis 76
Gardiner, Judith Kegan 27
gay liberation 87, 187
Gay Sweatshop 228, 232
gaze 22, 32–3, 157, 170; *see also* desire
Ghana 228
Giacomelli, Anne 62
God 3, 37–8, 118, 121, 156, 184, 185, 206, 207, 208, 209, 210, 211, 213, 214, 216, 218, 219, 220, 221–3; *see also* Baptists; Christianity; divinities; goddesses; gods; Quakers; Seekers
gods 3, 55, 56–7, 58, 157, 160, 196, 206, 207, 216
  see also divinities; God; goddesses; Hinduism; Ram
goddesses 3, 57, 58–64, 156, 246
  see also divinities; God; gods; Hinduism; Ida; Kali; Maya; Shiva; Sita, Urvashi
Gongyla 53
Gouge, William 213
governesses 91, 97, 99, 102; *see also* teachers
Grahn, Judy 243, 249
Greenham Common 245
Greer, Germaine 46, 203
Grewal, Shabnam 230–1, 232, 236, 237
Griffin, Gabriele 2, 3, 257
Griffin, Susan 34–5
Grosz, Elizabeth 28–9
Guardian 154
Gulf War, 1991 253

Gyrinno 53

HD, *see* Doolittle, Hilda
Hall, Radclyffe 2, 86–108
  The Well of Loneliness 86, 88–9, 90–2, 96, 97–9, 103, 104, 136–7, 140–1, 143, 143–4, 151, 243;
  The Unlit Lamp 89, 95, 96–9, 101–2
Hallett, Judith P 66
Hamilton, Roberta 224
Hammett, Dashiell 10, 11
Hanscombe, Gillian 2, 3
Harriss, Kathryn 202
headmistresses 15, 25, 134, 137, 143, 145
Hellman, Lillian 146
Hemming, Mary 258
Hennegan, Alison 143
Henrietta Maria 204
Hensman, Savitri 231
hermaphroditism *see* androgyny
Hesiod 67
heteropatriarchy 111, 112; *see also* heterosexuality; patriarchy
heterosexual: attitudes to lesbianism 1, 20, 24, 30, 45, 69, 70–5, 95–6, 146, 149, 190; language 30, 163–4; models of lesbianism 20, 50–1, 70–75, 94–5, 128, 131, 149, 156, 175–8, 188–9, 190, 244; religion 37, 70, 158; heterosexual sex 43, 96, 169, 211–12, 214–15, 248; *see also* heterosexuality; homophobia
heterosexuality: dissolution of 159–60; lesbian threat to 130; rejection of 135, 167, 196, 201; resistance to 52–3, 145, 216–17; structures of 205–6, 208–9, 211, 213
Hill, Christopher 202, 223, 224
Hinduism 155–79
Hinton, James 84
Hobby, Elaine 2, 3, 84, 224, 257, 260
Holland, Penny 253

Homer 57
homophobia 20, 41, 44; *see also* heterosexual
homosexuality: denial of 156; female 50, 147, 175–8; history of 3, 50–1, 63–4, 68, 69–71, 83, 94, 145, 184, 185–9, 202, 241; Indian 156, 157, 173–8; male 62, 68, 78, 79–80, 80–83, 102, 173–5, 217; promotion of 151; *see also* Clause 28; desire; inversion; inverts; lesbianism; Section 28
Hurcombe, Linda 47
husbands 68, 73, 95, 99, 114, 131, 185, 197, 213, 214, 218, 220

Ida 166, 167; *see also* goddesses
identity: and desire 30, 158, 177; formation of lesbian identity 28–49, 68, 89, 220; heterosexual 100; language and 29–30, 31–2, 36–8, 41, 45, 78, 80, 163; sexual 135–6, 140, 147, 187, 188; unified lesbian 88; *see also* subjectivity
incest 113, 114, 129
India 189, 230
individualism 16–17, 18, 49, 81, 152, 220
Indra 169
inversion 2, 68–9, 73–4, 75, 79–80, 80–83, 95–6, 98, 140; *see also* inverts; sexology
inverts 50, 76, 78, 244; *see also* inversion; sexology
Ireland 183, 193
Irigaray, Luce 29, 30, 32, 33, 34, 36; *see also* Irigarayan theory
Irigarayan theory 28–9; *see also* Irigaray, Luce
Isle of Man 241–2, 245
I-Spirit 235, 236

Jacobus, Mary 152
Jaiminiya Brahman 175
Jamaica 254

James, P D 15
Jeffreys, Sheila 107, 145
Jenkyns, Richard 66
Jesus Christ 209, 210, 214
Joreen 26–7
Judaism 206

Kali 155–9, 164
Kalika Khand 163–4, 177, 179
Kanter, Hannah 238
Kathak Samhita 173–4
Kay, Jackie 230, 232–3, 237
Kaplan, Cora 10, 25
Keats, John 135
Kennard, Jean E 152
Kirkwood, G M 65
Knight, Dame Jill 255
Knight, Stephen 26
Krafft-Ebing, Richard von 70
Kristeva, Julia 29
Kunjufu, Johari M 48

LM – *see* Baker, Ida
Lacan, Jacques 30, 36, 39
Lacanian theory 29, 30, 36, 39
Landor, Liliane 237
language: butch–femme 20; and desire 1, 2, 34, 142–3; erotic 43–4; and formation of identity 29–30, 31–2, 36–8, 41, 45, 78, 80, 163; heterosexual 30, 163–4; polysemy 142–3, 159, 161; and silence 162; struggle to create language 1, 2, 28, 34, 35, 38, 44–5, 78, 93, 159, 160; and subject–object relations 163–4; *see also* translation
Lawes, Henry 196
Lawrence, D H 99, 112, 122, 128; *see also* Lawrentian theory
Lawrence, Frieda 122
Lawrentian theory 102, 129 *see also* Lawrence, D H
Laws of Manu 175, 179
Leach, Edmund 223
Le Carré, John 11, 14
Le Comte, Edward 224

Lefanu, Sarah 238
lesbian feminism 9, 13, 19–20, 29,
    88; and spirituality 36–8, 42,
    43, 246;
    see also lesbianism; separatism
lesbianism: attitudes of
    heterosexuals to 1, 20, 24, 30,
    45, 69, 70–5, 90, 94–5, 128, 131,
    145, 146, 149, 156, 175–8, 190,
    241, 244; Blacklesbianism 3, 4,
    38–9, 88, 189, 249; and
    closetedness 2, 17, 20, 24, 105,
    134–54, 190, 201; definitions of
    50–1, 70–5, 79, 90, 140–1, 188–9,
    206, 226; history of 241; and
    incest 113, 114; relationship
    with feminism 3, 19–20, 21, 88,
    247; *see also* homosexuality;
    passing women; zamis
Lesbos 50, 51
Lewis, Gail 237
Light, Alison 145
Lilith 221, 222
literary criticism 1, 11, 52–3, 56,
    60–1, 103, 111, 112, 113–14,
    115–16, 123, 128–9, 190
Lobel, Edgar 64, 65
Lorde, Audre 43, 44–5, 48, 235,
    242, 248; *The Black Unicorn:
    Poems* 41–2, 45; *The Cancer
    Journal* 246; *Chosen Poems –
    Old and New* 39–40; 'My Words
    Will Be There' 40–1; *Sister
    Outsider* 42, 48; 'Uses of the
    Erotic – the Erotic as Power'
    42, 246–7; *Zami: A New
    Spelling of My Name* 45, 246,
    248, 249
Love, Barbara 140
Loy, Mina 112
Lucasia *see* Anne Owen

McDermid, Val, *Report for
    Murder* 15–16, 25
Mack, Phyllis 202
MacLachlan, Bonnie 67
MacRae, Lindsay 237

Mahabhagvat Puran 178
mainstream: academic curriculum
    3, 103, 112, 183; literary
    criticism 1, 11, 52–3, 56, 60–1,
    103, 111, 112, 115–16, 123,
    128–9, 190; literary tradition 9,
    136, 138, 142–3, 148, 150, 190,
    192–3, 195, 201, 215–16
Maitrani Samhita 173
Malekin, Peter, *Liberty and Love:
    English Literature and Society*
    204
Manchester University Press 3–4
Manning, Rosemary 2, 134–54;
    The Chinese Garden 134–54; *A
    Corridor of Mirrors* 150, 152; *A
    Time and a Time* 146–7, 150
Mansfield, Katherine 1, 2, 111–
    33; 'Bliss' 112, 113–15, 118,
    121, 122, 123–33; *Journal* 115,
    116–19, 129; letters 115, 119–
    22, 124–5, 131
March, Caeia 3, 21, 257–8
Marcovich, M 66, 67
Marriott, Charles 71–2
Mason, Libby 245
Maya 160, 163–4; *see also*
    goddesses
Meynell, Alice 148
middle class 14, 39, 147, 155; *see
    also* class
Migrant Film and Video
    Collective 231
Millett, Kate 46
Milton, John 205, 207, 211–12,
    217–18, 222; *Areopagitica* 219;
    Ars Logica 207; *De Doctrina
    Christiana* 222; *Doctrine and
    Discipline of Divorce* 211–12;
    Epithamium Damonis 217; *Of
    Education* 217; *Paradise Lost*
    207–25
Miners' Strike, 1984 255
Minshull, Elizabeth 212
misogyny 10, 15, 216
Mnasidica 53
Modernism 111, 112, 115

Mohin, Lilian 237
Moore, Lesley *see* Baker, Ida
Mort, Frank 76
Munt, Sally 10, 19, 21, 23
Murry, John Middleton 115, 116, 119–22, 124–5, 130–1
myths 40, 43, 114, 131, 205–6, 241, 242; African 45; Christian 116–17, 119, 205–6, 241, 242; male 29; Sanskrit 1, 2, 165

National Curriculum 86
National Front 76
Nazis 76
Nero (Nero Claudius Domitius) 198
Nestle, Joan 20
New Zealand 116
Ngcobo, Laura 238
Nichols, Grace 237
Nietzsche, Frederic 77
Nigeria 229
Nirrti 167, 170–1, 171–8
Noble, Vicki 43
Nyquist, Mary 224

O'Byrne, Deirdre 5
O'Flaherty, Wendy 156–7
Olsen, Tillie 46
Oram, Alison 108
Organisation of Women of African and Asian Descent (OWAAD) 236
Orinda *see* Philips, Katherine
O'Rourke, Rebecca 10, 13–14, 90, 91, 106
    Jumping the Cracks 9, 13–14, 17–18, 19, 22, 23–4, 25
Ostriker, Alicia Suskin 40
O'Sullivan, Sue 237
Ovid *Metamorphoses* 196
Oxford English Dictionary 50, 89, 192
Owen, Anne (Lucasia) 191–201

Page, Denys 60, 61, 64, 65, 66
Palestine 222

Palmer, Jerry 26
Palmer, Paulina 1, 3, 258
Parker, Pat 243
Parmar, Pratibha 237
Paskin, Sylvia 237, 238
passing women 20, 91–2
patriarchy: and death 170–8; discourses of 28, 29, 33, 44, 129, 158; and literary criticism 128–9; position of women in 32, 33–4, 69, 129, 147, 209–10, 245; and religion 37, 158, 205; subversion of 9, 12, 22, 23, 28, 147, 244; values of 10, 16, 30–1, 132; *see also* heteropatriarchy; heterosexuality
St Paul 210, 213, 217, 220
Pearse, Gabriela 226, 232, 233–4
Pearse, Jean 233–4
Philips, James 183, 191
Philips, Katherine (Orinda) 1, 2, 3, 183–204
Philophilippa 196
Phoebus 196
Piercy, Marge 46
Plutarch 67
Poe, Edgar Allan 24
politics 11, 69, 70, 150, 191, 192, 227, 245; of evasion 144; feminist 17, 78, 246–7; racial 12, 249; of religions 155, 246; sexual 12, 70, 78, 83, 156, 160, 211, 217, 218; sexual activity and 20, 42–3, 70, 78, 156; of translation 160; of writing 28, 29, 42, 104; *see also* feminism; racism
pornography 44, 210, 216, 246, 247, 255
Powell, Mary 211–12
psychiatry 12–13, 244
psychoanalysis 12–13, 23, 28–36, 39, 45, 56, 114, 119; *see also* Freud; psychology
psychology 11, 12, 13, 51, 95

Pururvas 166–71

Quakers 184–5

race 4, 12, 24, 33; *see also*
Blacklesbianism; racism; zamis
racism 10, 24, 38–9, 41, 76, 149,
189, 244–5, 249–51; *see also*
colonialism; eurocentrism
Ram 158
Ramsay, J 238
rape 10, 19, 102, 169, 170, 196
Raymond, Janice 249
reader, positioning of 11, 14, 19,
22, 23, 29–30, 38, 45, 51, 52, 56,
71, 94, 103, 136, 149, 151, 152,
160, 161, 192, 209
Reagan, Ronald 17
Rhodesia 116
Rich, Adrienne 34, 44;
'Compulsory Heterosexuality
and Lesbian Existence' 145;
*The Dream of a Common
Language* 42–4, 242; *On Lies,
Secrets and Silence* 29, 242;
*Origins and History of
Consciousness* 31–3
Richardson, Dorothy 112
Rig Ved 163, 165, 165–73, 176–7,
178, 179
Rilke, Rainer Maria 148
Robbins, Emmett 67
Rochester, John Wilmot, 2nd
Earl of 193
Rollason, Christopher 16
Roper, Lyndal 187–8, 202
Rosania *see* Mary Aubrey
Rose Bruford College 229, 231
Rose, Phyllis 103
Ross, Robert 85
Royal Court Theatre 229
Ruehl, Sonja 153
Rule, Jane *Lesbian Images* 139,
153, 243; *Desert of the Heart*
243
Rushdie, Salman 90
Ryan, Joanna 27

Sachs, Nelly 161–2, 178
Sackville-West, Vita 92, 94
sadomasochism 23, 197–9, 248;
see also domination and
submission
Saïd, Edward 149
St Hilaire, Patricia 229, 231–2
St Kitts 236
Salvation Army 78
Sands, Martin 21
Sappho 1, 2, 50–67, 153, 189–90,
259
Satan 206, 209, 218, 220
Sayan 159, 171, 178, 179
Sayers, Dorothy L 10
Scaliger, Joseph 66
Scarlet Harlots, The 244–5
schools: girls' boarding schools
15, 25, 134–54
Scotland 232, 235
Section 28 of the Local
Government Act 1988 4, 96; *see
also* Clause 28 of the Local
Government Act 1988
Seekers 184
selfhood *see* subjectivity
Sellers, Jan 4, 202, 258–9
Semple, Linda 26
sensuality 125–9, 131; *see also*
desire; eroticism; sex
separatism, lesbian 31, 219–20,
223
sex, lesbian: and desire 43, 186;
history of 20, 54, 186–7; and
identity formation 36–8, 41–2;
representation in literature 21–
2, 23–4, 28–49, 54, 93, 141–2,
192–3, 247–8; *see also* butch;
desire; eroticism
sexology 2, 68, 90, 244; *see also*
inversion; inverts
Shah, Shaila 238
Sharp, Jane, *The Midwives Book*
189, 203
Sheba Feminist Publishers 230,
232, 235, 237
Shelley, Percy Bysshe 135

Shepherd, Simon 4, 5, 84, 202
Shiva 163–4, 165; *see also* goddesses
Silva, J 238
Silverstolpe, Frederic 65–6, 84, 187
Sinfield, Alan 202
Sistahs in Song 228, 232, 234–5, 235, 236
Sistren Theatre Company 254
Sita 158; *see also* goddesses
Slade, Ruth 245
slavery 39, 189
Slawson, Eva 245
Smartt, Dorothea 3, 233, 234–5, 259
Souers, Philip 202
Southall Black Sisters 230, 236
Spedding, Carole 238
Speranza *see* Wilde, Lady Jane Francesca
spirituality, feminist 36–8, 42, 43, 234, 246; *see also* goddesses
Spillane, Mickey 10
Spraggs, Gillian 2, 3, 259
Spretnak, Charlene 47
Sri Lanka 231
Stein, Gertrude 112
Stigers, Eva Stehle 66
Styles, Morag 238
subjectivity: cultural specificity of 156–7, 227; fractured 16, 17, 72, 75; non-unified 19, 69, 72, 115; oppositional identity 70–1, 75, 83, 220; self and other 29, 31, 32, 36, 40, 48, 135, 156–8, 160, 163; self-denial 135, 145–6; subject-object relations and 32, 33–4, 163–4; unified 227; unstable 12, 69–70, 164; *see also* identity; Lacanian theory
Sulter, Maud 235–6
Symonds, John Addington 68
Symons, Julian 26

teachers 96, 99, 134, 135, 137, 138, 139, 144, 145, 146, 147,

teachers (cont.)
149, 150, 245; *see also* governesses; headmistresses
Teatro del'Angolo 228
Temba Theatre 228
Tey, Josephine 10, 11, 15: *Miss Pym Disposes* 15, 25
Thadani, Giti 2, 3, 259
Thatcher, Margaret 17
Theatre of Black Women (TBW) 229, 231–2, 233–4, 235, 236, 237, 244–5
Theatre Centre 228
Thompson, Tierl 245
The Times 98–9
translation: politics of 160; principles of 64; 160–1
Trefusis, Violet 94
Trinidad 233

Ulrichs, Karl Heinrich 70
unemployment 4, 13, 241
United States of America 19, 24, 39, 45, 51, 87, 227, 232, 235
Unwin Hyman 4
Urban Fox Press 235, 237
Urvashi 165–71; *see also* goddesses
Usha 168–9

Vaughan, Henry 192
Vicinus, Martha 152
Virgil (Publius Virgilius Maro) 135, 148
Voices for Oya 236; *see also* Sistahs in Song

Wales 183
Walker, Alice, *The Color Purple* 246; 'Porn' 255
Wallis, Mick 4, 5, 202
Wandor, Micheline 220–1
Weeks, Jeffrey 107
Weighall, Arthur 66
West, M L 61, 65
White, Antonia 147

White, Chris 2, 3, 187, 202, 257, 260
Whitlock, Gillian 90
Wilde, Lady Jane Francesca (Speranza) 80–2
Wilde, Oscar 80–1, 83
Wilde, Speranza *see* Wilde, Lady Jane Francesca
Williams, Carmen Tunde 233, 235, 236–7
Williams, Raymond 106
Wills, Garry 66–7
Wilson, Anna 21
Wilson, Barbara 12–13, 20; *Ambitious Women* 9; *Murder in the Collective* 12, 17, 18–19, 24; *Sisters of the Road* 13, 19, 25
Wings, Mary 10, 13, 14, 20, 22; *She Came Too Late* 9, 14–15, 22, 23, 24, 25
Winkler, John J 66
Winstanley, Gerrard 214
Wittgenstein, Ludwig 161–2, 178
Wittig, Monique 46, 221–2
Wollstonecraft, Mary 139, 153, 220
Women In Entertainment 254

women's liberation movement 17, 19–20, 21, 87, 242, 246; Blackwomen's movement 226–7
Women's Press, The 4, 240, 241
Women's Theatre Group, The 228, 229, 245
Woodcock, Katherine 212
Woolf, Leonard 95
Woolf, Virginia 1, 2, 86–108, 112; *Mrs Dalloway* 95, 97, 99–104, 105; *Orlando* 92, 104; *A Room of One's Own* 93–4
working class 13, 14, 78, 88, 248; *see also* class

Yajnavalkya 179
Yogini Hradya 179
Yorke, Liz 2, 3, 260

zamis 226–238; *see also* Blacklesbianism
Zeig, Sande 221–2
Zeus 59
Zimbabwe *see* Rhodesia
Zimmerman, Bonnie 148